Hybrid Fictions

Hybrid Fictions

American Literature and Generation X

Daniel Grassian

McFarland & Company, Inc., Publishers

Jefferson, North Carolina, and London

LIBRARY OF CONGRESS CATALOGUING-IN-PUBLICATION DATA

Grassian, Daniel, 1974–
    Hybrid fictions: American literature and Generation X /
Daniel Grassian.
        p.   cm.
    Includes bibliographical references and index.

    ISBN 0-7864-1632-7 (softcover : 50# alkaline paper) ∞

    1. American fiction—20th century—History and criticism.
2. Social change in literature.   3. Literature and society—
United States—History—20th century.   4. Pluralism (Social
sciences) in literature.   5. Hybridity (Social sciences) and
the arts.   6. Generation X—Intellectual life.   I. Title.
PS374.S67G73   2003
810.9'3552'09045—dc22   2003017625

British Library cataloguing data are available

On the cover: Ron Rozzelle, *Untitled (Man with Venetian Blinds)*,
80" × 50", oil and acrylic on canvas, 1992

Manufactured in the United States of America

McFarland & Company, Inc., Publishers
  Box 611, Jefferson, North Carolina 28640
   www.mcfarlandpub.com

Contents

Introduction

Chances are if you ask an average college student who his or her favorite author is you might receive a blank stare or an occasional Tom Clancy, J.K. Rowling, Scott Turow or Stephen King. Unfortunately, most people do not discover or rediscover literature after college. If anything, the average person reads increasingly less as he or she ages. How many college students, or twenty- or thirty-somethings can name, let alone have read, any fiction writer of their generation? Even a liberal estimate wouldn't be higher than 25 percent or 30 percent and a conservative estimate might be even below 5 percent. On the surface, this appears to be damning news for the future of American literature, confirming the worst fears of postmodern, literary doomsayers. Yet serious literary fiction has always reached only a small audience. What percentage of Americans knew about Thomas Pynchon and John Barth in the 1960s and 1970s? And what percentage of young Americans in the 1920s and 1930s knew of Ernest Hemingway and William Faulkner? I would not argue that a vastly greater number of Americans knew of those canonical writers than those who now have heard of or have read David Foster Wallace, Richard Powers, Neal Stephenson, William Vollmann, Sherman Alexie, Michele Serros or Douglas Coupland. This is not to suggest that there hasn't been a steady decrease in the number of serious literary readers in America, for indeed I believe there has been. But not enough, I would argue, to constitute a genuine literary crisis as some critics like Allan Bloom might contend.

Since the 1960s, academic critics have theorized that literature is well on its way to becoming obsolete or, at the very least, that it has lost a substantial amount of its power as an influential medium of social and cultural criticism. After all, we live in a visually attuned culture, and each successively younger generation appears to be less engaged with literature than the last. While having some merit, these speculations could lead to the belief that in the future, works of American literature will become historical artifacts relegated to lesser or even negligible roles in both the university and our public life. It also suggests that the quality

1

of serious contemporary American literature has so deteriorated that it is no longer worthy of academic or intellectual study. One of the primary objectives of *Hybrid Fictions* is to overturn this misconception and to argue that contemporary American literature is not only alive and well, but has mutated in exciting and important ways, reflecting the various, significant changes in American culture during the last twenty years. Furthermore, I will argue that we have reached a point at which we can no longer effectively describe a literary movement as being time bound (or dominating a certain time) as scholars often do with American realism, naturalism, modernism and even postmodernism.[1] It cannot be asserted with certainty that the period from 1980 to 2000 is the age of new realism, maximalism, minimalism or multiculturalism, though a case could be made for the application of each term. Because of the proliferation of writing styles from maximalism to minimalism, cultural pluralism and the diverse composition of the reading public, we have reached a point at which literary movements cannot effectively be defined or classified by time or era. Instead, we have entered a period of literary eclecticism and hybrid fictions, which utilize a wide variety of literary approaches, have conflicting viewpoints and blend media and technological forms.

I would like to clarify my use of the term "hybrid" in reference to two important literary and cultural critics who have frequently used the term: Homi Bhabha and Mikhail Bakhtin. As a postcolonial theorist, Bhabha embraces hybridity because it "entertains difference without an assumed or imposed hierarchy" (4). For Bhabha, hybridity "carries the burden of the meaning of culture," for he believes that identities are formed and cultures established in the in-between spaces of ethnic and cultural identities. Bhabha's concern is primarily ethnic, and, while I will address ethnic hybridity in Chapter 4, my definition and use of hybridity is nonethnically specific. Indeed, I feel that to focus solely upon ethnic hybridity in contemporary American literature is a constricting approach, for there are other forms as hybridity such as literary, psychological and technological hybridity, all of which I will explore in context with contemporary American literature and culture.

My use of the term "hybrid" is closer to that of Bahktin. For him, language is by definition a hybrid form, and literature (most specifically, the novel) is a form that allows writers to blend distinct and often opposing social languages (Bahktin xix, 358). Bahktin explains, "We may even say that language and languages change historically, primarily by means of hybridization, by means of [the] mixing of various 'languages' co-existing within the boundaries of a single dialect, a single national-language, a single branch, a single group of different branches or different groups of such branches" (359). The novel as a "supergenre" is the archetypal hybrid form through which to analyze culture and society because its "power consists in its ability to engulf and ingest all other genres" (xxix). In line with Bahktin, most of *Hybrid Fictions* focuses upon the contemporary novel, which I would submit is the ideal form through which to perceive American cultural and literary hybridity.

Bakhtin's distinction between intentional and unintentional hybridity is also useful to my argument. That is, an author may intentionally yoke together disparate characters, viewpoints and devices. However, in studying literature, we often find unintentional or unconscious hybridity and conflicts, as apparent in the revisionist studies of sexuality in Ernest Hemingway's fiction. Or, borrowing from Roland Barthes, we can find unintentional or unconscious hybridity if we look at the author as a microcosm of society. Indeed, writers often compose without conscious intellectual intentions, and in a good work of literature, we can often perceive larger social or cultural issues which go beyond the immediate scope of the narrative. In *Hybrid Fictions*, I identify both conscious and unconscious hybridity involved in contemporary American literature and culture along with conflicting desires and cultural messages.

Also, I will relate hybridity to contemporary cultural and technological developments in the 1990s and at the beginning of the new millennium. As Bhabha proposes, "In the fin de siècle, we find ourselves in the moment of transit where space and time cross to produce complex figures of difference and identity, past and present, inside and outside, inclusion and exclusion. For there is a sense of disorientation, a disturbance of direction, in the 'beyond'" (1). Indeed, here at the beginning of the twenty-first century, hybridity is an effective descriptive term for contemporary American culture. Once new cultures, media forms and technologies have been introduced into society, they often interbreed or fuse, thereby creating hybrid forms. Hybridity and the oppositions it feeds upon have significant political and social implications. On the one hand, we seem to be on the cusp of a revolutionary, technologically advanced age, but on the other hand, we are racked by continual ethnic conflict as well as environmental problems.

I am no pessimistic naysayer, nor is *Hybrid Fictions* the work of a grumpy young man who derides his own generation as worthless slackers. For we have both advanced and backtracked culturally and literarily in the past forty years. Many literary and social critics celebrate the 1960s as a golden era of social change, after which American culture has steadily plummeted downhill. For instance, in *The Real American Dream*, Andrew Delbanco contends that "Something died, or at least fell dormant, between the later 1960s, when the reform impulse subsided into solipsism, and the 1980s—two phases of our history that may seem far apart in political tone and personal style, but that finally cooperated in installing instant gratification as the hallmark of the good life, and in repudiating the interventionist state as a source of hope" (97). There is merit to Delbanco's point of view about contemporary youth culture. Indeed, in my second chapter, I argue that the most engaged of young American fiction writers rightly criticize their generation for having become too hedonistic, though not all of the blame should be placed on the shoulders of their generation as baby boomers sometimes do. One such person, baby boomer journalist and teacher Peter Sacks, complains in his book *Generation X Goes to College* that his students view a good class as one which entertains or personally pleases them rather than provides any substantial knowledge or insight (72). Taking Sacks's criticism a step further, Allan Bloom crystallizes the conservative backlash against youth culture in *The Closing of the American Mind*, emphasizing, "This gradual stilling of the old political and religious echoes in the souls of the young accounts for the difference between the students I knew at the beginning of my teaching career and those I face now. The loss of books has made them narrower and flatter. Narrower because they lack what is most necessary, a real basis for discontent with the present and awareness that there are alternatives to it" (61).

To some extent, Bloom, Sacks and Delbanco make rational and justifiable critiques of Generation X as not being literary minded enough and for being increasingly self-indulgent. However, their views are correspondingly narrow, and they tend to implicitly and unfairly place the blame upon Gen Xers themselves. In contrast to these theorists, while I would argue that being literary minded helps breed altruism, as well as historical and social consciousness, I would not contend that a person who is strongly "media minded" would necessarily be self-involved and intellectually disengaged. Indeed, people can hone their keen analytic skills by studying film, the Internet and even television and thereby become, in a way, more knowledgeable and insightful about the increasingly media-dominated country and world. Besides, even a bibliophile can become almost as obtuse as a television addict, both having forsaken empirical experience. However, one problem is that literature is often completely neglected in favor of virtually all other media forms, which provide easier, more passive, pleasures. Furthermore, if Gen Xers are too self-indulgent, then the elder generation ought to take at least some of the responsibility or accept some of the blame. For as both media and divorce pioneers, they are largely responsible for creating the familial and environmental atmosphere that helped produce their so-called monstrous offspring.

However, allied with Bloom, Sacks and Delbanco, I feel that literature does not play as large a cultural role as it could, for as Bahktin suggests, literature (specifically, the novel) surpasses any other art or media form in its ability to capture and interpret culture as a whole. It is not the case that young Americans have stopped writing fiction. The groundbreaking and socially important writings of a new, younger generation of Americans have already been published and will continue to be published in the future. My hope is that *Hybrid Fictions* will spark an interest, particularly in younger American Gen Xers, in fiction that speaks to them and the changing nature of their world. Consequently, *Hybrid Fictions* focuses almost exclusively upon American fiction writers born from the late 1950s to the early 1970s. Most of these writers fall under the vague rubric of "Generation X." Rather than classify their work as Generation X fiction, however, I have chosen "hybrid" fiction as a more appropriate term of classification. Hybridity does not conflict with theories of Generation X culture because Generation X is a generation that cannot be effectively described as a whole. Indeed, among the primary criteria underlying the concept of Generation X are heterogeneity and diversity. Thereby, hybridity as a literary development fits with sociological theories of Generation X.

Still, a cynical Gen Xer might ask: What does literature provide for us which other art forms or popular culture do not or cannot? As Margaret Doody argues in *The True Story of the Novel*, "The novel has been, as Lionel Trilling said, the chief agent of our moral imagination, the form that more than any other has taught us the virtues of understanding and forgiveness" (1). Understanding and forgiveness in addition to empathy are increasingly important and rare attributes in an age that has become increasingly self-indulgent and narcissistic. Furthermore, as Harold Bloom proposes, "Imaginative literature is otherness, and as such alleviates loneliness" (19). Indeed, despite our increased standard of living and despite the multifold pleasures of various media forms and popular culture, these may be the loneliest times in American history, with communities and families playing an ever decreasing role in our everyday lives. Furthermore, the media's emphasis upon the charismatic and impeccably attractive makes most people feel at least somewhat inadequate by comparison. Serious literature helps make readers feel less alone and does not cater solely to a person's prurient interests.

Furthermore, literature, like the best of other art forms, can have important social ramifications. I would not agree with Harold Bloom, who argues in *How to Read and Why*, that "the pleasures of reading indeed are selfish rather than social. You cannot directly improve anyone else's life by reading better or more deeply" (22). Rather, I would argue that literature can be both directly and indirectly beneficial as people become cognizant of historical contexts, as well as the contemporary meanings of events, and more understanding of differences among people. Therefore, one can become more compassionate, insightful and knowledgable and thereby capable of making better, more informed decisions, which can directly or indirectly affect the lives of others. It is true that one can never directly gauge the social benefits of any artwork, but that doesn't mean that art or fiction do not have significant social worth. In *Hybrid Fictions*, there is an implicit canonical argument and an intentional focus upon literature over that of theory and criticism. I concur with Joseph Tabbi, who argues, "one of the unfortunate effects of the modern information explosion is its re-direction of narrative energies and much of the academic reader's time toward works of scholarship rather than literary narratives" (3).

Finally, the format of *Hybrid Fictions* is in itself hybrid: part literary analysis, part cultural studies, part literary biography and part generational study. While most of *Hybrid Fictions* focuses on novels, in Chapter 2, I also investigate a memoir by Dave Eggers and briefly draw upon a memoir by Elizabeth Wurtzel to frame my argument about depression and mental illness. My justification for using these two memoirs is that they both blur the divisions between autobiography and fiction; they are hybrid memoirs that illustrate the shady ground between self-representation, self-promotion and self-distortion. In Chapter 4, I also briefly touch upon Michele Serros's prose poetry, which is not written in a demonstrably different fashion from her prose.

At the same time that I analyze literary works, I also make cross-cutting observations about contemporary American culture from mental illness to the effects of the media to artificial intelligence. Just as it is important to investigate the texts themselves, it is equally important to elucidate the cultural issues with which contemporary writers engage themselves, for no author writes in a social vacuum. This generation of American writers, having an almost symbiotic relationship with the media, is culturally savvy.

My primary intention is to convince the reader that a younger generation of American fiction writers offers pertinent, socially valuable commentary about late 1980s' and 1990s' American culture (and beyond). I also wish to demonstrate that these authors and their works deserve critical, academic attention and ought to be viewed in conjunction with one another as a new literary generation, in line with the modernist generation of writers, Cather, Faulkner, Dos Passos, Hemingway and Fitzgerald. Specifically, I investigate the writings of David Foster Wallace, Richard Powers, Neal Stephenson, William Vollmann, Douglas Coupland, Sherman Alexie, Michele Serros and Dave Eggers. I also argue that these American fiction writers are among the best and brightest of their generation (born after 1955) and that their works have important literary and cultural implications. Because there has been virtually no critical exploration of these young American fiction writers, I hope my exploration will lead to further academic research and writing.

1 *From Modernists to Gen Xers*

Virginia Woolf once declared that "Human character changed around 1910" (96).[1] While this is something of a sweeping generalization, Woolf's claim attests to the huge and significant transformation that occurred in the Western World after the turn of the century. During the subsequent modernist movement, artists such as James Joyce, Pablo Picasso, T.S. Eliot and Gertrude Stein rebelled against the previously dominant Victorian and Romanticist belief in divine order and harmony. To some extent, the modernist movement was the first worldwide revolution in art, philosophy and culture, whose reverberations we still feel today and whose artists are still considered to be among history's elite.[2] As significant as the changes were in Western society during and after the turn of the twentieth century, the Western world has been technologically and culturally advancing at an almost exponential rate in the past fifty years. With all due respect to Woolf, human life and Western society did not change overnight but seems to be in a process of progressive evolution. In this chapter, I briefly survey the historical developments of American literature in the twentieth century, and concurrently, the changes in American culture from the early part of the twentieth century to the present beginning of the twenty-first century. If human character did indeed change around 1910, then ever since, it has remained in flux, subject to fragmentation and the molding forces of cultural change.

In order to better comprehend our historical and literary position in the beginning of the twenty-first century, it is beneficial to take a wider, historical view of previous movements. I start with the development of modernism because modernism marks the first significant worldwide artistic movement in the twentieth century. It is now widely regarded as the pinnacle of American literature (with the possible exception of the Transcendental movement of the mid-nineteenth century). Although European and American modernist writers and artists developed along

7

parallel tracks, it wasn't until the early twentieth century that individual American writers and artists firmly asserted their own identities and distinct views of their home country in context with the larger world. While most prominent American modernist writers became expatriates for a time, settling in a Europe that they believed to be more receptive to their avant-garde views and philosophy, their primary focus was upon the United States or on the differences between Europe and America. So while the modernist movement was a movement toward American independence in the arts, it was not a clean break from the European tradition. Indeed, one of the key elements of modernist writing was a reliance on Greco-Roman-Anglican mythology.[3] Yet, at the same time, modernist artists were preoccupied with the present and inspired by a desire to be original, led by Ezra Pound's dictum, "Make it new." American modernist writers came to represent a distinct generation of Americans who were largely shaped by the vast technological changes brought about during the early twentieth century: the social upheaval of changing gender roles and mass industrialization, as well as the vast disillusion wrought by World War I. In a frightening world that threatened individuals and provided little or no emotional or moral sustenance, American modernists attempted to invent their own alternative ethos within their creative works. Over time, such American modernist writers as T.S. Eliot, Gertrude Stein, Ernest Hemingway, Willa Cather, William Faulkner and John Dos Passos rose in worldwide critical esteem, and America, in and of itself, was finally perceived as having a noteworthy literary culture with an identity and history distinct from that of Europe.

After the stock market crash of 1929 and subsequent 1930s' depression, American literature largely splintered off into new genres, such as the "proletarian" literature of John Steinbeck and Clifford Odets, the sprawling, self-invested narratives of Thomas Wolfe and the race-conscious "naturalistic" writing of Richard Wright and Zora Neale Hurston as well as the beginnings of "Black humor" in the works of Nathanael West. While modernist writers like Dos Passos and Hemingway continued to publish during the 1930s and 1940s, the end of World War II brought a new generation of writers to the forefront, such as Saul Bellow, Norman Mailer and Ralph Ellison as well as a number of new Southern writers, following in the lead of Thomas Wolfe and William Faulkner, such as Carson McCullers, Robert Penn Warren and Flannery O'Connor.

The most significant postwar literary movement, I would argue, was a new variety of rebellious, textually experimental, socially defiant writing that would eventually be described as "Beat" writing by one of its originators, Jack Kerouac. Much has been written about Beat writers, but not enough attention has been given to considering their place in the

American literary tradition, especially in context with that of modernist and subsequent postmodernist writing. In fact, some might agree with Truman Capote's oft-repeated derogatory comment about Beat writing, originally made on David Susskind's television show, "That's not writing. That's typing" (D'Orso, 118). However, to agree with Capote and summarily dismiss Beat writings would be to neglect one of the most important and influential literary developments in twentieth-century American literature.

In one way, Beat writing was a stepping-stone from modernist to postmodernist writing, but in another way, Beat writing was much more avant garde than most postmodern writing. With Jack Kerouac's stream of consciousness writing, William Burroughs's cut-up techniques and Ginsberg's Whitmanesque ebullient and passionate social critiques (not to mention Richard Brautigan's textually experimental environmentalism and Amiri Baraka's (aka, Leroi Jones's) emotionally charged race-conscious writing), the Beats rebelled against literary conventions and nearly all forms of social and intellectual constriction. More than they are given credit for, the Beats helped reshape the direction of American literature after World War II in their attempt to efface the distinction between life and art. Instead of art functioning as a refuge from life as it did for the modernists, art for the Beats served as an arena in which to record or contemplate transcendental life experiences. Instead of placing art above life, the Beats placed real life above art. But most importantly, the Beats emphasized the cultivation of personality and rebelled against any form of repression. In late 1940s and 1950s America, while the government and mainstream public viewed nonheterosexual practices as deviant and even criminal, the Beats championed almost all forms of sexual expression as healthy and life affirming. They became the first self-conscious literary icons, products of a new advertising-and consumer-based society that packaged and labeled them as "beatniks" (unlike the modernists, who weren't labeled as such until after the era of the writing had mostly passed). Unfortunately, as Thomas Pynchon so brilliantly satirizes in his first novel, *V.*, the Beat movement deteriorated into a media-generated subculture of "Beatniks" who perverted the original Beats' messages of freedom and self-expression into aggressive, and largely phony, fashion consciousness. The media helped transform the socially rebellious but intellectual Beats who sought religious or spiritual enlightenment and sought to breed compassion and tolerance into aimless, less than coherent, leather-wearing asocial miscreants played so brilliantly by Marlon Brando in *The Wild One* (1954) and James Dean in *Rebel without a Cause* (1955).[4] This transformation is significant because it was the first but not the last time that the media would pervert or shape the direction of social and literary generations.

The Beat heyday was a brief pocket in time, gradually overtaken by a new literary movement.[5] Indeed, in the preface to his short-story collection, *Slow Learner*, Thomas Pynchon argues that during the early 1960s, "We were at a transition point, a strange post–Beat passage of cultural time, with our loyalties divided" (2). In the late 1950s and early 1960s, the post–Beat era quickly transformed into the postmodern literary era with the first publications and subsequent critical acclaim of the now-canonical John Barth, Thomas Pynchon, Robert Coover, Donald Barthelme and William Gass. Following the lead of the experimental, daring Beats in the 1950s, these writers further pushed literary and linguistic boundaries with their use of metanarrative, parody, historical deconstruction and abstract juxtapositions. Modernism placed high emphasis on interiority, or the capacity of the individual consciousness—usually that of the poet—to make meaning from a fragmented and enervated exterior social reality. However, the next generation of American artists and writers rejected the modernist goal of making meaning and achieving transcendence and even regarded the push to do so as potentially destructive and possibly fascist in its implicit totalitarianism (in line with Ezra Pound's eventual Fascist leanings). If modernists looked for new epistemological foundations, their literary descendants, postmodernists, rejected the supposed benefits of or even philosophical basis for this sort of search, reveling instead in multiple forms of narrative and competing, equally valid theories and perspectives.

With the beginnings of the postmodern movement in the 1960s, fiction writers began to look at fiction in different ways. Postmodernism revealed a general mistrust of the epistemological authority of the interpretative novel largely because the complexities of contemporary society made all interpretations of reality arbitrary and therefore simultaneously accurate and absurd. The main assertion in postmodernism was that literature is its own reality and that fiction need not address any realities other than its own internal consciousness. Just as one of the chief inventions of the modernist movement was stream of consciousness, one of the chief innovations of postmodern literature was the metanarrative. In the *Postmodern Condition*, Jean François Lyotard argues that by the late twentieth century, Western culture had gradually abandoned grand, unified theories in favor of smaller, competing narratives or metanarratives (57). These metanarratives purportedly upset the hegemony of standard linear narrative and decentered the author, subject and plot. Fiction thereby became more of a battleground of competing voices and viewpoints, polyphonous texts without either a clear center or an exact interpretation.

However, as postmodern philosophers and multicultural perspectives began to grow at American universities during the 1970s and 1980s (replacing the new critical, structural, psychoanalytical and existential schools of criticism of the 1950s and 1960s), contemporary American "serious fiction" largely diverged from postmodernism to so-called minimalism or retrorealistic writing. While art theorists use the term "minimalism" to name the style of art in which objects are stripped down to their elemental, geometric form and presented in an impersonal manner, literary critics adopted the artistic term "minimalism" to describe a new kind of fictional movement or genre beginning in the 1970s.[6] In fact, it is one of the leading writers and essayists of literary postmodernism, John Barth, who first used the word "minimalism" as a contemporary literary trend to summarily describe the fiction of Raymond Carver, Ann Beattie, Richard Ford, Tobias Wolff and others who began publishing in the 1970s and 1980s[7]. At the same time, Barth championed his own writing (and that of others like William Gaddis) as "maximalist," which he compared to "life at its best" (Barth, *Further Fridays,* 88). Responding (or not responding) to the postmodern insistence on a lack of epistemological or existential certainties, these so-called minimalist writers championed and focused upon empirical or emotional reality filtered through individual subjectivity (in that sense, their writing "regressed" or reverted to modernistic forms). Of these writers, none has been more significant than Raymond Carver, whose heart-wrenching short stories about the desperate working class and ubiquitous American loneliness struck a chord with readers and virtually resuscitated the short story, opening the doors for writers like Richard Ford, Bobbie Ann Mason, Fredric Barthelme, and Tobias Woolf.

With the resuscitation of the short-story form and a new reader interest in plot-driven, nonexperimental narrative also came the first wave of new fiction writers born a generation after most American postmodern writers. The 1980s saw the rise of the media-dubbed literary brat pack of Bret Easton Ellis, Jay McInerney and Tama Janowitz. While still in their twenties and early thirties, Ellis, McInerney and Janowitz became minor celebrities with their largely dismal caricatures of vapid middle- and upper-class white American life, primarily focused in the twin urban centers of Los Angeles and New York. Their most significant and lasting work is McInerney's *Bright Lights, Big City* (1984), Ellis's *Less than Zero* (1985) and Janowitz's *Slaves of New York* (1987), all of which were subsequently coopted by Hollywood and made into movies, starring celebrities such as Michael J. Fox, Andrew McCarthy and Robert Downey Jr. Thereby, Ellis's, McInerney's and Janowitz's works became affiliated with the media-labeled brat pack of young Hollywood actors and actresses such as Fox, McCarthy, Downey, Molly Ringwald, Ally Sheedy, Rob Lowe and Demi Moore. Indeed, their work was summarily labeled by critics as "brat-pack" fiction.

While I would not argue that the work of Ellis, McInerney and Janowitz is brilliant or groundbreaking in either content or form, these writers mark an important transition from the previous generation of American postmodern writers like John Barth, Thomas Pynchon and Robert Coover to the subjects of *Hybrid Fictions*. Ellis, McInerney and Janowitz wrote fiction that made literature relevant once more for a new generation of Americans. All three writers argue that most Americans, especially younger Americans who have more of a symbiotic relationship with televisual and audio media than previous generations, suffer from desensitization and a lack of emotional affect. They cast a wary, accusatory finger at the totalizing effects of popular culture which champions artifice and breeds emotional desensitization and frigidity, as well as the common dysfunctions of contemporary American families. They also show a jaded media sensibility and a renewed interest in the modernist search for epistemological certainties. Furthermore, the works of these writers also introduced a new form of ironic satire, a hallmark of Generation Xers, a tactic still used by many young American writers.

Should the fiction of McInerney, Ellis and Janowitz be considered postmodern literature? To address this question, I want to clarify the meaning of the word "postmodernism." Fredric Jameson has argued that "postmodernism" arose from late capitalism and the globalization of the world market after World War II. However, Jameson's argument does not identify the psychological and social effects of world globalization or consumerism. I would add to Jameson's theory that by the mid to late 1980s and certainly by the 1990s, there was a revelation of the social and individual effects of a global, rampant capitalism based on consumerism. The 1980s ushered in a new phase of American capitalism that involved the cultural domination of an "individual," whose "identity" became largely determined by consumer/popular/postmodern culture. This is what Ellis, McInerney, Janowitz and like-minded novelists such as Mark Lindquist, Walter Kirn and Jeff Gomez all sternly critique, and this is one reason characters often appear flat and two dimensional. It is not that the writers and their characters are dull, as some critics have proposed. Rather, the world of the characters (and even authors) revolves around the popular culture forms of television, film, music, fashion and consumer products. To show a level of insight or sophistication, a character might perform a compelling analysis of musical groups such as Patrick Bateman does in the narrative interludes of Bret Easton Ellis's *American Psycho* (1991) or have penetrating thoughts about tabloid stories as "You" does in *Bright Lights, Big City*. However, I would argue that their work is narrow minded and reflects only a segment of American culture in the 1980s. Still, their fiction should be seen as stepping away from postmodernity and toward contemporary hybrid fictions.

During the 1990s, a new generation of American fiction writers grew in prominence. The largely pop-culture-influenced work of these writers is not postmodern, or if it is, then there has evolved a new brand of postmodernity which differs from that of twenty or thirty years ago. The term "postmodernism" grew in popularity during the 1980s to the point of overuse and virtually blanketed the study of contemporary literature. Indeed, the label of postmodernism does not lend itself well to intellectual scrutiny. In a sense, the term perfectly reflects the dogma of deconstruction, which champions substitution, uncertainty and questioning. Postmodernism is interchangeably used as a philosophy (or antiphilosophy), a cultural epoch and a literary movement. Following its own disordered ethos, postmodernism purposely or accidentally puzzles academics and the general public through its inherent linguistic ambiguity and confusion. Yet, out of its amorphous confusion, postmodernism has been adopted by contemporary American media and culture as a form of anarchic entertainment. From the playful self-reflexivity of Kevin Willamson's *Scream* films, which deconstruct formulaic horror movies, the self-parodying David Letterman, and the pastiche and fusion of "alternative" musicians like Beck to the meta-watching, self-reflexive Simpsons, postmodernism and deconstruction have become part and parcel of American pop culture, which has in turn become a primary area of inquiry for a new generation of American fiction writers who realize that the technomedia landscape from film to television to the Internet has become our primary environment, our primary field of reference, artificial though it may be.[8]

While these new writers are still young, ranging from their early thirties to their mid-forties and will no doubt produce a significant body of work in the years to come, I feel that the time has come to begin considering the literary and cultural implications of their already impressive and substantial corpus of work. These recent novelists are largely members of the American generation considered today as Generation X, consisting of individuals born between 1961 and 1981.[9] Cognizant of the resistance and hostility to the label Generation X, I feel much of the hostility is warranted. As Douglas Brinkley argues:

> The term Generation X has become a derisive media catchphrase, a snide put-down for those, like me, who were born between 1961 and 1981. It is important to ask who is doing the labeling. When Gertrude Stein told Ernest Hemingway, "You're all a lost generation," she was part of it. When Jack Kerouac coined the term "the beat generation," he saw himself as a "beat." Although "X" was meant to refer to the '60s generation, by the time the term came to the United States it began to be used by the Boomers to explain their own bewildering children [1].

Nevertheless, "Generation X" has some value as a term of classification in that it aptly describes a diverse generation that cannot be simply defined. One significant problem is overcoming the lingering stereotypes of Generation X as being slackers, emotionally and intellectually stagnant and vapid, apathetic, brainwashed creations of popular culture. Even Douglas Coupland, whose 1991 novel, *Generation X*, helped define a generation, has distanced himself from categorization and stereotypes that support his basic belief that Generation X is paradoxically defined by its lack of commonality and indeterminacy. He encourages people to "continue defying labels: Once people think they've pigeonholed you, they'll also think they can exploit and use you.... Let X = X" ("Generation X'd," 72). With due respect to Coupland, Generation X is not completely eclectic or indeterminate. Rather, there is some cohesion amongst the generation, especially in terms of the central and common ground of media-focused historical and political events, as well as television shows, films and music that frequently serve as their common frames of reference.

While *Hybrid Fictions* is not a study in Gen X literature, I contend that during the time that American postmodernism has been canonized (beginning in the mid–1980s), a new literary genre has been developed primarily by Generation X writers, dating back to the mid–1980s with the first publications from the literary brat pack of Ellis, McInerney and Janowitz. In addition to brat-pack fiction, others have called the fiction of young contemporary writers anything from post-postmodernism, image fiction, punk fiction, downtown writing, and neorealism, to minimalism.

The wide naming differentiation shows the increasing difficulty in coming up with agreeable labels. To some extent, labeling a literary movement or generation has always been something of a guessing game. Certainly, there is great distinction among various modernist, postmodernist and Beat writers, but there is sufficient similarity and common ground in order to classify them as distinct literary movements. However, the most recent generation of American fiction writers is even more difficult to label or classify, in part because their wide range defies precise labeling. Furthermore, young fiction writers themselves appear resistant to any form of labeling or classification. As products of a media-savvy, consumer-based society, they recognize that labeling of any sorts tends to be used by self-interested media to capture the viewer/listener's attention and money. Most tellingly, in his short-story collection, *Girl with Curious Hair*, David Foster Wallace explains his resistance toward fictional categories:

> Dividing this fiction business into realistic and naturalistic and surrealistic and modern and postmodern and new-realistic and meta is

> like dividing history into cosmic and tragic and prophetic and apoc-
> alyptic, is like dividing human beings into white and black and brown
> and yellow and orange. It atomizes, does not bind crowds, and, like
> everything timelessly dumb, leads to blind hatred, blind loyalty, blind
> supplication. Difference is no lover [346].

While I would not agree with Wallace that genre labeling is "timelessly dumb," it does have significant drawbacks, most notably in increasing the prejudicial attitudes toward writers who become fenced into categories and classifications. At the same time, there are common conventions in a literary category or movement, and while the description of any category will necessarily be a generalization, there is normally enough common ground in most literary movements to make them useful methods of categorization.

The primary area in which there is sufficient common ground to effectively categorize the most recent generation of American writers as a cohesive generation is in popular culture. There has arisen a symbiosis between popular culture and identity in contemporary postmodern America. As Larry McCaffery argues, there has been "a prodigious expansion of culture throughout the social realm, to the point at which everything in our social life—from economic value and state power practice to the very structure of the psyche—can be said to have become cultural in some original and yet untheorized sense" ("Introductory Ways," 39). Popular culture has become the primary text of reference for young, contemporary, American fiction writers. Whereas John Barth claimed in his postmodern treatise "The Literature of Replenishment" that a true postmodern writer has "a foot in the narrative past" (*The Friday Book*, 204), most hybrid fiction writers have both feet firmly planted in the cultural present. Popular culture, allied with mass media, has set up rival histories of its own, complete with modernist and postmodernist forms. Contemporary American fiction writers typically rely on popular cultural history rather than on narrative or literary history as substance for their works.

Canonized postmodern writers tend to revel in postmodern (dis)integration as literarily and culturally liberating, but postmodern (dis)integration has the serious potential to become a personally destructive form of empty decadence. In recent fiction, young American fiction writers often portray popular culture as a prison of postmodern fragmentary thought, responsible for the production of either manipulated, emotionally impoverished persons or cognizant disgruntled consumers, who recognize their emotional and psychic isolation in a dissolute, consumer-based, postmodern culture (often called "slackers" for their attempt to live economically unfettered by America's consumer/corporate system). Indeed, there has been a shift in how to regard popular culture as evidenced by the title of two books, one considered postmodern (*White Noise*, written by Don DeLillo, born in 1936), and the other considered Gen X (*Our Noise*, written by Jeff Gomez, born in 1970). Popular culture has moved from being "white noise" to "our noise," from the socially distant to the personally immediate. Like it or not, popular culture has become the dominant culture and dominant history of the most recent generation of American fiction writers, and literature must make sense of it.

There also appears to be a significant generational gap, even conflict, between the younger generation of American fiction writers and their postmodern "elders." Some younger American fiction writers appear almost actively hostile, if not murderously Oedipal, to their literary elders, whose work they perceive as dominated by formal gimmicks with little pertinence to more significant, contemporary, social and cultural issues. To younger writers like David Foster Wallace, postmodern writers appear to be savvy comedians and erudite thinkers, but ultimately arrogant, their difficult and allusive fiction lacking substantial social or emotional depth or insight. Postmodern writers like John Barth and Thomas Pynchon contend that they are being more open and honest through their use of metanarratives, which helped break down the hegemony of the narrative and the author by providing a window onto composition. However, Wallace argues that theirs was more of "a sham honesty, aimed to get you to like them" (*Brief Interviews with Hideous Men* 145). In response, writers like Wallace aim to write directly relevant fiction with more emotional substance and social application.

Wallace, who, with his impressive corpus of work and literary showmanship, is somewhat of a spokesperson for his literary generation, convincingly argues that some postmodern literary techniques are self-serving and have lost their social relevance (and that in some cases, they may have had little to begin with). In line with Wallace, I feel that the work of young, contemporary American fiction writers combines the best of modernism and postmodernism. Their texts display active hybridity between opposites and extremes: between the highbrow and the lowbrow, between the literary and the popular, and between competing ethnicities and conflicting desires. They forge a middle ground between the emotionally jarring but intellectually thin writings of minimalist writers like Raymond Carver and the brilliant, but often obfuscating, protoacademic writing of Thomas Pynchon and John Barth. If the precise, image-based language of modernist literature was chosen as a means of protecting these writers from incomplete knowledge of their forebears, new novelists often let the floodgates loose, contending that in an age of information, there is more to incorporate, discuss and debate in their fiction. Hence, they often write huge, informationally savvy and erudite novels: Wallace's 1100-page *Infinite Jest*, Vollmann's 700-page *You Bright and Risen Angels*, Richard Powers's 650-page *Goldbug Variations*, Neal Stephenson's 900-page *Cryptonomicon* and Jonathan Franzen's 600-page *Corrections*. Writers whose aim it is to make broad, crosscutting statements about contemporary American culture or even writers who want to investigate certain topics are like contemporary scholars and web surfers. They must plow through an incredible amount of information and competing theories, much of which they incorporate into their fiction.

If modernists tried to write about situating themselves and constructing foundations or codes while postmodernists tried to write about dislocating themselves and fragmented or competing foundations, then hybrid fiction writers argue that both viewpoints are oversimplifications. If one tries to construct exact foundations, one becomes prey to totalitarianism or fundamentalism, but if one rejects foundations, one risks chaos. I do not wish to argue that the next wave of fiction writing is post-postmodernism because that term suggests we have moved past postmodernism. However, we still grapple with the issues of both modernism and postmodernism in contemporary America and in contemporary American fiction.

Still, with the beginning of the 1990s, American literary fiction has been experiencing a renaissance. From the somewhat meager beginnings of Ellis, McInerney and Janowitz, there has now emerged a substantial number of young American fiction writers whose work deserves academic study and who offer important and relevant commentary concerning contemporary America.[10] American fiction writers have kept pace with the rapid cultural and technological changes of the 1980s and 1990s, and their work has grown serious and significant with pertinent cultural commentary. Already, young American fiction writers have undertaken socially important topics with their exploration of contemporary American culture. Arguably the most critically acclaimed or socially important American fiction writers of this new generation (born after 1955) are David Foster Wallace, Richard Powers, William Vollmann, Neal Stephenson, Sherman Alexie, Douglas Coupland (Canadian by birth), Dave Eggers, Michele Serros, Mark Leyner, Michael Chabon, Susan Daitch, Rick Moody, Katherine Harrison, A.M. Homes, Jonathan Franzen, Donald Antrim, Jennifer Egan and Colson Whitehead.[11] (At the same time, many fascinating young writers such as Hal Hartley, Todd Solondz, Steven Soderberg, Paul Thomas Anderson, Quentin Tarantino, Gus Van Sant and Darren Aronofsky have migrated to film and become independent screenwriters and directors). Of all of these talented writers, I contend that the most significant fiction writers are David Foster Wallace and Richard Powers, with Vollmann, Stephenson, Alexie, Coupland, Serros and Eggers as strong second-tier writers whose work deserves critical study.[12]

So far there has been little critical exploration of Wallace, Powers or any young, contemporary American fiction writer with the exception of a few book reviews and random journal articles about selected works. To date, only one critic, James Annesley, in his *Blank Fictions,* has attempted a full-length study of this new generation of American writers. However, Annesley's portrait of young American fiction writers as preferring "blank, atonal perspectives, and fragile, glassy visions" (3) is a gross generalization that carries a derogatory connotation of insubstantiality. In contrast to Annesley, I argue that the writings of young American fiction writers are not blank but, rather, intellectually and culturally rich. One of the first, established literary critics to acknowledge the importance of Wallace and Powers is Tom LeClair, author of *In the Loop: Don DeLillo and the Systems Novel* (1987) and *The Art of Excess: Mastery in Contemporary American Fiction* (1989). However, in an article titled "The Prodigious Fiction of Richard Powers, William Vollmann and David Foster Wallace," LeClair merely scratches the surface of their work by limiting himself to only one novel by each: Powers's *Goldbug Variations,* Vollmann's *You Bright and Risen Angels* and Wallace's *Infinite Jest.* While LeClair does a fine job of summarizing the plots of these novels, he does not attempt to place these writers within the American literary tradition, nor does he undertake a sufficient critical analysis. However, he does enthusiastically endorse their work: "Among writers who set their fiction on this planet, those three novelists are, I think, most advanced in their knowledge of and most sophisticated in their use of information" (22). Since there has as yet been little academic exploration of young American fiction writers, I would like to provide some biographical and general critical background on the primary subjects of *Hybrid Fictions,* with the exception of Dave Eggers, as his biography comes out in my analysis of his memoir, *A Heartbreaking Work of Staggering Genius* (2000), in Chapter 2.

The son of a philosophy professor who was a student of Ludwig Wittgenstein's biographer and a grammar instructor, David Foster Wallace was raised in the small town of Philo, Illinois.[13] Despite being physically small and weak as a child, Wallace excelled at tennis and rose to become a nationally ranked teenage player. However, the rampant, aggressive competition disturbed young Wallace, who claims, "Midwest tennis was also my initiation into true adult sadness" (*A Supposedly Fun Thing I'll Never Do Again,* 12). While attending Amherst College in Massachusetts, Wallace transformed from "jock to math-wienie" (13), specializing in math and philosophy. He recalls: "For most of my college career I was a hard-core syntax wienie, a philosophy major with a specialization in math and logic" (McCaffery, "An Interview with David Foster Wallace," 132). While Wallace was exceptionally talented in his chosen field, he found the work largely unsatisfying and had what he calls an early, midlife crisis after his junior year in college. He promptly took a year off from college, during which he went back to Illinois and drove a bus in Urbana. During this time, Wallace read a prodigious amount of fiction,[14] and when he returned to Amherst for his senior year, he decided to switch his focus to creative writing. Subsequently, he began work on a creative writing honors thesis, which eventually turned into his first novel, *The Broom of the System*. After graduating from Amherst in 1985, Wallace entered the graduate creative writing program at the University of Arizona, where he received an M.F.A. in 1987. By Wallace's own accounts, his experiences at UA were not wholly positive. While his instructors championed John Cheever–style realism, Wallace wrote in a more colloquial, popular-culture-infused style, which clashed with the ideals and standards of his faculty mentors (McCaffery, "An Interview with David Foster Wallace," 140). Despite this, in 1987, Avon Books published *The Broom of the System*, which combines popular culture, postmodern philosophy and technology.

In the late 1980s, Wallace moved to Boston, where he continued to write fiction and also spent a semester in Harvard's graduate philosophy department. By his own account, the late 1980s and early 1990s were troubled times for Wallace, who used various kinds of drugs and suffered from clinical depression. His fast-paced lifestyle caught up with him quickly, resulting in some hospitalizations and a reported near-death scare (ibid., 130). While Wallace published his next fictional work, *Girl with Curious Hair* (1989), during this time, and for his collaboration with Mark Costello on rap music, *Signifying Rappers* (1990), he would eventually use many of his personal troubles as the basis for his magnum opus, *Infinite Jest* (1996). To halt his downward spiral, Wallace opted for a quieter lifestyle and accepted a position in the English department at the University of Illinois at Normal in 1993, where he remained until autumn 2002, at which time he joined the English department at Pomona College in Southern California. *Infinite Jest*, a 1079-page novel which was promoted by its publisher, Little, Brown, and Company, as being a late-twentieth-century *Ulysses*, catapulted Wallace into the literary spotlight. In recent years, Wallace has published a book of essays and nonfiction, *A Supposedly Fun Thing I'll Never Do Again* (1997) and a collection of shortstories and fictional interviews, *Brief Interviews with Hideous Men* (1999). Already, Wallace has won several prestigious writing awards, including the MacArthur Fellowship, the Lannan Award for Fiction, the Paris Review's Aga Khan Prize, the John Train Prize for Humor and the O. Henry Award.

Wallace's staggering range is encyclopedic in scope. He has a Dos Passos–like ambition to describe in totality the manifold voices and developments in American society, a considerably more formidable task in the 1990s than it was in the 1930s. Wallace's diverse subject matter includes linguistics, sports, rap music, television, independent film, psychotherapy, mathematics, literary theory, drug addiction and sexuality. Like his contemporary Richard Powers, Wallace heavily researches his subjects, and his fiction is informationally dense. For instance, in *Infinite Jest*, there are tens of pages of text and footnotes that give almost infinitesimal detail of things such as the precise working and effects of a huge number of drugs from bromide to marijuana and the use of tongue scrapers. When Wallace describes a person dying of "ventricular restenosis," he places a footnote next to the clinical description and in the footnote describes this medical condition as being "the progressive asymmetrical narrowing of one or more cardiac sinuses; can be either atherosclerotic or neoplastic" (995).

Wallace's knowledge of medicine and drugs reads much like a medical encyclopedia. For instance, he demonstrates his wealth of knowledge on other subjects, such as mathematics. In one footnote, he describes the founder of transfinite mathematics (George Cantor) in the early 1970s. An extended footnote explains in great detail the thirty-odd independent films of James Incandenza, from *The Man Who Suspected He Was Made of Glass* to the six different versions of the film *Infinite Jest* with an insider's knowledge of cinematography and film technique. Events that other novelists might have described in a sentence or two take Wallace pages to describe precisely. For instance, he spends a couple of pages alone describing the mathematical angles of a bed frame that is being moved. While this might seem like overindulgence, it is Wallace's aim to write from the psychological perspective of his characters, with this character (James Incandenza) being a mathematical prodigy. Wallace's narrators range from nearly illiterate drug addicts to mid–Southeastern hillbillies, from African Americans to Saudi Arabians, to lexical prodigies like Hal Incandenza, who submits seven college essays to the University of Arizona with titles like "Neoclassical Assumptions in Contemporary Prescriptive Grammar" and "The Implications of Post-Fourier Transformations for a Holographically Mimetic Cinema" (7).

Wallace has an impressive ability to describe different characters using their own diverse speech and thought patterns. Like an accomplished actor, he writes from the perspectives of hugely varying individuals. In *Infinite Jest*, he ranges from the nearly illiterate "Poor Tony Krause" to the highly cerebral postmodern übermensch James Incandenza, who is overly analytical and mechanistic.[15] Wallace rarely seems content to focus on just one character for very long, but through his character studies, a reader can find some common ground. For instance, in *Brief Interviews with Hideous Men*, Wallace details the sexual perversions and difficulties of male characters throughout America, and while each speaks differently and has a different story, they all reflect Wallace's belief that there are increasing difficulties in fostering and establishing satisfactory romantic and sexual relationships in an increasingly isolated, politically correct America.

In his own omniscient narrating voice, Wallace writes in a sprawling, freewheeling style, a cross between the brainy antics of Thomas Pynchon and the manic, spontaneous prose of Jack Kerouac. Especially conscious of his critical reception, Wallace has accordingly developed a stage persona that corresponds with his language use. As if to keep up with the brimming thoughts of his febrile mind, he also frequently uses abbreviations such as P.G.O.A.T. (for Prettiest Girl of All Time) and U.H.I.D. for (Union of the Hideously and Improbably Deformed) that mirror the abbreviations used in cyberspace, like LOL, for "laughing out loud." In addition, Wallace also uses a prodigious amount of popular-culture infused slang, including the Southern California "like" and "eliminating map" for suicide.

Like his contemporary Douglas Coupland, Wallace places much of the blame for the problems facing his generation upon the preceding baby boomers. He is among the most literate and historically cognizant of his contemporaries, in terms of his and their place in the American literary tradition. While Wallace appreciates the breakthroughs made by postmodernist writers, he sternly critiques them for the uneven legacy they have given to the next generation. In much of Wallace's fiction, there is a remote, paternalistic protopostmodern figure who becomes crippled by his own rampant cerebralism, largely unable to express himself emotionally. These figures typically fall into self-destructive behavior or become damaging to those that surround them. For instance, in *The Broom of the System*, the ineffectual father-figure is Rick Vigorous, editor of Frequent and Vigorous publications. Rick is a quintessential postmodernist, believing in nothing specific, completely immersed in a world of his imagination. For Rick, the world is a text, which makes him unable to respond emotionally to his younger girlfriend, twenty-four-year-old Lenore Beadsman, except through fiction.

Similarly, in *Infinite Jest*, Wallace portrays James Incandenza, the founder of Enfield Tennis Academy and avant-garde (or après-garde as Wallace calls him) filmmaker as the archetypal, postmodern father-figure who is destroyed by his inability to find meaning in life. The Incandenza children call their father "The Sad Stork" and "Himself," illustrating his unearthly emotional dissociation: "The man was so blankly and irretrievably hidden that Orin [one of James's sons] said he'd come to see him as like autistic, almost catatonic" (737). Orin's girlfriend, Joelle van Dyne, the P.G.O.A.T., who becomes the lead actress in most of James's later films, including the film *Infinite Jest*, describes Jim's work as "more like the work of a brilliant optician and technician, who was an amateur at any kind of real communication. Technically gorgeous but oddly hollow, empty, no sense of dramatic towardness—no narrative movement toward a real story, no emotional movement toward an audience" (740). Like the worst of postmodern artists, Jim is preoccupied with form to the expense of content. Despite his prodigious intelligence, Jim is stunted emotionally and can communicate with his sons only with the help of an intermediary (usually his wife Avril). That James eventually commits suicide, leaving an inheritance of sadness and confusion for his emotionally damaged sons, points to Wallace's main critique of the postmodern movement. In its cool, nihilistic cerebralism, postmodernism denies the efficacy of human emotions and adds to general feelings of despair and meaninglessness.

Wallace's rebellion against postmodernity is most biting in his novella, "Westward the Course of the Empire Makes Its Way," included in *Girl with Curious Hair*. "Westward" begins in a creative writing program at fictional East Chesapeake Trade School, a class which is taught by Professor Ambrose, an obvious caricature of John Barth (Ambrose is the name of Barth's protagonist in his seminal, postmodern bildungsroman *Lost in the Funhouse* [1967]). Ambrose's students gradually grow disgruntled with Dr. Ambrose/Barth, culminating with one student, D.L. (Drew-Lynn), writing a savage limerick directed in response to Ambrose/Barth's question in *Lost in the Funhouse*, "For whom is the Funhouse fun?" She scrawls on the chalkboard before class:

> For lovers, the Funhouse is fun.
> For phonies, the Funhouse is love.
> But for whom, the proles grouse,
> Is the Funhouse a house?
> Who lives there, when push comes to shove? [239].

At another point, D.L. continues her savage attack on Professor Ambrose/Barth by claiming that "the professor's whole 'art' is nothing more than the closet of a klepto with really good taste" (293).

To an extent, "Westward" is the centerpiece of Wallace's critique of American postmodern fiction writing. In it, Professor Ambrose/Barth sells his fictional idea of a funhouse to advertisers from McDonald's, who co-opt Ambrose/Barth's idea of the funhouse into "the new Funhouse franchise flagship discotheque" (235). Most of Wallace's criticism is targeted at metafiction, which he describes in the story as:

a required postmodern convention aimed at drawing the poor old reader's emotional attention to the fact that the narrative bought and paid for and now under time-consuming scrutiny is not in fact a barely-there window onto a different and truly diverting world, but rather in fact an "artifact," an object. Thus in a "deep" sense just an opaque forgery of a transfiguring window, not a real window, a gag which opens the door to a fetid closetful of gratuitous cleverness, jazzing around, self-indulgence, no hands-ism ... the ultimate odium for any would-be passionate virtuoso [265].

While John Barth describes his purpose in *Lost in the Funhouse* as creating a space for lovers, Wallace claims that it is "a story that does not love" (331).

Wallace continues his damning of metafiction in the story "Pop Quiz," contained in *Brief Interviews with Hideous Men*. He accuses metafiction writers of projecting a false honesty which is "actually a highly rhetorical sham—honesty that's designed to get you to like him and approve of him (i.e., of the "meta"-type writer) and feel flattered that he apparently thinks you're enough of a grownup to handle being reminded that what you're in the middle of is artificial" (125). To his credit, what clearly separates Wallace's writing from that of postmodern fiction writers is his passionate concern with emotional reality and his contention that there is an emotional reality that underlies the façade of everyday lives.

Wallace argues that we live in a culture that shuns seriousness and sadness, favoring instead humor, entertainment and nonchalance. Most tellingly, Wallace claims, "In most other cultures, if you hurt, if you have a symptom that's causing you to suffer, they view this as basically healthy and natural, a sign that your nervous system knows something's wrong. For these cultures, getting rid of the pain without addressing the deeper cause would be like shutting off a fire alarm while the fire's still going" (McCaffery, "An Interview with David Foster Wallace," 132). Wallace demands that people acknowledge the hidden or latent pain and suffering in our lives, part of which is inevitable in being mortal, but another often unacknowledged part of which is fostered by a culture which parades its winners and shuffles its losers underneath the carpet, a culture which he believes to be too self-absorbed.

While Wallace's fiction is informationally rich and technological astute, it is his grounding in the emotional reality (or lack thereof) of his generation that makes his work so important. Wallace's somewhat disturbing subject matter (sometimes concerning drug addiction and sexual perversion) and erudite writing style might prevent him from gaining a large following among the serious, literary mainstream, which may mean that his contemporary Richard Powers, whose work is equally brilliant but more subdued in content and form, may be the first American fiction writer of his generation to be widely studied.

Like Wallace, Richard Powers is a Midwesterner. Powers was born in Chicago in 1957 and, at the age of eleven, moved with his family to Bangkok. He then returned to the United States at sixteen and finished high school in a rural Illinois town. Powers subsequently attended the University of Illinois, where he dabbled in many fields but showed talent and great interest in the sciences. However, Powers tried to avoid specialization. He recalls: "The difficulty for me growing up was this constant sensation that every decision to commit myself more deeply to any of these areas meant closing several doors.... I just wanted to arrive somewhere where I could be the last generalist and do that in good faith. I thought for a long time that physics might be that place.... It's a great field to be in if you want the aerial view of how things work" (Williams, "The Last Generalist," 52). Although Powers's use of the modifier "last" for generalist seems a little apocalyptic, he shares with David Foster Wallace a voracious, encyclopedic desire to know all that a person can know. Physics proved to be not so dynamic a field as literature; hence, Powers, like Wallace, turned to English rather than the sciences. Unlike Wallace, who immediately tried his hand at creative writing, Powers first turned to the study of literature. After completing his bachelor's degree, Powers continued on at the University of Illinois, receiving a master's degree in English.

Literary criticism didn't turn out to be the all-encompassing field that Powers thought it would be. He recalls: "It didn't take me long to realize that the professionalization of literary criticism has taken reductionism as its model, and that it too can lead to learning more and more about less and less until you're in danger of knowing everything there is to know about nothing" (Williams, 53). After receiving his master's degree, Powers then moved to Boston, where he worked as a computer programmer. Subsequently, he lived in the Netherlands for about ten years, before moving back to Urbana-Champaign, Illinois, where he is a member of the English department of the University of Illinois, teaching courses in multimedia authoring and publishing as well as fiction writing.

To date (2002), Powers has written seven novels. His first, *Three Farmers on Their Way to a Dance* (1985), is a revisionist novel set during World War I, sparked by a photograph of three playful German soldiers going off to war. After *Three Farmers*, Powers published *Prisoner's Dilemma* in 1988, a loosely autobiographical account of Powers's family and his father's death. Although his first two novels received almost uniform critical praise, I would argue that they are mediocre works with a somewhat narrow scope. With his third novel, *The Goldbug Variations*

(1991), Powers showed a new depth and maturity in content and style. *The GoldbugVariations* concerns a research librarian who tracks down and unfolds the story of the man who cracked the genetic code in the 1950s, Dr. Stuart Ressler. Tying musical theory to biology, *Goldbug* is astonishing in its scope. In his semiautobiographical *Galatea 2.2*, (1995) concerning his move back to the United States and his work on artificial intelligence with a cognitive scientist, Powers recalls what inspired him: "I wanted to write an encyclopedia of the Information Age" (215). He later explains: "I hoped my molecular genetics might transcribe, if not an encyclopedia of successful solutions to experience, at least some fossil record of the questions. I wanted my extended metaphors to mirror speculation in the widest lens" (257). Powers's efforts were met with critical praise as both *Galatea 2.2* and *The GoldbugVariations* were honored with a nomination from the National Book Critics Circle Award.

Powers's next novel, *Operation Wandering Soul* (1993), which concerns a disillusioned doctor in a pediatrics clinic and the sick children in his ward, was nominated for a National Book Award. In 1998, Powers published *Gain*, a novel which details the development of Clare Soap and Chemical, a huge corporation, over a hundred and fifty years, which intersects with the domestic narrative about a forty-two-year-old mother who is diagnosed with ovarian cancer due to her exposure to chemicals from the nearby Clare factory. *Gain* won the James Fenimore Cooper Prize for historical fiction from the Society of American Historians. Powers's most recent novel is *Plowing the Dark* (2000), which also tells two intersecting stories: one of a virtual reality laboratory in Seattle and the other of a kidnapped hostage in Lebanon. Like David Foster Wallace, Richard Powers has received the MacArthur "genius" grant and was the recipient of a Lannan Literary Award in 1999. As literary critic Laura Miller notes, "Powers has earned an as-yet-modest, but devoted readership (David Foster Wallace has called him one of the greatest novelists working today) writing brainy, intricate novels drunk on the delights of thought itself" (Miller, "The Salon Interview: Richard Powers" online).

While Wallace concerns himself more with the flotsam and jetsam of popular culture and entertainment, Richard Powers is more of an encyclopedic scientist turned novelist, who, like Wallace, changed directions in college from math and science to literature. In part due to his ten-year stay in Europe, Powers is much less attuned to American media and popular culture than Wallace. Still, Powers's narratives are distinctly hybrid, typically involving two competing narratives: one highly scientific and technical in the style of Thomas Pynchon and the other, a domestic and emotional account of "ordinary" people put in extraordinary circumstances, reminiscent of Raymond Carver. Powers notes, "So many of my books are dialogues between the little and big. There's this desire to see how the parts of the whole can see the whole, come to know it, suffer the consequences of it" (Miller, online). Like Wallace, Powers rebels against categories and conventions and maintains that "a book can either be a heart book or a head book" (ibid.). His ambition is admirable and enormous, nothing less than "to write something that's like us, namely all in one. There's this sense of wanting to get the big picture. Wanting to really see, get the aerial view.... That's a monumental thing that fiction can do" (ibid.).

For Powers, it is imperative that a contemporary novelist deal with the "utter technological transformation" in recent years and the "incredible turmoil that these technological revolutions are working on us" (Williams, "The Last Generalist," 54). Still, he sees the artistic benefits of vast and quick technological change. He emphasizes: "The turmoil is creating a kind of artistic renaissance.... American fiction at the present amazes me in its unprecedented innovation and range, its diversity and eclecticism. It's doing everything, all at once: There are so many good people writing, and it's hard to believe that they all belong to the same country" (ibid., 55). Like Wallace's, Powers's fiction is an alluring blend of comprehensive knowledge and emotional engagement. Powers seeks to elevate the novel into a superior cultural position in the contemporary world. He emphasizes: "I think that the novel's task is to describe where we find ourselves and how we live now. The novelist must take a good, hard look at the most central facts of contemporary life—technology and science. The 'information novel' shouldn't be a curiosity. It should be absolutely mainstream" (Blume online).

While I consider Wallace and Powers the most promising writers of their generation, I do not want to dismiss the many other, talented young American fiction writers whose work deserves critical exploration. Often grouped with Powers and Wallace in book reviews and praised by *The New Yorker* in 1998 as one of the twenty most talented American writers under forty, William T. Vollmann has produced a significant corpus of work since the late 1980s. In an recent ebullient review of Vollmann's most recent novel, *The Royal Family* (2000), Melvin Bukiet of Sarah Lawrence College claims: "I'll take him sentence for sentence over just about any writer in the country" (31).

Vollmann is a gifted hybrid journalist and fiction writer whose ambition and determination are impressive. Although now only in his early forties, Vollmann has already published seven novels, two short-story/nonfiction collections and two collections of travel writing. Unlike Wallace and Powers, whose novels rarely stray from America's shores, Vollmann's writing spans the world. He shares with Beat writers a predilection for travel and a fascination with those who stray from societal and sexual mores. Vollmann's worldwide fiction reached a pinnacle with his impressive travel collection, *The Atlas* (1998), a thematically linked compilation of vignettes and short stories set in every continent in the world, from the Northwest Territories in Canada to Outer Mongolia to Madagascar.

Vollmann is more daring and explorative than his contemporaries Wallace and Powers, and his global travels make for fascinating reading that is part memoir, part fiction and part autobiography. Born in Los Angeles in 1959, Vollmann attended Deep Springs College in California, a small agriculturally based school, for a year before transferring to Cornell University, where he graduated with a degree in Comparative Literature. Subsequently, the Hemingwayesque Vollmann traveled to Afghanistan, where he attempted to assist the Afghan rebels in their fight against the formerly communist Soviet Union. Vollmann details his failed and somewhat naive efforts in his nonfiction book, *An Afghanistan Picture Show* (1992). Still, Vollmann is especially prescient in identifying ethnic conflict and anti–American sentiment that helped lead to the establishment of the Taliban and was the primary breeding ground of Al Qaeda.

Since the mid–1980s, Vollmann has periodically been on the move. His home base in America is San Francisco, and a fair amount of his writing takes place in the decrepit "Tenderloin" region—*The Rainbow Stories* (1989), *Whores for Gloria* (1991) and *The Royal Family*. Within San Francisco and for that matter throughout the world, Vollmann gravitates toward and focuses upon the socially excluded or detritus of late capitalism: prostitutes, drug addicts, alcoholics, violence, hate groups along with the dead and the dying. He describes his attraction to the seedier side of life in his preface to *The Rainbow Stories*: "the prettiest thing is darkest darkness" (3). A muckraker, Vollmann uncovers the dismal lives of the lower class in order to create understanding for the socially stigmatized. Like his predecessor Hunter S. Thompson, Vollmann functions as a journalistic actor, a participant in the madness and despair that he witnesses and details. While his active journalism may not be innovative, his commentary is socially important.

Still, there is an element of self-absorption and egotism in Vollmann's approach which prevents me from grouping him with Wallace and Powers as a first-tier American fiction writer. In a way, Vollmann's work suffers from the same failings as that of Bret Easton Ellis. Both tend to focus on a rather narrow cross-section of American society. Ellis focuses upon the spectrum opposite that of Vollmann: young, wealthy, careless, emotionally deficient Americans (the Tom and Daisy Buchanans of the late twentieth century). However, to his credit, what should place him above Ellis is that Vollmann sees himself as something of a social redeemer and continually tries to broaden his horizons. Yet his social and political views are not always clear to the reader and hardly an asset to those around him. For instance, in *An Afghanistan Picture Show*, Vollmann admits that his assistance to the Afghan rebels was negligible (3). Yet in *The Atlas*, Vollmann describes a real-life circumstance in which he and a friend rescued an abused Cambodian prostitute. In the end, Vollmann's ethical intentions are ambiguous as he has admittedly procured the services of a number of prostitutes, who have become material for his fiction and nonfiction.

In prostitution, Vollmann sees and utilizes an overarching metaphor for contemporary life. In an interview, he emphasizes, "I think we're all prostitutes. We all do things that we otherwise wouldn't choose to do, for the sake of getting somewhere else" (McCaffery, "Interview with William Vollmann," 18). In a corrupt and amoral world dictated by greed, Vollmann sees prostitution as an exchange system no different from any other monetary exchange system and also a clear expression of the monetary economics he believes to be involved in all personal relationships. Hence, in the preface to *The Butterfly Stories* (1993), he calls prostitution "that most honest form of love" (2). For Vollmann, romantic idealized "love" is sorely lacking in the contemporary world and may never have existed except as a fictional concept. Vollmann's characters are typically lonely isolates, hanging by a thread financially and emotionally with little or no stable belief system or community to sustain them in a hostile world.

Vollmann's strengths as a writer outweigh his weakness in focusing on a narrow segment of contemporary American society. Among his strengths is his journalistic wanderlust to detail the entire world, like a roaming documentary filmmaker. Reminiscent of William Burroughs, who proclaimed in *Naked Lunch*, "there is only one thing a writer can write about: what is in front of his senses at the moment of writing.... I am a recording instrument" (221), Vollmann also declares in *The Rainbow Stories* that his function as a writer is also to be "a recording instrument" (3). With few exceptions, the bleak world Vollmann details is poverty stricken, war torn, nearly amoral, and governed almost entirely by economics. Still, Vollmann captures a hidden beauty, an altruism or basic goodness amongst the social and economic outcasts of the world. He points an accusatory finger at the negative ramifications of democratic free enterprise run amuck. The world which Vollmann perceives is one in which moderately wealthy Americans can dominate others with the almighty dollar and become ensnared in a Kurtz-like primitive locus of sex and violence. Indeed, Vollmann suggests that there is a cancer eating away at the core of the Western world.

Vollmann tries to explore the origins of this cancer of violence and greed he sees in the contemporary world within his ambitious revisionist history of the first settlements in North America. As Sven Birkets notes, the so-called Seven Dreams series (*The Ice Shirt, Fathers and Crows, The Rifles* and *Argall* published so far) are "large scale, deeply researched and energetically executed panels from North American history. They reflect, respectively, the tenth-century encounter of the Norse explorers and the indigenous Indian populations; the seventeenth-century Jesuit missions in Canada and the early nineteenth-century search by traders for the Northwest passage" (Birkets, 45). Vollmann's most significant contributions thus far are his journalistic fictions, which I explore in Chapter 2.

The next tier of young American fiction writers haven't yet produced as large and notable a body of work as Wallace, Powers and Vollmann, but their work is worthy of academic exploration. Among these writers, Neal Stephenson (b. 1959) is perhaps the most impressive. Stephenson is even more scientifically astute than Powers, especially in the burgeoning fields of computer technology and information theory. Stephenson's first two novels received little critical attention. *The Big U* (1984) is an insider's account of life at a major research university thrown into pandemonium by violent riots, and *Zodiac: An Eco-Thriller* (1988) is an account of a renegade James Bond–like environmental savior who tries to protect the world from toxin-spewing corporations. Stephenson's real breakthrough came with *Snow Crash* in 1992. Set in the not-so-distant future, *Snow Crash* envisions an America (and world) teetering on the edge of environmental collapse, in which a virtual reality space, the Metaverse, rivals the "real world" for precedence. Stephenson's follow-up, *The Diamond Age* (1995), continues in his scientific exploration of the possible future and the impact of media and technological advances. Set in a neo–Victorian society, *The Diamond Age* displays a world in which nanotechnology, the concept of using microscopic computers to create virtually anything, has become possible. In this futuristic landscape, the distance has grown between the haves and the have-nots. One nanotech engineer, John Hackworth, steals a copy of "A Young Lady's Illustrated Primer" for his daughter, Fiona. The nanotechnology primer, a virtual reality interactive education for children, falls into the hands of a poor and abused child, Nell, and Stephenson describes her educational adventures while he spotlights the futuristic dystopia.

Stephenson's most recent novel is *Cryptonomicon* (1999), a 900-plus page novel reminiscent of Pynchon's *Gravity's Rainbow*. One of the two narratives focuses upon several mathematicians and scientists during World War II (among them Alan Turing) who are trying to break Axis communication codes. The present-day narrative centers upon the grandchildren of the World War II codebreakers who create an offshore data haven in Southeast Asia. To top off Stephenson's already impressive writing resume, his most recent publication is *In the Beginning ... Was the Command Line* (2000), a 150-page nonfiction essay which discusses the status of personal computing systems and in which Stephenson evaluates the four main systems currently operating (Mac OS, Windows, Linux, BeOs).

Stephenson has justly received a good deal of critical praise since the publication of *Snow Crash*. As one reviewer notes, "When it comes to depicting the nerd mind-set, no one tops Stephenson. His predecessors in the cyberpunk science-fiction movement (writers like William Gibson and Bruce Sterling) depicted hackers as moody James Deans in leather. Stephenson lays out the way they really think and act—awkward, chatty mensches whose insistence on logic makes them borderline nut cases" (Levy, 92). His influence extends from the general public to hardcore tech workers. "Everyone reads Neal Stephenson here," says Mike Paul, a manger in Microsoft's hardware division, "He's our inspiration" (ibid.).

Although not so technologically astute as Neal Stephenson, Douglas Coupland (b. 1961) has already published several culturally and literarily significant works. He achieved immediate commercial success with his first novel, *Generation X* (1991), an account of three overeducated, angst-ridden twenty-somethings who effectively drop out of corporate society and try to live unfettered by American culture. Part of *Generation X*'s success had to do with the coemergence of "grunge" music from the Pacific Northwest during the early 1990s and the unexpected critical and commercial success of independent films such as Steven Soderburgh's *Sex, Lies and Videotape* (1989) and Richard Linklater's *Slacker* (1991). Along with Coupland's novel, these cultural phenomena contributed to the now seemingly accepted label of an entire American generation as Generation X.[16]

However, Coupland rebelled against the label, and after another popular-culture-savvy novel, *Shampoo Planet* (1992), he turned moralizer and more serious fiction writer. Beginning with *Life After God* (1994), a collection of bleak but touching vignettes and short stories about young people searching for meaning in an isolating culture, Coupland investigated ways to frame contemporary lives other than by religion, family or community. One possible frame, Coupland determined, is computer technology, which he investigated in his next novel, *Microserfs* (1995). *Microserfs* depicts a group of renegade Microsoft workers who try to start a new company and achieve satisfying social lives. Coupland's most recent novels, *Girlfriend in a Coma* (1998), *Miss Wyoming* (2000) and *All Families Are Psychotic* (2001), continue in his search for meaning amidst the popular-culture detritus of North America.

Coming from a vastly different background, Native American writer

Sherman Alexie has already published an impressive body of work, despite his youth. Alexie, a Spokane/Coeur d'Alene Native American, was born on an Indian reservation in 1966. He has already published three novels, nine books of poetry and two collections of short stories. Alexie's most recent fiction depicts the conflicts and intersection points between American popular culture and Native American folklore and culture. The result is a hybrid culture, populated by individuals with hybrid identities. In *Reservation Blues* (1995), legendary bluesman Robert Johnson arrives at a Spokane reservation, giving his guitar to Native American Thomas-Builds-a-Fire, whose rock 'n' roll band subsequently achieves widespread success. Alexie's *Indian Killer* (1996) details a serial killer who scalps white men in Seattle.

The multitalented Alexie has also written and coproduced an independent film, *Smoke Signals* (1998), loosely based on his short-story collection, *The Lone Ranger and Tonto Fistfight in Heaven* (1993). *Smoke Signals* won the audience award for the most popular film at the Sundance film festival. He also wrote and directed the film *The Business of Fancy Dancing* (2002), which premiered at the Sundance film festival. Alexie's recent *The Toughest Indian in the World* (2000) explores urban Indians who work as lawyers, writers and other professionals. As Alexie comments, "I'm the first practitioner of the Brady Bunch school of Native American literature.... I'm a twenty-first century Indian who believes in the twenty-first century" (Brewster, 23).

Similar to Sherman Alexie, Michele Serros is a young, multitalented fiction writer, poet and performer whose writings investigate and detail the hybrid identities forged from the merging of Latino culture and American popular culture. Born in 1966 in Oxnard, California, Serros attended Santa Monica Community College and UCLA for seven years, while concurrently working at a number of service and media jobs which she describes in some of her stories. While an undergraduate at UCLA, Serros published a collection of her poems and short stories, *Chicana Falsa: Stories of Love, Death and Oxnard* (1993). *Chicana Falsa* sold slowly at first and then gradually gained a devoted following through California (and beyond), especially within Latino literature circles. Her books are now frequently used in high school and college classrooms throughout California (Sherwin online). She was also "selected by the Poetry Society of America and the Getty Research Institute to have her poetry placed on MTA buses throughout Los Angeles County" ("Michelle Serros" online). Serros's most recent publication is *How to Be a Chicana Role Model* (2000), which continues her quest toward the reinterpretation of ethnicity in contemporary America. In addition to her writing and frequent speaking engagements throughout California classrooms, Serros is also a frequent contributor to National Public Radio and has released a spoken word CD, "Selected Stories from *Chicana Falsa*" on Mouth Almighty/Mercury Records ("Michelle Serros" online).

Now that I have introduced the major subjects of my discussion, I would like to begin a closer examination of their works in the context of contemporary American culture.

2 *Hybrid Desires*

Although I am a young professional with limited financial resources, I am neither destitute nor deprived. With a relatively meager income, I am able to rent a modest apartment, which objectively can be seen as an opulent pleasure dome with a wide variety of creature comforts. Whereas during their youth, my parents had to suffer through brutal Eastern summers, central heat and air conditioning keep the temperature in my apartment at a pleasant seventy degrees year-round; my cable television provides me with sixty channels of everything from science fiction to sports; my modem connects me to the seemingly limitless information scope of the Internet. My bountiful CD collection provides me with a wide variety of musical choices from Mahler to the Clash. If I grow hungry, I need not cook or even shop. I can order food and groceries to be delivered to my doorstep. Aside from the times I teach and work, I need not leave my apartment.

Compared to people's lives of fifty or a hundred years ago, my life is unimaginably luxurious, but I take my luxuries for granted. In fact, I would argue that those same luxuries can be dangerous. Instead of appreciating what I already have, I desire more and consider these years in training to be a financial sacrifice. I want a larger home, a better car, more creature comforts, and greater financial security. Am I selfish, greedy, even unappreciative? Perhaps, but if so, I am no different from most young Americans. In fact, because I have rejected a financially lucrative career in favor of academics, I consider myself to be less materialistic than most.

As I believe my case to be typical, I want to begin by claiming that never before has such a large proportion of Americans lived such pleasurable, easy lives as we do now, especially those from my generation, Generation X, who have never really known deprivation or great social upheaval. Throughout Western history from Plato and Socrates to the eighteenth-century philosophers Jeremy Bentham and John Stuart Mill, intellectuals have debated and discussed the changing nature and ethics of pleasure and desire. These issues still affect contemporary American literature and culture and play a large role in the fiction of the authors I'm investigating.

Since the 1950s, critics have argued that there exists a growing generational shift in America, signified by homogeneity and passive acceptance of socially mediated identities. In his groundbreaking sociological text, *The Lonely Crowd* (1950), David Riesman suggests that the post–World War II generation has become more peer oriented or other directed than earlier, inner-directed generations, who were "mainly assured by the internalization of adult authority" (v). Implicit in Riesman's argument is that the post–World War II generation lacks character and a firm sense of their own individual identity. These new other-directed people "live in a group milieu and lack the inner-directed person's capacity to go it alone" (26). For Riesman, this new mold of American is preoccupied with being liked and securely fitting into a social network.

Riesman's claims are insightful when placed in context with the largely conformist mentality of the 1950s, which helped spark McCarthy's Communist witch hunts and lauded the benefits of the aptly named "organization man." However, the social activists of the 1960s fought against the very conformity that Riesman identifies, and their work helped recenter focus upon individuals, who seemingly became more inner directed through their pursuit of self-actualization. Were the 1960s really the beginning of a brave new socially aware and equal America? Certainly, there were great leaps forward made in civil, gender and race rights, but the revolutionary idealism of the 1960s did not last, rather, giving way to the more hollow, self-indulgent 1970s.

In the late 1970s, Christopher Lasch followed in David Riesman's footsteps of overarching social critique of America in *The Culture of Narcissism* (1978). Lasch begins by proposing that the Vietnam War, economic stagnation and a loss of belief in political leaders led to mass malaise and pessimism in late 1970s' America. In some ways Lasch's critique is prescient and pertains to today, especially in his claim that the contemporary narcissist "demands immediate gratification and lives in a state of restless, perpetually unsatisfied desire" (xvi). Lasch bemoans our preoccupation with the present as contributing to a lack of regard for the past and future. In fact, he claims that "Our culture's indifference to the past—which easily shades over into active hostility and rejection—furnishes the most telling proof of that culture's bankruptcy" (xviii). Still, Lasch's scathing critique of Americans as overwhelmingly hedonistic and self-absorbed reeks of arrogance and condescension. Turn-of-the-millennium American culture is not bankrupt; yet the ample opportunity for satisfying personal desires results in many hidden, even unacknowledged costs, which, taken together, could lead to future cultural decay.

However, I will not suggest or agree with Lasch that hedonism or narcissism is an unqualified evil, with no redeeming ramifications what-soever. Indeed, to some extent the subjects of *Hybrid Fictions* are great, self-indulgent narcissists who are so confident of their abilities that they often write gargantuan, encyclopedic fictions, tackling a huge number of subjects or composing self-involved, Norman Mailer–style narratives in the tradition of *Advertisements for Myself* (1959).[1] Following Lasch, I want to propose that in the 1990s, the media and popular culture exaggerated our natural inclinations toward narcissism and self-indulgence. Further-more, the atmosphere of political correctness caused individuals to repress their own narcissistic tendencies.

In contemporary America, it has become easier than ever to satisfy personal desires, complicated by a culture-wide demand for instanta-neous personal happiness and a rejection of nearly all forms of sorrow and depression as correctable mental illnesses. At the cost of ignoring eudemonistic happiness, contentment based more on one's character and actions, many choose solely to pursue hedonistic pleasures. However, preoccupation with hedonistic desires leads to a range of larger, culture-wide problems, from social isolation to environmental damage to ethnic and class conflicts.

One goal common to several of the authors I'm investigating is that they (especially Wallace, Eggers, Vollmann and Powers) want to awaken complacent Americans from their self-focused pursuit of hedonistic plea-sures. If that is not possible, then their desire is to make more people, at the very least, cognizant of the larger forces that can dominate and even destroy them. Their target audience is not only amoral, reckless pleasure seekers, but also "normal," everyday consumers, the very backbone of American society. In the first two-thirds of this chapter, I will investigate the different manners in which these four authors approach the prob-lems of pleasure, desire and happiness, both in terms of form and content. Then, for the remaining portion of this chapter, I will address contem-porary theories of depression in reference to culture and literature.

Dave Eggers, a Generation X enfant terrible, represents hedonistic desire run amuck, but he realizes his own self-absorption and wishes to break down the wall not only between himself and the reader, but between himself and his entire generation. David Foster Wallace, meanwhile, takes the role of cultural critic, observing but distancing himself from the ram-pant consumer and consumption ethos he perceives to be governing and increasing American appetites. William Vollmann shows how hedonistic pleasures can exacerbate loneliness and isolation and lead to death through drug addiction and AIDS from promiscuous sexual behavior. Finally, Richard Powers takes the role of a new historicist and focuses on the role of corporations, from the mid-nineteenth century to the pre-sent time, in nurturing consumerism that exacerbates personal desires.

While all four writers are on similar moral high ground in that they crit-icize American culture for its preoccupation with the fulfillment of hedo-nistic desires, they employ different fictional techniques. Eggers plays with the memoir form, while Wallace toys with journalism. Vollmann's writings are globally expansive, sexually explicit and shocking, while Powers is serious, historical, scientific and erudite. No one approach is intrinsically superior. Taken together, these four writers provide a com-prehensive critique of one of the chief problems facing contemporary American society.

Resisting and Questioning Desire: How to Enjoy Being Awkward and Miserable with David Foster Wallace

Two key essays by David Foster Wallace illustrate his main cultural critique. This is not to suggest that cultural critique is the only force at work in these essays, for Wallace also employs important formalistic devices such as his minute-observation-style journalism often written in diary for-mat. He also offers caustic comedy through scathing critiques of self-indul-gent pleasure seekers. However, Wallace is not a grumpy nouveau Puritan who rationalizes or projects his own repressive tendencies onto others. Indeed, as I have established in my previous chapter, Wallace has personal knowledge of the dangers of drug excess and self-indulgence. Rather, there are conflicting forces at work within these essays (and possibly within Wallace as well) in which he struggles with battling his personal desire for passive hedonistic pleasures, wanting to please his audience, and try-ing to convince his audience not to be preoccupied with the self-inter-ested pursuit of hedonistic pleasures. Wallace's trifold goals are somewhat contradictory. How can a writer please the reader and at the same time convince readers not to give in so easily to their own personal pleasures? Wallace walks a thin line between personal self-absorption and near mis-anthropic derision. Still, by complicating the issue beyond a simplistic binary of pleasure and misery, as well as happiness and depression, he uncovers a middle ground between hedonism and asceticism.

Wallace's essays "Getting Away from Already Pretty Much Being Away from It All" and "A Supposedly Fun Thing I'll Never Do Again" (both contained in *A Supposedly Fun Thing I'll Never Do Again*) best illus-trate his central concerns. In the most seemingly "normal" of situations, Wallace finds at work the duplicitous forces of contemporary American society and insists that we not give ourselves over to personal pleasures so easily because there is little difference between hedonistic happiness and subsequent mindlessness. Here, Wallace is at his most convincing: In contemporary America, the desire to satisfy one's self has superceded the desire to be socially aware, largely due to the multiplicity of pleasurable entertainment forms in contemporary America. In essence, Wallace encourages eudemonistic happiness as a morally and personally superior alternative to hedonism.

Because Wallace has the difficult task of trying to convince the reader to resist or question personal desire, he uses the pleasurable form of comedy along with insightful, minute observation, interspersed with social critique. However, he aims not to seduce the audience into consumerism or personal pleasure as an advertiser would, but into self- and social evaluation and criticism. In that sense, Wallace is an antiadvertiser. Another way for an author to please the reader is by appealing to the reader's ego and by looking down upon less-informed others. Thereby, the reader can feel superior and more enlightened than others. Wallace doesn't want to be regarded as an arrogant grouse, so he presents himself in an unflattering manner to set the reader at ease.

In "Getting Away from Pretty Much Being Away from It All," Wallace describes the ongoings at an Illinois state fair. Wallace's immediately implicit, although never stated desire, is to gain the trust of the readers. To do this, he appears to be indifferent and nonthreatening, claiming that his real interest in covering the story for a "swanky East-coast" magazine is "getting into rides and stuff for free" (83). Furthermore, Wallace distinguishes and emphasizes his difference from the others. While the press room swarms with well-dressed reporters and is buttressed by farm hands, Wallace mentions his nondescript, sporty dress (84). Wallace's portrayal of himself as an everyman figure makes him seem a credible, trustworthy source.

During the fair, Wallace literally stands at the sidelines, observing, marveling and ridiculing the antics of such fairgoers as the atavistic, sexually suggestive male barkers, who yell in microphones, "You got to get it up to get it in" and "testes" instead of "testing" (97). Also, a few of the barkers purposely stop a ride in midflight to look up the dress of Wallace's female companion, whom Wallace says they look at "like she's food" (ibid.). As time passes, it becomes clear that Wallace views the fairgoers as being the true "exhibit" and he describes them in less kind terms than the animals he sees. In part, Wallace's attitude seems to be fueled by near-misanthropic scorn, but these fairgoers seem to be the casualties of consumerism and contemporary America, as they have become extraordinarily self-absorbed, almost to the point of complete passivity. Indeed, his apocalyptic vision of a consumer-driven America appears to be typical low- to middle-class rural Midwesterners, whom he calls "K-Mart People." According to Wallace, they "are sharp-voiced and snap at their families. They're the type you see slapping their kids in supermarket checkouts (120–21). Wallace's snide and somewhat condescending attitude toward "K-Mart people" might not work if he didn't self-deprecatingly portray himself as an aloof, disengaged person who cannot participate in the activity around him (especially the amusement rides) because he is, as his sister has described him, "lifesick" (106).

Because part of Wallace's aim is to provoke thought and closer scrutiny, he provides minute, critical observations of the fair and its ongoing activities.[2] Wallace's targeted audience seems to be urban professionals, unfamiliar with rural America or the Midwest. He acts as an inquisitive tour guide to rural life, relating a huge number of observations and anecdotes about animals. He compares the faces of horses to "coffins" (92), gives an in-depth description of the nostrils of a cow and proudly discovers that "Swine have fur!" (94). With his characteristic humor, Wallace describes the face of one cow as being "eerily reminiscent of former British P.M. Winston Churchill" (93). Thereby, Wallace writes like a human camera, zooming in upon people and objects and then zooming out, with an almost inexhaustible curiosity to discover the inner workings of people and places, but also to discover how they fit into the larger picture. Wallace's technique is that of voyeur who wants to give the reader as full a description and interpretation as possible of the action. The reader is thereby encouraged to dig deeper, to think more and to contemplate his or her surroundings.

In part, Wallace searches for a villain or at least an entity responsible for the rampant consumption ethic; accordingly, he casts an accusatory figure toward corporations. He sees the state fair as a microcosm of the larger themes of consumerism and consumption. Even in a seemingly innocuous setting, Wallace uncovers the rampant effects and hidden, but staggering, power of American capitalism and industry. Everywhere Wallace looks, he sees the evidence of corporate sponsors from McDonald's to Miller Genuine Draft to Morton Commercial Structure Corporation (87). The state fair then merely becomes an opportunity for corporations to showcase their supplies and lure visitors into another monetary exchange system. Instead of family farmers showing off their products and animals, corporations lord over the state fair, the atmosphere and depersonalizing the land, which Wallace claims has become a "factory" (92). Reading the essay, one becomes aware of how American appetites have literally and figuratively grown and that in a country of plenty, the main choices seem to be the selection of exchange systems according to their potential for personal pleasure. Wallace notes:

> There is, in this state with its origin and reason in food, a strong digestive subtheme running all through the '93 Fair. In a way, we're

all here to be swallowed up. The Main Gate's maw admits us, slow tight-packed masses move peristaltically along complex systems of branching paths, engaging in complex cash-and-energy transfers at the villi alongside the paths, and are finally—both filled and depleted—expelled out of exits designed for heavy flow [131].

Not only is there a strong digestive subtheme, but that there are also economic, monetary and even Marxist implications in Wallace's choices of metaphor and analysis. In this essay, he wants to awaken readers to the knowledge that they are one in a much larger corporation dominated country and that individuals can be dehumanized by mass industrialization and privatization.

For Wallace, the enemy is wealth, privilege and the relentless pursuit of hedonistic happiness. He argues that a substantial number of Americans have been pampered (himself no exception), and for many, the only important decisions in life are determining which choices will be the most personally pleasurable. Wallace fears that in their pursuit of hedonistic happiness, now more realizable than ever, many Americans are gradually losing their critical-thinking skills. Nowhere is this more apparent than in Wallace's account of his week-long adventures on a luxury cruise ship, courtesy of a never-named magazine in the title essay, "A Supposedly Fun Thing I'll Never Do Again." In "Getting Away from Already Being Pretty Much Away from It All," Wallace uses the relatively innocuous setting of the Illinois state fair as a site for philosophical discussion of the rampant corporation based consumerism endemic in contemporary American culture. Similarly, on board the cruise ship, Wallace catalogs the dangerous excesses of wealthy Americans who seem to be secretly dominated by the ever-present corporate world in which resides real, Foucaultian power. From the very beginning of the essay, Wallace's manifold voices of ennui, anger, disgust and humor compete as he catalogs his observations at the end of the cruise:

> I have smelled what suntan lotion smells like spread over 21000 pounds of hot flesh. I have been addressed as "Mon" in three different nations. I have watched 500 upscale Americans dance the Electric Slide.... I have been thoroughly, professionally, and as promised beforehand—pampered. I have, in dark moods, viewed and logged every type of erythema, keratinosis, pre-melanomic lesion, liver spot, eczema, wart, papular cyst, potbelly, femoral cellulite, varicosity, collagen and silicone enhancement, bad tint, hair transplants that have not taken.... I have felt as bleak as I've felt since puberty, and have filled almost three Mead notebooks trying to figure out whether it was Them or just Me [256–58].

I would argue that it is not merely Wallace. His snide cynicism is a Generation X hallmark, yet there is intelligent reason behind the sarcasm.

Wallace implicates the other passengers for their mindless willingness to give themselves over completely to the hedonistic pursuit of happiness. For Wallace, underneath the social niceties, the cruise is ultimately a cold, economic venture, engineered by corporate minds whose sole purpose is to produce economic profits, using any legal methods at their disposal, no matter how devious. Rather than most guests who treat the staff as animalistic servants, Wallace cannot ignore the oppressive class structure of the cruise staff, the majority of whom work themselves to the bone to please the passengers, presumably because they fear the wrath of their less numerous but much more wealthy and powerful superiors.

As time progresses, Wallace uses the cruise to show the extent to which self-serving greed and self-absorption have come to dominate American lives. Although he never states it, Wallace implicitly argues that the largest danger facing Americans is their desire for pure physical or sensual pleasure, which requires that a person be essentially mindless, not cognizant of the larger world and certainly not sympathetic or compassionate, which leaves them prey to outside domination (or hypnotization). The purported main objective of the cruise is to fulfill the passenger's every need or desire without any effort on the part of the passengers. While the passengers claim that they are there to relax, Wallace argues that they are merely rationalizing due to their shame of self-indulgence. Examining the cruise brochure, Wallace sees that not only are the passengers promised pleasure, but their cruise experiences have already been interpreted for them: "In the cruise brochure's ads, you are excused from doing the work of constructing the fantasy. The ads do it for you. The ads, therefore, don't flatter your adult agency, or even ignore it—they supplant it.... The promise is not that you can experience great pleasure, but that you will. That they'll make certain of it" (267). Essentially, the cruise promises passengers the ability to do "absolutely nothing" (268), which greatly disturbs Wallace, who comically asks the reader:

> How long has it been since you did Absolutely Nothing? I know exactly how long it's been for me. I know how long it's been since I had every need met choicelessly from someplace outside me, without my having to ask or even acknowledge that I needed. And that time I was floating, too, and the fluid was salty, and warm but not too-, and if I was conscious at all, I'm sure I felt dreadless, and was having a really good time, and would have sent postcards to everyone wishing they were here [268].

In essence, the cruise offers the passengers, many of whom are elderly, the ability to become completely passive infants once again. In our psychologically sensitive era that emphasizes nurturing "the inner child," returning to an infantile state can seem appealing, but Wallace asks us to resist the urge to give ourselves over to this form of intellectually devastating pleasure. While the cruise claims to be able to satiate the infantile part of a person that wants indiscriminately, Wallace retorts, "but the Infantile part of me is insatiable—in fact its whole essence or dasein or whatever lies in its apriori [*sic*] insatiability" (317).

Indeed, the cruise ship works as a form of tyranny or mental slavery and serves as a microcosm of a greater societal problem of the easy accessibility of hedonistic pleasures and the intellectual damage that focusing primarily upon personal pleasure can do. Wallace also becomes bothered by what he believes to be the phony kindness and consideration offered to him by the crewmates. As an example, he describes what he calls "the professional smile," which he notices during the cruise and elsewhere in American society. Wallace pinpoints fraudulence inherent in an increasingly isolated country that provides a false sense of intimacy and concern in order to manipulate customers or lull them into a false sense of security. He describes the professional smile as:

> The smile that doesn't quite reach the smiler's eyes and that signifies nothing more than a calculated attempt to advance the smiler's own interests by pretending to like the smilee.... This is dishonest, but what's sinister is the cumulative effect that such dishonesty has on us: since it offers a perfect facsimile or simulacrum of goodwill without goodwill's real spirit, it messes with our heads and eventually starts upping our defenses even in cases of genuine smiles and real art and true goodwill. It makes us feel confused and lonely and impotent and angry and scared. It causes despair [289].

In a consumer-oriented society, people have become further duplicitous. Thereby, it has become increasingly difficult to trust others if they appear kind and considerate when it may actually be a self-serving façade. Yet, in advertisements and commercials, corporations contend that their primary objective is to please the customer. For instance, McDonald's current slogan is "We love to see you smile," combined with snapshots of employees who flash Wallace's very "professional smile." In truth, though, what the owners of McDonald's truly mean by their slogan is that "we want you to be happy so you will come back to buy more food and make our corporation stronger and each of us more independently wealthy." Along similar lines, Wallace finds himself unable to enjoy the cruise because it, like the brochure, "seems to care about me. But it doesn't, not really, because first and foremost it wants something from me" (290).

In his essay on the cruise ship, Wallace focuses on people with wealth or power as the focus for his cultural criticism. Specifically, Wallace targets one specific spoiled passenger, eighteen-year-old Mona, as an example of how wealth and privilege can intellectually and emotionally damage a person. Not only does Mona only agree to attend Penn State if she would receive a car with four-wheel drive, she is actively hostile and demeaning to others around her, including her wealthy grandparents, who give her a hundred dollars every night to spend however she chooses. Wallace explains: "Mona never once said thank you for the money. She also rolled her eyes at just about everything her grandparents said, a habit that quickly drove me up the wall" (282).

At the same time, Wallace doesn't excuse himself from the negative aftereffects of being spoiled. After only a few days of the luxurious cruise, he becomes easily habituated and even begins to believe that his room isn't cleaned spotlessly enough, that room service doesn't come quickly enough, and that his food and cabin, which he thought to be exquisite the first couple of days, have substantial imperfections. Furthermore, when Wallace's cruise ship docks at a Caribbean country with other cruise ships, he longingly looks at the other ships and bitterly imagines how life on one of the other ships must be better. In the end, though, he declares: "a subsequent re-entry into the adult demands of landlocked real-world life wasn't nearly as bad as a week of absolutely nothing had led me to fear" (353). While Wallace chooses the trials and tribulations of the real world, he suggests that most of the wealthy, self-absorbed passengers will continue in their relentless and socially damaging, hedonistic pursuit of happiness, with little or no concern for the social and personal welfare of others. The reader then is left with Wallace's cynical, derisive but pleasing prose, which encourages thought and questioning rather than apathy and passive acceptance.

Henderson, the Generation X King: Dave Eggers's Hybrid, Narcissistic Memoir

To a key extent, Wallace is caught between a rock and a hard place, wanting to be both sincere and serious but also feeling compelled to be cynical and sarcastic, in order to address and possibly even entertain a wary audience. He might want to be regarded as authentic, but he is also well aware that postmodernity denies the efficacy of literary realism. Just as Wallace appears torn between the desire to please and socially awaken his audience, Dave Eggers consciously or unconsciously battles with these same conflicting impulses in his hybrid memoir/novel/cultural critique, *A Heartbreaking Work of Staggering Genius* (2000).

While Wallace takes the role of a cultural critic, attempting to at least intellectually distance himself from the hedonistic self-indulgence he perceives to be running rampant in American society, Eggers gives into his hedonistic desires, wanting to be front and center rather than lurking in the periphery as Wallace does. Born in 1970, Eggers is a quintessential Generation X writer, if not a Generation X enfant terrible. He represents hedonistic desire run amuck, but he realizes his own self-absorption and wishes to break down the wall not only between himself and the reader, but between himself and his entire generation.

In a sense, Eggers's memoir, a coming-of-age story in which a twenty-something tries to reconcile his idealism and passion to the demands of the real world, describes the common compromises that many postcollegiate Americans make. Indeed, Eggers works hard to maintain his "everyman" status, but he cannot mask his desire to distinguish himself from most people and become a celebrated public figure. His title alone, with its qualifier "staggering," is part shameless promotion, part ironic statement and part boastful arrogance. Eggers is David Riesman's archetypal other-directed person, whose primary purpose is to be liked and appreciated. Eggers even goes so far as to criticize himself and his book in order to avoid intimidating the reader. I certainly would not argue that Eggers is a bona-fide genius or that his story is completely heartbreaking, yet I don't think he believes either outlandish claim himself. Or does he? Eggers's narrative works on many levels, and his seemingly modest self-effacement may actually be a front for his true narcissism. In the preface, Eggers describes what led to his decision to use the title and immediately preempts criticism about it by absolving himself of complete responsibility. While first acknowledging the reader's possible reservations about the title, Eggers describes the different titles considered for the book, such as *A Heartbreaking Work of Death and Embarrassment, An Astounding Work of Courage and Strength* and *Memories of a Catholic Boyhood*, along with reasons for why each was dismissed and why *A Heartbreaking Work of Staggering Genius* was eventually chosen. He anticipates the reader's attraction to the title:

> Yes, it caught your eye. First you took it at face value, and picked it up immediately. "This is just the sort of book for which I have been looking!" Many of you, particularly those among you who seek out the maudlin and melodramatic, were struck by the "Heartbreaking" part. Others thought the "Staggering Genius" element seemed like a pretty good recommendation.... In the end, one's only logical interpretation of the title's intent is as a) a cheap kind of joke b) buttressed by an interest in lamely executed titular innovation (employed, one suspects, only to shock) which is c) undermined of course by the cheap joke aspect and d) confused by the creeping feeling one gets that the author is dead serious in his feeling that the title is an accurate description of the content, intent, and quality of the book [xxiii].

Eggers's hyperbole is a Generation X blend of ironic exaggeration, sarcasm, and self-deprecation, all of which are concurrently self-serving and self-effacing.[3] He is well aware of the importance of marketing techniques, and his "genius" may very well be his ability to maintain a sense of disequilibrium, whereby the reader cannot ascertain which of the four logical interpretations to choose. At the same time, Eggers's title is a serious manifestation of the hopes of his literary generation in their common quest to bridge what they perceive to be the growing gap between popular and serious literature, believing that the former is too melodramatic and flimsy and that the latter is too cerebral and distanced. Like most hybrid writers of his generation, Eggers aims to efface or blur the distinction between the highbrow and the lowbrow, which many believe to have been further exaggerated by the ascension of literary theory and postmodernity.

A.H.W.O.S.G. is Eggers's account of his early to mid-twenties, a period in which both of his parents died from cancer and he was left to care for his eight-year-old brother, Christopher, or Toph. A hundred and fifty years ago, Eggers's story would have made for an appropriately bleak Dickensian tale, but Eggers is himself a product of America's televisual culture. Consequently, he follows the now accepted media device of mixing comedy with drama, in order to appeal to a larger audience and reflect the ever-shifting mood of American culture. The result is a half-mocking, half-serious memoir, written in a manic-depressive style. As a person schooled in various media forms, Eggers demonstrates an impressive knowledge of marketing and self-promotion. Unlike Norman Mailer's self-promotion as intellectually and physically macho, Eggers shamelessly promotes and then demolishes his own self-image. Concurrently, Eggers straddles a thin line between the tragic descriptions of the pain and suffering involved in the death of his parents along with the comic and manic highs and anxiety-fraught lows involved in trying to raise his young brother and start a magazine and change the world for the better. He is weighed down by amazingly large desires and emotions.

At times, it is difficult to evaluate the seemingly protean Eggers, whose positions and moods seem to switch like television channels. Should his vibrancy and energy be respected or considered as rampant self-interest? Eggers does appear to be a virtual fountainhead of emotion. However, he doesn't seem to have a proper channel for his intense passion. Consequently, his frustrated passion often borders on anger at times, such as when he describes driving with his brother, Toph, on Highway 1, near San Francisco. In part, Eggers's anger might understandably be motivated by the death of his parents, but it can also be seen as a young American's ubiquitous, desperate cry for fulfillment in a culture which creates and feeds on desires but offers no guarantees of satisfaction. In a sense, Eggers is a perfect example of the kind of greedy, self-absorbed hedonist whom David Foster Wallace criticizes in his essays. Yet, Eggers has suffered a great familial loss and is faced with the great responsibility of caring for his eight-year-old brother.

> Look at us, goddamn it, the two of us slingshoted from the back side of the moon, greedily cartwheeling toward everything we are owed. Every day we are collecting on what's coming to us, each day we're being paid back for what is owed, what we deserve, with interest, with some extra motherfucking consideration—we are *owed*, goddamn it— and so we are expecting everything, everything [43].

Of course, Eggers isn't owed anything and his expectations are unrealizable and unwarranted. While this description sounds adolescent and self-absorbed, it also a vivid, emotionally wrought description of the aftermath of the loss of loved ones and Eggers's passionate desire for freedom.

However, Eggers's almost revolutionary fervor to forge social change separates him from the hedonistic mass of his generation and gives his narrative intellectual weight. Free from his parents, he becomes more determined to create a new and improved world. However, it is difficult to determine how exactly Eggers believes that he and his generation could help change the country for the better except in minor ways. Once again, his supposed revolutionary fervor may be fueled by arrogant self-absorption. After moving to San Francisco and starting up his 'zine, *Might Magazine*, Eggers declares of the community of youth-fueled magazines/ 'zines/e-journals in San Francisco:

> It's like the 60s! Look! Look, we say to one another, at the imbalances, the glaring flaws of the world, aghast, amazed. Look at how things are! Look at how, for instance, there are all these homeless people! Look at how they have to defecate all over the streets, where we have to walk! Look at how high rents are! Look at how banks charge these hidden fees when you use their ATM's! And Ticketmaster! Have you heard about these service charges? How if you charge your tickets over the phone, they charge you, like $2 for every goddamn ticket? [155].

However noble and inspiring Eggers's passion is, his desire to change nominal fees is hardly revolutionary and rather trivial. Furthermore, Eggers's use of exclamation points undercuts any serious analysis of his proposal. He mentions the homeless only inasmuch as they affect him. Is Eggers unwilling to be serious because it might compromise his audience? He is still playing the role of a showman and doesn't seem willing or able to let his guard down. Rather, he offers a laundry list of complaints.

Yet, to be fair, Eggers desires more to inspire or awaken his readers emotionally than to forge social changes. In part, he does not play the role of a serious social revolutionary because he and his generation have grown up wary of any and all real or would-be political figures.

Eggers partially wants to be an Abbie Hoffman for the 1990s, but he realizes that social activism and fervor-inspiring social issues have tapered off since the 1960s. Like Wallace, he implicitly recognizes that one of the biggest threats facing young Americans is their own self-indulgence. Thereby, as a person with revolutionary fervor but without the exact issues or means to forge social change, Eggers battles both himself and his intended audience. Like many of his generation, Eggers is pulled in several different directions simultaneously. He wants to be tender and emotionally honest but is suspicious of sentiment. Eggers is boastful but self-deprecating; he projects a manic joy but has a gnawing sense of loss and loneliness, manifest in his almost desperate attempts to reach the audience with his use of gimmicks. He is greedily self-absorbed but hopelessly devoted to the well-being of his brother. Eggers is caught in a dilemma between sincerity and skepticism that is endemic to writers of his generation.

Like Wallace, Eggers's sincere skepticism and earnest, confessional writing style reflect his desire to be regarded as a trustworthy narrator. However, he also wants to please his audience. Insightfully, Eggers recognizes that self-debasing confession appeals to readers, who are able to feel better about themselves and their personal shortcomings after an author confesses his or her own gross judgment errors. Indeed, Eggers pushes the envelope on "confessional" autobiography with a virtual tell-all in which he confesses the exact number of sexual partners he has had, his masturbatory habits and the precise recipes of the dinners he cooks for his brother. He even lists the phone numbers of his friends, using presumably real numbers (not the 555 prefix). He admits shameful secrets such as that he made love to his girlfriend the night of his father's funeral, that he sometimes engages in unsafe sex and that he fears he has contracted the HIV virus. Eggers opens his life up to the reader, so that the reader feels that he or she has been awarded a certain intimacy. This is one of the appeals of Eggers's memoir—it feeds on our voyeuristic desire as readers or watchers to know the most intimate (usually sexual) details of a person's life. Eggers is ready and willing to bare his life to the reader and feels no remorse for doing so:

> We feel that to reveal embarrassing or private things, like say masturbatory habits (for me, once a day, usually in the shower), we have given someone something, that like a primitive person fearing that a photographer will steal his soul, we identify our secrets, our pasts and their blotches, with our identity, that revealing our habits or

losses or deeds somehow makes one less of oneself. But it's just the opposite, more is more—more bleeding, more giving [188].

In a way, Eggers is correct in that revealing personal secrets helps make a person seem more human and trustworthy and gives the reader/viewer a more concrete image of the person. Eggers's memoir demonstrates the importance of tell-all in a memoir and that the more that a person has to tell and the more a person reveals, the more he or she will be remembered and, in a way, rewarded.

Despite the gravity of his subject matter, Eggers offers the reader further pleasures. Unlike David Foster Wallace, who tends to appeal to an intelligent, well-educated reader's ego while frequently forcing the reader to work hard to interpret the narrative, Eggers feels no shame in catering to passive individuals with short attention spans. Hence, *A.H.W.O.S.G.* begins with a list of six "Rules and Suggestions for Enjoyment of This Book." Eggers acts as a self-deprecating comedian with his comments, "There is no overwhelming need to read the preface. Really. It exists mostly for the author, and those who, after finishing the rest of the book, have for some reason found themselves stuck with nothing else to read" (vii). By doing this, Eggers helps to make general readers feel at ease. He is on their level, speaking to them, not at them. In fact, Eggers goes as far as telling the reader that he or she can skip the first three or four chapters and that the book thereafter is "kind of uneven" (vii). Furthermore, he emphasizes: "The author wishes to acknowledge that because this book is occasionally haha, you are permitted to dismiss it" (xxii). Again, Eggers's motives are questionable, for it is doubtful that he really wants his readers to dismiss his book as trivial. Rather, he is trying to sucker his audience into believing him to be somewhat inept. It may be that Eggers wants to gain the trust of cynical readers. In order to curry the favor of cynics, there is no better tactic than to mirror their sentiments, by being self-deprecating and emphasizing, as Eggers does, that the author "is like you" (xxiv).

While Eggers often appears to be sarcastic and careless, he concurrently appears sincere and serious. This leaves the reader with unresolved questions such as: Should Eggers be condemned for trivializing the death of his parents with comedy and sarcasm, or should his ability to find life-affirming mirth and laughter in an emotionally trying situation be applauded? In either case, like most hybrid writers of his generation, Eggers purposely and rebelliously defies categories and conventions, leaving important, unresolved questions of whether *A.H.W.O.S.G.* is tragedy or comedy or whether it is even a true memoir, considering Eggers admits that "this is not, actually, a work of pure nonfiction. Many parts have been fictionalized in varying degrees, for varying purposes" (ix).

Still, *A.H.W.O.S.G.* purports to be primarily a nonfiction memoir and, as such, derives a significant portion of its power from its supposed basis in truth. In the preface, Eggers takes the role of a vaudeville entertainer who offers gifts and gimmicks to the reader such as a digital version of his book with names changed according to the reader's desires (xxiii). Somewhat sophomoric in his attempt to cater to the reader's desires, Eggers also comprehends that memories are often appealing in the extent to which the reader can relate the narrative to his or her life. He offers his life as public domain or public property, and in that sense, his memoir could be interpreted as an altruistic gift to the reader. In yet another game-show-like gimmick in the preface, Eggers offers to send the reader an 18" × 24" chart which "maps out the entire book" for five dollars. Again, it is difficult to determine whether this is a genuine offer. Eggers does include a legitimate address for the publisher, Simon and Schuster, and there is no footnote indicating that the offers are made in jest. On the one hand, Eggers seems to be shamelessly scouring for additional money. Yet, on the other hand, he also mocks the excessive marketing and advertising tools that so many organizations use to lure consumers. Besides, it is doubtful that Eggers would get much demand for five-dollar thematic charts of his book, and it would take a bounty of buyers to create a significant profit. Furthermore, Eggers makes a seemingly ridiculous, but possibly genuine, offer of a five-dollar check to each of the first 200 readers of the book who write and prove to him that they understand the "many lessons" of his book (xxxv). All of these comedic ploys aim to lessen the distance between reader and writer and draw the reader into the narrative. His derision of marketing tools ironically helps market his own book.

While Eggers walks a thin line between self-effacement and self-deprecation, he is dramatically other directed and feels no guilt for his self-indulgent hedonism. He admits wanting to display his suffering because he hopes to gain sympathy and be acknowledged for his sufferings (xxvii). *A.H.W.O.S.G.* is not a self-help book focusing upon how to best come to grips with the loss of one's parents or loved ones. Although the aftereffects of the loss of his parents reverberate through his memoir, Eggers details the painful deaths of his parents only in the first forty pages. His memoir is more a bildungsroman of a typical young American (male) coming of age in a media-saturated society, familiar with and entrenched in popular culture, but also trying to forge some personal meaning.

That Eggers wishes to be the voice of his generation becomes apparent in the second half of his memoir. Like Douglas Coupland's exiles in *Generation X*, Eggers, his brother, his older sister and his friends move to California with the hope of reinventing their lives (and that of their generation) according to their own ethos. Despite his revolutionary zeal, Eggers does not devote himself to a nobler goal such as eradicating homelessness or improving urban life in San Francisco. Rather, his desire is to further his own narcissistic desires. However, Eggers's narcissism is kept somewhat in check by his role as a parent to his younger brother, Toph. Still, I would argue that Eggers's devotion to his brother is sparked in part by a desire to be even better liked. In fact, he admits to occasionally using his appearance of parental maturity to attract women.

While Eggers tries to raise his younger brother, he delves into the media world by starting up a 'zine called *Might Magazine*. A collection of twenty-somethings, the *Might Magazine* staff, headed by Eggers, attempt to be hipper and flashier than their competitors like *Wired Magazine* in part by promoting their magazine as reflecting their generation (Generation X). While Eggers's passion and determination are admirable, *Might Magazine* fizzles out after about a year. During that time, he tries many techniques to gain attention and a devoted readership, including taking a snapshot of several staff members and friends streaking on the beach and using it for the cover of an issue. Eggers also stages a faked celebrity death of former *Eight Is Enough* child star, Adam Rich, with the help of Rich himself. Even though *Might Magazine* praises the best and brightest of Eggers's generation such as the founders of Teach for America and the founders of Organize or Emigrate!, it is more of an outlet for Eggers's revolutionary idealism and energy. He describes some of the objectives of *Might Magazine* as deriding the "artifice" of student loads, college, work, marriage, makeup and the Grateful Dead (265). Cynicism sells to Eggers's target market, but his points of contention are dubious at best.

However much Eggers might enjoy his work on *Might Magazine*, his true desire is to become a celebrity. Eggers's self-indulgent narcissism becomes apparent when he applies for and secures an interview to star in a season of MTV's *The Real World*, a seminal "reality" television show dating from the early '90s, in which eight twenty-somethings from different backgrounds cohabit and supposedly face real-world conflicts and demands. In *A.H.W.O.S.G.*, Eggers includes over forty pages of dialogue between himself and the casting scout, during which he rattles his qualifications as a potential media star. Eggers's active and unabashed self-indulgence translates into long, detailed descriptions of his childhood, his friends, the deaths of his family members, and his sexual history.

In the interview, Eggers describes his childhood in Lake Forest, Illinois, an upscale, racially homogeneous suburb of Chicago. He insists that the "main by-product" of his sheltered upbringing is "a pure, insinuating solipsism," which converges with *The Real World* in that *The Real*

World wants solipsistic individuals who project an extremely strong sense of self and identity. Furthermore, he argues that self-obsession reigns in contemporary America because of "the absence of struggle against anything in the way of a common enemy—whether that's poverty, Communists, whatever" (175).[4] Eggers shrewdly identifies his own marketability as a television star. He tells the interviewer that he can be The Tragic Guy and that he can also emphasize his work on *Might Magazine*, thereby "defining the zeitgeist, inspiring the world's youth to greatness" (178). Eggers's self-confidence is almost unbelievable. The reader wonders whether he truly believes what he says. Eggers emphasizes that he is "one whose tragic past touches everyone's heart, whose struggles become universal and inspiring" (179). Yet, aside from the death of his parents, Eggers's past is hardly tragic, as he never had to struggle with poverty or oppression. He is certainly not the first young adult to lose his parents.

One of the most important claims Eggers makes in his monologue to *The Real World* talent scout is that his hedonistic narcissism is typical of his generation. Because of the totalizing power of popular culture and the championing of celebrity, his age-group has grown up to believe that "the idea of anonymity is existentially irrational, indefensible" (176). In a way, Eggers rightly identifies the media as the culprit for encouraging desire and self-absorption, an idea I will explore in my next chapter. Furthermore, he tells the interviewer that he perceives his generation as a lattice (184). In increasingly manic hyperbole, Eggers declares his hybridity and the essential hybridity that I believe characterizes Generation X. This Whitmanseque passage shows a writer who is seriously conflicted by his own personal desire:

> I will be sad and hopeful. I will be the conduit. I will be the beating heart. Please see this! I am the common multiplier for 47 million! I am the perfect amalgam! I was born of stability and chaos. I have seen nothing and everything. I am twenty-four but feel ten thousand years old.... I am bursting with the hopes of a generation, their hopes surge through me, threaten to burst my hardened heart! Can you not see this? I am at once pitiful and monstrous, I know, and this is all my own making. I know—not the fault of my parents but all my own creation, yes, but I am the product of my environment, and thus representative, must be exhibited, as inspiration and cautionary tale [207–8].

On one level, Eggers is being completely narcissistic in his contention that he can be the center and voice of his generation. Yet, Eggers may purposely be exaggerating for dramatic effect. After all, his monologue is geared to convince a talent scout to put him on *The Real World*. Furthermore, Eggers's seemingly boundless desire gets the better of him as he contradicts himself. How can he be all his "own creation" and also the product of his environment? At the same time, Eggers also truly and passionately wants to reawaken a culture of young people who, I would argue, are largely socially apathetic and emotionally blunted. The remaining problem is that Eggers doesn't really know what he wants or what changes he would like to see come about.

In order to shock a jaded audience, Eggers rightly uses emotionally charged language. In a sense, his confessional memoir is a sacrificial offering to the reader. Yet all his energy, passion and good intentions do little good, for his memoir often reads more like a catalog of failures and disappointments. By the end, Eggers seems to be at rock bottom, playing frisbee on the beach with his brother while he recounts the final moments of his mother's life. Still, after the failure of his magazine and the failures of his many relationships, along with the trials involved in being a surrogate parent to Toph and his near miss with celebrity as a cast member of *The Real World*, Eggers does not compromise his passionate desire to be a surrogate parent, social activist, and generational mouthpiece. Finally, Eggers ends by directly addressing his generational "lattice" in a stream-of-consciousness monologue. Out of frustration, passion and desire, he makes a desperate emotional plea:

> Don't you know that I am connected to you? Don't you know that I'm trying to pump blood to you, that this is for you, that I hate you people, so many of you motherfuckers.... if you're going to fucking sleep all day fuck you motherfuckers oh when you're all sleeping so many sleeping I am somewhere on some stupid rickety scaffolding and I'm trying to get your stupid fucking attention I've been trying to show you this, just been trying to show you this—What the fuck does it take to show you motherfuckers, what does it fucking take what do you want how much do you want because I am willing and I'll stand before you and I'll raise my arms and give you my chest and my throat [375].

Eggers's impassioned, angry, vulgar and accusatory ending leaves the reader unclear as to what the author wants members of his generation to do. Like other hybrid fiction writers of his generation, he feels almost torn apart by conflicting desires and passions. In his final monologue, Eggers attempts to tear the wall down between himself and the reader. Torn between love and hatred, self-absorption and self-effacement, life and death, Eggers ends with writing that is more akin to a scream that wants to be heard around the world, to wrest a generation from apathetic complacency or a cry for attention.

Eggers's memoir also demonstrates how writers feel increasingly strained to come up with innovative methods in order to capture readers' and critics' attention in a competitive publishing industry. Furthermore, Eggers, like Wallace, embraces his "average" qualities and writes in a fierce, impassioned manner about the world we have unwittingly come to accept without truly contemplating its many features, with the hope he can bring new light to world-weary eyes. Also similar to Wallace, Eggers demonstrates the importance of self-deprecating humor as a literary method to achieve credibility with his largely cynical and untrusting audience. However, these attributes leave the reader with many unanswered questions. What does Eggers really want? Is he serious in his revolutionary fervor? Is he a pure solipsist or is he self-effacing? I would submit that even Eggers doesn't know the answer to these questions. However, there is one thing which he seems certain about and which I find convincing: his belief that his generation, Generation X, lacks a cohesive, binding center and has become far too self preoccupied for their own good and for the good of the country. However, the comedy in Eggers and Wallace somewhat counteracts their serious social criticism. While they investigate parallel issues, their contemporary, William Vollmann, is a noncomic, serious muckraking writer/journalist who does not try to please or entertain the audience but rather provides shocking and supposedly unadulterated evidence of the destructive aftereffects of mass cultural hedonism.

The Dark Side of Hedonism:
William Vollmann's American Inferno

While Wallace and Eggers concentrate on a wide cross-section of mainstream America, William Vollmann investigates the gritty recesses of American society and countries beyond, specifically focusing on the lower class and socially shunned. In his relentless desire to portray the socially excluded, Vollmann works as a muckraking journalist in order to give the reader faithful accounts of his subjects. While Wallace implicates the wealthy and privileged for their selfish pursuit of hedonistic pleasure and Eggers barely sees beyond his own desires, Vollmann typically focuses on the lower class and does not judge their meager attempts to satisfy their personal desires, mostly through drugs and sex.

Regardless of their economic class, the hedonistic appetites of Vollmann's subjects often turn into violence, disease and addiction, which subsequently can become either psychologically or physically destructive. Vollmann does not place himself on a moral pedestal above the subjects of his narratives; rather, he portrays himself as a hedonistic purveyor of pleasure, an American in a global economy dominated by popular culture, money and goods.

Spanning the globe, Vollmann's worldwide fiction often is set in second- or third-world countries, where "ugly Americans" can become almost omnipotent thanks to the power of king dollar. It is hard to read Vollmann's writings and not feel guilty as an American at how privileged and secure a life most of us have compared to people in the rest of the world. Furthermore, Vollmann wants us to be appalled at the negligent and harmful behavior of Americans in foreign countries, who show little shame in using the natives for their own devices. Vollmann, like Eggers and Wallace, wants to awaken complacent Americans from social apathy and from the mindless pursuit of hedonistic pleasures. But he adds an additional dimension; he wants us to perceive our privileged and pampered position as self-indulgent Americans in contrast to the larger world, in which most people struggle, at least indirectly, because of American prosperity.

Vollmann showcases the horrific consequences of hedonistic, self-indulgent lifestyles of certain Americans in his novel *The Butterfly Stories* (1993), a graphic depiction of an American journalist and a photographer who "set out to whore their way across Asia" (43). While both shamelessly regard the Asian prostitutes they meet in Cambodia as consumer goods, Vollmann makes a crucial distinction between the callous, amoral photographer and the seemingly gentler journalist. The photographer treats the prostitutes as objects whose only purpose is to please him sexually. The wanton cruelty of the photographer becomes apparent in his casual comments to the journalist, such as "You don't have to give 'em anything after you buy 'em out. I remember one time this bitch kept pestering me for money; I sent her away with nothing, man. She was crying; it was GREAT!" (46). When the journalist confesses his moral reserve about their frequent use of prostitutes, the photographer replies, "Well, we're giving 'em money, aren't we? How else they gonna eat? That's their job. That's what they do. What's more, we're paying 'em real well, a lot better than most guys would" (51). In a way, the photographer's logic is irrefutable, for the money the prostitutes receive from the two is significantly greater than they would otherwise make as farm or retail workers, which would barely support them individually, not to mention their families. However, the photographer misses the crucial problem in that it is precisely the wealth disequilibrium between America and third-world nations that gives Americans power over foreigners and feeds their often callous disregard of others.

Throughout *The Butterfly Stories* and in other of Vollmann's works, he contrasts the tragic, difficult lives of the natives of poorer, war-torn countries with that of wealthy, pampered Americans. In contrast to their own peaceful upbringing, the journalist and the photographer meet Cambodians whose entire families were killed by the Khmer Rouge. Living

as spendthrifts, the two feed upon the unrealizable desires of the prostitutes, who dream of marrying wealthy foreigners. The two are gluttonous, ugly Americans, and their casual disregard of others makes them
appear morally deficient in comparison to the nobler, struggling Cambodians, whose only function to the journalist and photographer is to literally service them. Vollmann implicitly asks the question: What good do
Americans provide for third-world nations? In the *Butterfly Stories*, other
than weapons and the money spent on prostitutes by amoral tourists like
the journalist and photographer, the only other significant American
export seems to be television and film, which work as soporific drugs,
lulling the poor into complacency. Vollmann writes of a city in Cambodia: "Every little chessboard restaurant has become a movie theater of
chairs with mothers and children raptly watching a TV" (71).

However, Vollmann complicates matters in that while the amoral
photographer seems addicted to casual sex, the more sensitive journalist becomes addicted to his somewhat perverted idea of love. Implicitly,
Vollmann wants the journalist to be seen as a representation of the
patronizing, self-serving attitudes which Americans tend to have toward
third-world countries, whose inhabitants used to be called "our little
friends," a derogatory, paternalistic moniker. The rationalizing journalist claims that he feels genuine love and affection for the prostitutes.
While the journalist may not be entirely deluded in his belief that he
makes the prostitutes happy with his money, he is naïve if he believes
that they truly love him. His naivety parallels the naivety of many Americans pre–September 11, 2001, who thought their country to be almost
universally admired. If the journalist is being "loved," it is only for his
money.

Furthermore, the journalist at least secretly longs for omnipotence,
which I would argue, is the frightening result of narcissistic hedonism.
At one point, while riding through the Cambodian streets in a tank, the
journalist has an epiphany: "He felt like a God—a loving God, moreover;
he loved everyone he saluted; he wanted to love the whole world, which
(it now seemed to him) was all he'd ever wanted when he had whores.
All he wanted to do with people was hug them and kiss them and give
them money" (99). However, the journalist cannot see that his idea of
love is a kind of domination, involved in unequal power relationships.
Vollmann recognizes the duplicity of the journalist: "Interesting that the
photographer, who wanted to break as many hearts as possible, and the
journalist, who wanted to make as many happy as possible, accomplished
the same results! Does that prove that the journalist was lying to himself?" (102). The journalist hasn't so much been lying to himself as confusing physical intimacy with love. Indeed, as privileged Americans, the
journalist and the photographer are not capable of experiencing a selfless,

altruistic love, as they have grown accustomed to living in a world that caters to their physical desires. Even the journalist recognizes his own ridiculous search for love from the Cambodian prostitutes, since he "wanted to love any and all of them even though loving any of them would only make him more lonely because loving them wasn't really loving them" (141).

The journalist's hypocritical and naïve behavior becomes more apparent after he claims to fall in love with one prostitute, Vanna. But their "relationship" is defined almost entirely by conversation-less, physical intimacy, which appeals to the journalist, who had been miserably married for the past eleven years. Still, the journalist appears misguided as he continues rationalizing his sexual promiscuity even after he has "fallen in love" with Vanna. He argues:

> There was nothing wrong with sleeping around if you loved everybody; you could be faithful to a hundred wives—But how much can you really love them (our interlocutor might have said) if one is as good as another? More to the point, are you happy and are they happy? As it happened, there was an answer for that, too. The husband loved Vanna the best. He'd keep being promiscuous only until he had her forever. Then he wouldn't need anyone but her. And if it turned out then that he was still unfaithful after all, surely a whore would be used to it [186].

While the journalist seems devoted to Vanna and spends an inordinate amount of money to try to find her after he returns to the United States, his efforts are in vain, and he pays a steep price for his mindless promiscuity when he discovers that he has contracted the HIV virus. Thereby, for Vollmann, the consequence of hedonism and self-indulgence is the subsequent demise of love, which is only possible through at least partial self-restraint and self-denial. Yet, paradoxically, as David Foster Wallace personally discovered while on board the luxurious cruise ship, an individual's obsessive desire for hedonistic pleasures can create further emptiness and isolation. Thereby, Vollmann's characters are like boat wreck survivors who resort to drinking salt water, which only serves to exacerbate their thirst. Still, Vollmann suggests that the entire concept of romantic love may be a fraud. In a way, he also criticizes the addiction to romantic love as the most destructive of all addictions, because romantic love rarely has the power to be the cure-all that Hollywood films and mainstream American media promote.

Set in the gritty "Tenderloin" region of San Francisco, Vollmann's novel *Whores for Gloria* explores the darker and obsessive side of romantic love. It focuses upon alcoholic, Vietnam veteran Jimmy, who is addicted not only to alcohol and prostitutes, but most importantly, to his idea of romantic love. Vollmann wants our sympathies to lie with Jimmy as a casualty of contemporary free-market democracy and the current hedonistic trends that play a larger role in contemporary American culture. Jimmy is a man without family, community or employment, subsisting on his disability checks and possessing only one "friend," another alcoholic Vietnam veteran named Code Six. Jimmy's exaggerated needs may in fact help produce psychosis, for his obsessive love is for at least a partial figment of his imagination. In his relentless attempt to both mentally and physically create Gloria, Jimmy tries to combat his intense feelings of isolation, which he exacerbates through drinking and casual sex.

From the first pages of *Whores for Gloria*, the reader becomes aware of the extent of Jimmy's obsessive love for Gloria. Our first introduction to Jimmy occurs as an undercover police officer watches him talking into a pay phone, "holding the receiver tight in both hands" (2). The police officer notices that Jimmy is "saying Gloria and Gloria and Gloria" (3). Jimmy's desperate desire for Gloria becomes immediately clear to the reader as does his meek, but sad, demeanor. Vollmann writes: "Once upon a time a man made a phone call, and the man was crying.... What else did the doctor say? the man asked gently—Gloria? Gloria, what did the doctor say? Are you crying, Gloria? If I can buy you a plane ticket tonight will you come tonight?" (5–6). However, the undercover policewoman "knew that the pay phone had been broken for weeks. And she knew that the man was still crying" (7). Throughout the novel, the reader tries to determine whether Gloria is real or a figment of Jimmy's imagination. In addition to being an alcoholic, subject to alcohol-fueled delusions, Jimmy may also have posttraumatic stress disorder or schizophrenia, which would explain his "hallucinations" of Gloria. Furthermore, Jimmy's encounters with prostitutes are his only real experiences of intimacy. Instead of judging Jimmy or criticizing him for his "whore-hunting" (7), Vollmann humanizes Jimmy through his misguided and desperate longings for love and affection: "In his dreams of Gloria he was hammering at Being, hammering at lightness to shape someone who would not turn her face away from him the way the whores he flatbacked did" (81). After a cold, isolating experience with a prostitute, Jimmy decides to give himself over to his visions of Gloria: "Well James he said to himself it's time to turn over a new leaf and really work at thinking about Gloria and remember how she appeared to me and ask of her that she give me love.... He admitted that he hadn't been taking Gloria very seriously. But Gloria is all I have, he said" (18).

Although *Whores for Gloria* is graphically realistic, Vollmann's aim is also to document the heartbreaking conditions of America's downtrodden. Furthermore, Vollmann also argues for the emotional importance of narrative and imagination to sustain emotionally fraught people like Jimmy. This would seem like a positive transformation, except that Jimmy gradually loses the ability to distinguish between reality and fantasy. However, there is a thin line between the healing power of the imagination and its destructive powers. As Jimmy gradually gives himself over to his dreams of Gloria, he loses touch with reality and becomes more withdrawn and aloof. Gradually, Jimmy grows from being a self-centered pleasure seeker to a person in search of transcendence through narrative and through his own imagination. Jimmy is still self-centered in the sense that he uses narrative and stories solely to help him create a fuller mental image of Gloria. Since his own memory and imagination appear to be debilitated by alcohol, he pays prostitutes to tell him their past stories. After one prostitute, Melissa, tells Jimmy about a long train trip she took as a child and the excitement she used to feel before seeing movies in a theater as a child, Jimmy uses Melissa's stories as his own. Jimmy puts Gloria and himself in Melissa's place, adding description and color to her narrative, so that he can claim it as his memory, not Melissa's.

Subsequently, Jimmy goes on a quest to create Gloria out of his own imagination and from the stories that he pays various prostitutes to tell him. However, most of the stories that the prostitutes tell Jimmy are horrendous tales of sexual abuse, molestation and rape. Vollmann describes Jimmy at this point: "Jimmy was very downcast. He knew life was going to get worse. Maybe stories aren't enough, he thought. But no; they *have* to be" (96). Jimmy tries to take these stories and edit them into happier ones with him and Gloria in place of the storyteller. With each story, Gloria comes into sharper focus. "Jimmy looked at Gloria again and she cast a shadow now and her flesh had the firmness of flesh; she was completely opaque to the streetlights now, and he understood that when he got up to leave she would walk away with him and be visible beside him forever.... He knew that she knew all that he had done to clothe and adorn her with memories" (94).

Nevertheless, Jimmy cannot stave off either the sadness of the stories or his own personal isolation: "The problem he said to himself is how can I put one foot ahead of the other day after day for the rest of my life" (107). As time passes, Jimmy grows more detached and mentally unstable to the point that he buys hair from a prostitute who supposedly has the same hair as Gloria. Jimmy gets the hair converted into a wig and tries to get another prostitute to wear it, but she destroys the wig and humiliates Jimmy, who retreats to his invented memories and imagination of Gloria. Just how misguided Jimmy was becomes clear in the last monologue in the novel by Jimmy's Vietnam buddy, Code Six, who tells the reader that Jimmy was shot and killed by the real Gloria:

"She killed him dead right in front of the goddamn restaurant, and there were about twenty people in there, cooks and all" (138).

Throughout *Whores for Gloria*, Vollmann portrays the Tenderloin as a human wasteland. However, its damaged residents still cling to dreams of love, affection and acceptance. Underneath the violence and sexual perversion, Vollmann finds a core of forlorn people (mainly prostitutes) like Jimmy, who in their own way try to brighten or salvage their desolate lives with their own imagination and memories. Still, Vollmann forces the reader to confront the horrific aftereffects of hedonistic desire. In other of Vollmann's works, his lower-class, American characters feel cheated of the "good," life and their frustrated desire frequently motivates them to join hate groups like the Skinheads and/or to become addicted to harder drugs which they use to combat their sense of worthlessness and frustrated desire. For in consumer society, those who do not have much money are denied the agency to become consumers and thereby feel that they have lost the ability to realize a pleasurable, satisfying life. If these frustrated desires are at least partially motivated by consumerism and advertising as I believe they are, then who is responsible for setting the series of dominoes in motion? Richard Powers undertakes this question in his novel *Gain* (1998).

Pleasure Is Their Business: Corporations, Consumerism and Cancer in Richard Powers's *Gain*

While Wallace, Eggers, and Vollmann focus on the immediate personal and social ramifications of American hedonistic appetites, Richard Powers employs a new historicist approach to these pressing problems. Powers rightly does not argue that the contemporary emphasis on consumption and gain spontaneously appeared in the 1980s. Rather, he argues that over the past two hundred years, consumption and self-indulgence have been gradually amplified, largely by corporations and their consumer products that have shaped our lives and desires.

In *Gain*, Powers tells two interrelated stories. The first concerns the Clare corporation (or Clare Soap and Chemical as it is later called). Powers traces the history of Clare from its creation in the early 1830s by three Clare brothers to its 1990 status as a multinational and multibillion-dollar conglomerate. He pits the rise and development of Clare with the story of Laura Bodey, a forty-two-year-old, single mother of two and lifelong resident of Lacewood, Illinois, which is also home to one of Clare's primary manufacturing facilities. Powers suggests that there are forces (corporate, chemical, technological) beyond our acknowledgement, and to a large extent, beyond our control, which not only shape our lives, but also forge and exaggerate our personal desires. Throughout *Gain*, Laura battles ovarian cancer. Part of the suspense of *Gain* involves Laura's attempt to determine whether or not the nearby Clare facilities are responsible for her cancer. *Gain* is Powers's attempt to shock the reader with the possible consequences of blind consumerism. That Laura is an everywoman, no more self-absorbed or hedonistic than most Americans, makes *Gain* even more frightening in scope, for the creature comforts and goods which we often regard as necessities and which we purchase to make our lives easier and more pleasurable can ultimately turn lethal.

Although similar to Stephen Soderbergh's recent film, *Erin Brockovich* (2000), *Gain* illustrates how much more instructive, comprehensive and wider in scope contemporary literature can be than film. Whereas *Erin Brockovich* (the film) clearly sets up a division between the individual heroine, Erin Brockovich, the villain, Pacific Gas and Electric Company, and the residential victims, Powers complicates the matter by not setting up an easy division between good and evil. Furthermore, *Erin Brockovich* relies on witty one-liners and the almost irresistible charisma of Julia Roberts, who unabashedly uses her sexuality to manipulate others (and the audience), whereas Powers's Laura is middle aged, not as self-possessed and a more realistic depiction of a typical woman. Furthermore, *Erin Brockovich*, while a depiction of a real event and person, offers little or no insight into the connection between corporations and individuals or into the place of corporations in American history. Rather, it gives the viewer an easy villain to despise and a clear instance of an unethical act by a shady corporation. However, rarely is anything as morally or ethically clear as it in the film. Have corporations and corporate leaders grown too powerful and self-serving? Powers suggests possibly so, but his purpose is to show that such a view is only a small part of the picture. Furthermore, he asks us to resist making hasty, dismissive judgments about corporations before we are able to consider the larger picture.

To provide a more comprehensive description of a typical, large, American corporation and the power of corporations in America, Powers gives a complete historical account of the development of Clare from its beginnings in the 1830s as the tiny Clare and Sons. Along the way, Powers highlights Clare's benefits as well as its drawbacks. While Clare is fictional, Powers reportedly used several real-life corporations as models, which aids in the urgent documentary realism of his "novel." He states in an interview: "As far as researching, I went to several consumer-product companies, not all agricultural chemistry companies or soap

manufacturers" (Miller, "The Salon Interview: Richard Powers," online).
In addition, Powers emphasizes the direct personal relevance of Laura's
personal fight with cancer, which, "arose out of the deaths of five people very close to me, within the last eight years, by cancer, and this very
local sense that we're living in the middle of an epidemic of our own
devising" (Miller "The Salon Interview: Richard Powers" online). If we
are indeed living in an epidemic of our creation, Powers implicitly argues
that it is due to our exaggerated desires and needs for products that corporations provide. Powers argues that all Americans should share partial responsibility for the negative aftereffects of technological and
corporate development. He wants us to accept the Clare corporation as
a realistic representation of a contemporary, multibillion-dollar conglomerate, which largely comprises the essential infrastructure of contemporary America. To understand our place and future as Americans,
we must be cognizant that corporations are the hidden power that defines
and drives our lives.

Powers uses Laura's hometown of Lacewood, Illinois, as an example of how corporations and the products they produce have become
deeply entrenched in our lives and in the very infrastructure of communities. At the beginning of *Gain*, he emphasizes, "There must have
been a time when Lacewood did not mean Clare, Incorporation. But no
one remembered. No one alive was old enough to recall. The two names
always came joined in the same breath" (4). In the late nineteenth century, the Clare corporation single-handedly resuscitated the sleepy town
and has continued to serve as its economic infrastructure: Indeed, Powers states that "Without Claire, the town would have dozed forever" (5)
and proceeds to give a historical account of the development of a typical, multiglomerate corporation, because the status, role and power of
American corporations have changed over time. From the start of the
novel, corporations gain and increase their power through creating and
exacerbating the desires and insecurities of people, an activity that they
still undertake to an even larger degree.

To generate a demand for soap, the Clares place a needed emphasis upon marketing and thereby create a desire for soap which didn't previously exist. This, in essence, opens up a Pandora's box of advertising
and consumerism, whereby Clare and other corporations keep devising
new ways to create and exaggerate desires. Above all, though, it is the
scholarly, Harvard-educated Ben Clare whose ingenuity and creativity
laid the foundations for the eventual runaway financial success of Clare
and Sons. Ben's marketing genius was especially important because, as
Powers points out, in the early nineteenth century, there was no interest
in buying imported soap. By connecting soap with the Puritan ideals of
cleanliness, the Clares "cured an itch that Americans didn't know they

had until the scratch announced it" (20). In an image-conscious America, Clare's soap allows individuals to elevate themselves above the physical dirt and grime of the city and the lower class: "It emitted a whiff of purity that one could smell even above the crust of horse drippings that fouled ankles from Noodle Island to Southie" (44).

Because the objective of the Clares is to make money, they spare no resource in creating a greater demand for soap, even resorting to openly duplicitous methods. Scholarly Ben Clare stumbles upon the perfect advertising connection of soap to Native Americans, during a time of great nostalgia for Native Americans, by imprinting an Indian warrior on Clare soap. Furthermore, Ben comes up with an advertising slogan, which he affixes to a picture of hygienically clean Native Americans. But there is a hidden duplicity in Clare's advertising in that there is no basis for a connection between cleanliness and Native Americans. However, the soap sells a "state of worry-free grace" (132) and eventually becomes the most popular brand of soap in America. In a modern society in which people increasingly obsess about their personal appearance, Clare's advertisements feed perfectly on latent insecurities. While Powers seems to be vilifying Clare, the insecurities and desires which they help to create actually prove to be socially important by spawning a needed increase in sanitation and personal hygiene: "In a world that washed up with death, soap was the chief weapon against disease and fever" (ibid.).

As Powers details the beginnings of Clare, he switches back to 1990s' America to relate Laura's story. Through Powers's description of Laura's household, we witness the disconcerting repercussions of corporate and technologically advanced, postindustrial America. Laura's teenage children are absorbed in their own worlds. Her sixteen-year-old daughter, Ellen, "buries her grief in fan 'zines, music with deeply suggestive lyrics that Laura doesn't understand and long phone conversations" (48), while twelve-year-old Tim plays interactive computer games. Meanwhile, Laura engages in an off-and-on-again relationship with a married man. While in the hospital after a biopsy, Laura comes to a realization: "The three of them live in a house trapped in its own made things, hard on the coast of a man-made ocean. A house whose uses she only sees tonight because she is not there" (50–51). Even in Laura's small hometown, there is little or no community. Laura's house and most American houses have become isolated, technologically advanced islands unto themselves.

While postmodern theorists might contend that we live in an artificial world, their contention is largely irrelevant as we have given a physical shape to our environment, which greatly affects and often isolates us. Gradually, during Laura's story, we witness the dehumanization of the individual in technologically advanced, postindustrial America. While Laura is in the hospital during her biopsy, Powers brings attention to the cold, impersonal nature of the technologically advanced hospital: "Around her mechanical bed hum meters and dials, each cold with purpose" (51). To make matters worse, Laura's unnaturally cheery gynecologist surgeon puts on a false front of concerned optimism and flashes what David Foster Wallace might call the "professional smile" after telling Laura that she has ovarian cancer and discussing possible treatments.

Powers pits the life-affirming and life-changing developments of Clare in the mid-nineteenth century with Laura's realization that she has cancer and her subsequent treatment. The two narratives go along opposite and parallel trajectories simultaneously. While Laura gets sicker, Powers relates how Clare grows stronger. However, at the same time, Clare becomes an all-absorptive, amorphous mass, a correlative to Laura's cancer. Laura's body becomes its own conglomerate of destructive, parasitical cancer cells which mimic corporations in their desire for expansion, or gain. Powers uses economic metaphors to emphasize the link between cancer and corporations: "Junior, floating tumors may be loose in her system, ready to anchor and flare back into production" (84).

To complicate matters, Clare's duplicitous and materialistic actions are continually offset by their practical benefits. Ironically, Laura undergoes chemotherapy with chemicals produced by Clare, whose very same chemicals probably caused her cancer in the first place. So Clare may be at once killing and saving Laura. Further complicating matters, Laura's son, Tim, was born prematurely, and machines and chemical antiseptics, produced by Clare, saved his life. To aid Clare's reputation and credibility, Powers includes a third narrative in *Gain* of Dos Passos–like news advertisements that detail the successes of the contemporary Clare Corporation. One such advertisement from a subdivision of Clare, the Biological Materials Group, reads:

> This year, Melissa blew out all the candles. In one breath. By herself. Last year, just humming along while the other kids sang Happy Birthday left her gasping for air. Until Respulin appeared among the rest of her life's presents, each new candle taxed her lungs to the breaking point. She could not run, sing, shout or even jump a rope. She lived in constant fear. A spring day felt like being buried alive. Melissa turned nine today. Maybe she still can't spell oral leukotriene D4, receptor antagonist. But she does know how to spell happiness [115].

Indeed, it is very difficult to deny Clare's claim that "Because of what we do in Lacewood, people the world over eat better, live longer, and enjoy healthier lives" (140).

In the period after the Civil War, Clare and Sons becomes a many tiered corporation. For Powers, this is the turning point in American business history, in part due to mass production and mass invention at a scale never realized, but also because Clare and other corporations start diffusing responsibility amongst various company heads. Still, the monetary benefits of becoming a corporation are too alluring for the Clares to pass up. Consequently, J. Clare and Sons becomes Clare Soap and Chemical Company with stocks and a board of directors. Most tellingly, the heir apparent of Clare Soap and Chemical, Douglas Clare, Samuel's son, finds an entry for corporation in the Devil's Dictionary as "an ingenious device for obtaining individual profit without individual responsibility" (159). The faceless corporation becomes a behemoth which dwarfs individuals. For the last three decades of the nineteenth century, Clare grows by leaps and bounds and outgrows singular leadership (165).

Furthermore, as Clare grows as a corporation, it loses its scruples and becomes increasingly materialistic. By the turn of the twentieth century, advertising plays a larger role in corporate and public life as public image becomes increasingly important and other corporations threaten Clare. Peter Clare, brother of Douglas Clare, a "genius of the mundane," leads Clare's advertising charge during the latter part of the nineteenth century. As more consumer products become available and cheaper, capturing the consumer's attention through advertising becomes increasingly important. To capture more consumers, Peter Clare emphasizes aesthetics. He wraps the soap to make it seem more elegant and promotes it as "cleaner, surer, purer" (196). He also plans gimmicks like hiding a gold dollar in a soap bar contained in every tenth crate. Peter's marketing techniques work amazingly well, generating huge profits for Clare Soap and Chemical. For Powers, the late nineteenth century was a pivotal time in American history and in the history of corporations because having conquered and dominated the landscape and geographical distances, Americans now could completely turn themselves over to personal pleasures and luxuries. Instead of focusing their collective energies on conquering and taming the environment, Americans could focus more upon self-improvement.

While Powers describes the moral downfall of Clare, it is important to recognize that he does not place Laura Bodey on much higher moral ground. In a way, Laura's job as a real estate agent mirrors the work of the speculators and advertisers of Clare Soap and Chemical in that both somewhat coldly try to analyze and appeal to the hidden desires of their clients in order to achieve personal profit. In her personal desire for financial gain, Laura mirrors the self-aggrandizing techniques of corporations like Clare. By not portraying Laura as a humanitarian, Powers prevents his readers from making a simplistic distinction between good and evil. Furthermore, he argues that from an early age, Americans have been brainwashed into believing in the all-importance of personal gain and self-aggrandizement. Laura's twelve-year-old-son, Tim, seems to have subtly incorporated American society's push toward personal aggrandization. Tim becomes virtually addicted to a never-named interactive computer game in which the object is to "Build the best civilization. Cream everyone else" (202).[5]

Meanwhile, with the turn of the twentieth century, the next generation of Clares, led by Douglas Clare, takes over the company. As Clare grows, it becomes increasingly self-sufficient and interrelated. Essentially, Clare becomes a minicountry within America, and its self-sufficiency allows the company to self- govern effectively. Concurrent with Douglas Clare's ascension to chief executive of Clare Soap and Chemical, the director of promotion, Hirum Nagel, rises to become the most significant figure in the corporation. Powers emphasizes his value in that, "Here was a man who understood popular craving and anxiety. Nagel felt the new American appetites deep down, in the barometer of his own ample belly" (222). Nagel amplifies the important correlation of soap with godliness by using apostles to help market Clare's soap. Hirum begins a new line of soap, which he calls Snowdrop Soap, and promotes it as superior to Native Balm: "Native Balm bespoke a Nature pungent, arcane and enchanted. Snowdrop delineated the new face of Nature: immaculate, measured, managed, purity incarnate" (235).

Powers further emphasizes the positive ramifications of Clare's products in the Progressive Era as "liberating women from drudgery" and improving the living conditions of the poor. He emphasizes: "Everywhere, the corporation proved to be the greatest extension of human prowess since the spear and the most flexible one since the baseball mitt" (290). With the end of World War I and the subsequent need for mass production, Powers argues that corporations became entrenched in American society. While this occurs, the director of promotion, Hirum Nagel becomes the chief executive of Clare Soap and Chemical, displacing the Clares themselves. For Powers, the changing of the guard is a symbolic moment in that the Clare corporation has grown almost of its own accord, now dwarfing its own makers like a corporate Frankenstein's monster.

Meanwhile, as her cancer worsens, Laura goes on a personal crusade to discern whether or not Clare is responsible for causing her disease. In her library and personal research, she becomes overwhelmed by the realization that many of the products which she has used or consumed from hair spray to diet sodas to maraschino cherries could be carcinogenic: After reading a book titled *Shopping for Safety*, Laura desperately comes to the conclusion that "nothing is safe" and that the whole planet is "a superfund site" (284). This shocking revelation is crucial to the narrative because Powers wants us to acknowledge the possible costs of consumerism.

The products that Laura uses are products that most Americans use and take for granted as being safe. However, most of these same products are unnecessary luxuries, and their dangers aren't commonly acknowledged.

Still, as time progresses and more people in the Lacewood area are diagnosed with cancer, Laura becomes steadily convinced that Clare contributed to if not caused, her cancer. In response she "vows a consumer boycott, a full spring cleaning. But the house is full of them [Clare's products].... They paper her cabinets. They perch on her microwave, camp in her stove, hang from her shower head. Clare hiding under the sink, swarming [in] her medicine chest, lining the shelves in her basement, parked out in the garage, piled up in the shed" (304). However, instead of entirely blaming Clare, Laura acknowledges at least partial responsibility. She decides "She cannot sue the company for raiding her house. She brought them in, by choice, toted them in a shopping bag. And she'd do it all over again, given the choice. Would have to" (ibid.).

At this point, Laura realizes how dependent and reliant she has been on consumer products made by Clare. All of the little things she uses without thought and which have made her life easier and more pleasurable have backfired against her. While Laura initially gets angry at Clare, her anger gradually subsides as she has "a weird dream of peace. It makes no difference whether this business gave her cancer. They have given her everything else. Taken her life and molded it in every way imaginable, plus six degrees beyond imagining" (320). Perhaps Laura's acceptance comes too easily, but the fact is that Clare has not only made Laura's life much more pleasurable, it has also helped save the life of her son, Tim. The implicit question though is whether the consumer pleasures which corporations like Clare provide are worth their potential, hidden costs. That is a question which very few would consider until put into a position like Laura's.

By the time the narrative of the Clare corporation reaches the present, Laura is close to death, and the residents of Lacewood take legal action against Clare. Their suit is eventually settled out of court, but their moderate monetary settlement is a small victory and hardly affects the Clare corporation or the contemporary power of corporations in America. In fact, the new CEO of Clare, Franklin Kennibar, goes on a wide publicity tour across America in which he delivers a speech which emphasizes the importance of corporations in contemporary America: "Corporations pay for a quarter of public undertakings at all levels, provide half of all jobs, produce two thirds of all payroll, and an even greater proportion of total national wealth. By scrambling to win consumer votes and avoid consumer censure, business becomes the best tool we have for building the world that people want" (338). It is difficult to deny Kennibar's strong claims as corporations do stand responsible to the general public and need to appear somewhat trustworthy in order to be successful. However, Powers implicitly argues that corporations have gotten so large as to avoid individual responsibility. The "situation" at Lacewood hardly tarnishes the reputation of Clare Soap and Chemical. Furthermore, as Laura realizes, a huge number of her consumer products which could be potentially dangerous are manufactured by the same corporation— Clare Soap and Chemical.

Right before her death, Laura pinpoints what I believe to be part of Powers's main purpose in *Gain*, when she tells her husband: "People want everything. That's their problem" (343). While Francis Kennibar may be correct in claiming that corporations merely provide the structure and form of the world which people want, through Laura's story (and Laura's words) Powers asks us to think more before giving into our frequently mindless desires and not to be a slave to our hedonistic wants. In that sense, Powers and David Foster Wallace are on the same moral high ground in that they both argue that most Americans need to be more conscious of, and even resistant to, the ways their desires have been amplified and spurred on by consumerism, corporations and the media.

Powers's account of the Clare corporation is fatalistic in the sense that Clare appears insatiable in its seemingly inexhaustible desire for gain and its continual attempt to up the ante by exaggerating human desires and its insecurities. Powers argues that in a capitalist society, the desire for monetary self-aggrandizement is inevitable: "Forced to pick between liberty and equality, the market had no choice. Production was already a sealed contract. Wealth's job was to make more of the same, let the chips fall where they may" (263). Still, Powers is not a complete fatalist.

The ending of *Gain* indicates that he still maintains some belief in the power of the individual over the many and the potential for science to be further beneficial, helping to eradicate the problems it has caused. After Laura's death, her son, Tim, the former computer-game junkie, goes to graduate school at Harvard in chemical engineering. After a couple of years, Tim begins work with a research think-tank. Collectively, they make an amazing breakthrough in which they put together "a universal chemical assembly plant at the level of the human cell" which "promised to make anything the damaged cell called out for" (355). Guided by Tim's sense of loss at losing his mother, the research group immediately works on developing a cure for cancer. In an act of poetic justice, Tim uses Laura's settlement money from Clare, which he had not touched after her death, to finance the think-tank's chemical assembly plant, which Powers suggests, will produce the cure for cancer.

While Powers's hopeful ending might be an act of wishful thinking, he undercuts this note of optimism by the fact that Tim and his think-tank might have helped beget a new corporation. That is, despite his best intentions, Tim might have helped found a new Clare. With this in mind, Powers's main purpose in *Gain* becomes evident: to demonstrate how deeply contemporary American lives have become entrenched in larger economic and technological systems which have grown more powerful than any single individual, due in a large part to our own exaggerated, personal and hedonistic desires. At the same time, Powers emphasizes the remaining importance of the individual at the beginning of the twenty-first century. Even in the face of behemoth corporations and economic structures, an individual or a small group of individuals can still forge genuine change for the better, as Tim does, or fight against the powers that be. Powers promotes scientific research more than anything else as the arena in which individuals can make that life-altering change. The question he leaves the reader with is, is it inevitable that a corporation will counteract the best intentions of individuals, or can the two be mutually beneficial? In the case of Clare, the answer is a resounding "no," but it remains to be seen what will occur with Tim and his think-tank.

All four of the authors I have explored in this chapter offer important, relevant commentary concerning the dangerous consequences of the amplifications of personal desires in contemporary America. Their main objective is to make readers aware of the frequently hidden costs of self-absorption. Still, they are not Puritans, arguing for the dismantlement of corporate and technological society. These authors leave us with questions about the individual's place in contemporary America and how a person can find his or her inner self in a fragmented, postmodern world. In addition to questioning the contemporary emphasis placed upon the hedonistic pursuit of happiness, they also question the parallel backlash and redefinition of virtually all forms of sadness and melancholia as unnatural, treatable illnesses, conveniently placed under the incredibly vague term "depression."

Don't Worry, Be Happy? A False, American Complacency

Many people, if asked, will say that the goal of human life is to achieve happiness. However, as I have already established, there are many different forms of happiness, and younger Americans have more opportunities to pursue and fulfill their hedonistic desires, which consequently lessens the appeal and opportunities to achieve a less immediately gratifying, but more socially important, eudemonistic happiness. Being aware of the negative consequence of self-indulgence and also of one's own tendencies toward self-absorption as an American consumer is not something that many would like to consider, for such thoughts might understandably lead a person to feelings of sadness, melancholia, or even depression. I would argue that we live in a culture which tends to shun seriousness and considers sadness and melancholia as annoying, eradicable forms of mental illness. Contrary to this belief, I wish to show that there is definite social value in sadness and melancholia. Indeed, the major subjects of *Hybrid Fictions* are involved in an important backlash against an American culture-wide rejection and scorn of sadness and melancholia, which have unfairly been categorized along with clinical depression as forms of mental illness. I concur with Stephen Braun, who argues in *The Science of Happiness*:

> The prevailing notion that depression is a dysfunction caused by unbalanced neurotransmitters has become so deeply entrenched that it's hard to grasp the notion that a capacity for unhappiness—even depression—might be good for us, just as a capacity for pain is good for us, even though it is unpleasant. But in fact, as heretical as it sounds, the pain of depression can indeed be every bit as vital as the pain of injury....Most often, depressive moods are telling us that something is wrong with our intimate relationships, our life situation, or our efforts to achieve a goal [89–90].

To be sure, there is an important difference between mood-based melancholia and clinical depression, and I am not suggesting that clinical, largely physiologically based depression has great social value. Those who have suffered from severe clinical depression and lived to tell their tale, such as William Styron in *Darkness Visible*, attest to how completely devastating and crippling a disease it can be. However, I would argue that by nature, many healthy people are at least somewhat moody, and a normal person will experience moods of sadness and depression from time to time. For the most part, these moods are not pleasurable, and we now have a wide arsenal of antidepressants at our disposal, which are available for virtually anyone who complains of depression to a medical professional.[6] Still, the lines have been unfairly blurred between mood-based depression and clinical depression. As psychiatrist Patricia Ainsworth argues in *Understanding Depression* (2000), "Depression is not moodiness. Moodiness is a transient, unpleasant feeling that often occurs in association with some physical or environmental irritant, and it is never debilitating. Depression is to moodiness as a hurricane is to a whirlwind" (ix). To a key extent, the "revolution" in antidepressants is the next frontier in consumerism, which suggests that happiness, or at least the basic chemical infrastructure to achieve happiness, can be bought. As Braun suggests, "Unhappiness is being redefined from a normal pole of a human mood to a distinct disease state. Sometimes the message from drug companies or popular advertising seems to be that no unhappiness is normal—that unhappiness, as well as true depression, is like diabetes, a biological dysfunction correctable with drugs" (8). The underlying issue which isn't being addressed is that depression and happiness are not easily definable matters.

Many young, contemporary fiction writers implicate American culture for denigrating most forms of sadness and melancholia into the neat catch-all category of a mental illness known as clinical depression. How has this come about? In part, it is due to unconsciously adopting the aesthetics of television and popular culture. Indeed, I would argue that many younger Americans, especially the so called "latchkey kids" for whom television played a large formative role, have been spoiled and pampered by television and popular culture, which in turn, inform their aesthetics. As David Foster Wallace argues, "I think it's impossible to spend that many slack-jawed, spittle-chinned, formative hours in front of commercial art [TV] without internalizing the idea that one of the main goals of art is simply to entertain, give people sheer pleasure" (McCaffery, "An Interview with David Foster Wallace," 145). For very few people does "sheer pleasure" denote work or effort. This puts serious fiction in a difficult position because most of us consider serious fiction to be in direct opposition to the more visceral and vicarious thrills of humor or sexual stimulation.

Most tellingly, Wallace argues that he suffers from an inability to be completely serious. He argues that his generation has become too skeptical and cynical for its own good. In an informationally savvy culture, naivety or ignorance has become a greater liability, and being sentimental is often thought to be naive. In opposition to this widely held sentiment, Wallace argues that the hip transcendence of sentiment is really a manifestation of the fear of being human, "since to be really human is probably to be unavoidably sentimental and naive and goo-prone ... in some basic interior way forever infantile" (Wallace, *Infinite Jest*, 695).

One might contend that the Generation X emphasis on humor and sarcasm is life affirming and stands in contrast to gloomy, contemplative, depressive nay-sayers, who should be more properly medicated so they can experience the primal joy and hilarity of life. However, one of the problems of irony and relentless sarcasm is that it undermines sincerity. Indeed, this form of comedy often comes out of buried and unacknowledged hostility, anger and an inability to trust others. For instance, at the present time, a young person who says that he or she believes in the honesty and integrity of politicians would be thought to be naive. A gifted ironist might belittle the pretensions of public figures, but at the same time, the individual might internally feel that no one is really trustworthy or that the foundations of American society are based on lies and hyperbole.

While this is a perfectly valid viewpoint to hold and could theoretically help create a better society, there are significant problems with the rampant sarcasm and irony that have become almost ubiquitous in postmodern society. Irony and sarcasm aim to destroy or dismantle, not to create. In addition, irony and sarcasm undermine virtually all beliefs and trust. As Wallace claims, "Irony, entertaining as it is, serves an almost exclusively negative function. It's critical and destructive, a ground-clearing" (Wallace, *A Supposedly Fun Thing I'll Never Do Again*, 67). The resulting problem is that it has become increasingly difficult for people to be taken seriously or to trust in the words of others. Therefore, in order to gain trust, authors use irony, sarcasm and self-deprecation. However, they thereby put themselves in a double bind. For instance, a gifted ironic comedian might begin a stand-up routine by emphasizing, "I am such a liar. I lie all the time about everything," and then proceed to discuss the various situations in which he lies to better himself. I would argue that a hypothetical comedian such as this one would be praised and appreciated by a young, cynical American audience who would applaud the comedian's honesty in revealing how much people lie. Yet, how can the cynical audience then trust the comedian, who is a self-proclaimed sarcastic liar? Still, whether or not the audience would completely trust the comedian is not crucial as the hypothetical, young, media-savvy audience would be more interested in destroying the façades of others (usually public figures and celebrities) rather than staking their hopes upon a presumably unreliable hero figure.

Depression might understandably follow from a growing disbelief in the world's foundations and in the trustworthiness of others, a logical conclusion if one accepts the central tenets of postmodernity. Perhaps what many people describe as "depression" is a more realistic way of looking at one's imperfect self or a world that is not fair and composed of people who might be regarded, for the most part, as untrustworthy and self-interested. Indeed, as Stephen Braun suggests:

> Research shows that depressed people have a realistic—but maladaptive—awareness of their limitations. They better predict their performance relative to others on a task; they better understand the limits of their control over the outcome of games of chance; they are more accurate at monitoring and assessing their own skilled and unskilled social behavior, and they judge themselves responsible for both past successes and failures rather than seeing themselves as more responsible for their successes than for their failures [Braun 50].

Indeed, "normal" happier people typically have higher self-esteem and consider themselves to be, if not successful, at least intelligent and worthy of lavish praise rather than unfortunate or cheated. While it is true that individuals with an inflated sense of personal worth probably will be more content with their lives, it is doubtful that they will put in the energy to change themselves or help others as would individuals who are at least partially malcontent.

It is tempting to give in to the utilitarian chimera that the primary goal of human life is to maximize personal happiness and minimize unpleasant emotions like sadness and melancholia, and I would argue, this has become an even greater temptation in today's "Prozac era," in which most people have come to accept or acknowledge a chemical-based explanation for emotional behavior and personality. Contrary to this idea, I want to argue that sadness or melancholia, at least in a mild, somewhat transient state, can sometimes be personally and socially rewarding. To some extent, there is a relation between the study of literature and melancholia. One of the benefits of writing and reading literature is that it can encourage a mild level of melancholia at our mortal limitations and/or at social or personal injustices. Indeed, the process of writing itself, Julie Kristeva would argue, is by definition melancholic as there is an inevitable division between a person and the world and one can never perfectly capture a thought or image in writing.[7]

In line with Kristeva, several young, contemporary American writers criticize the current definitions of mental illness and depression. For instance, in her autobiography, *Prozac Nation* (1994), young, Harvard-educated Elizabeth Wurtzel depicts her lifelong struggle with chronic depression and her attempts to cope with her illness. There should be little doubt that Wurtzel's emotionally fraught, suicidal bouts with depression fall under the definition of "clinical depression" and must be in part biologically or chemically based. After all, she does admit that her life and general emotional state have significantly improved thanks to various antidepressants. However, Wurtzel claims that beginning in the late 1980s and 1990s, youth culture has tended to glorify depression as an understandable reaction to an unfulfilling world which cannot be trusted. Consequently, she argues that depression, "a state of mind once considered tragic has become completely commonplace, even worthy of comedy.... This private world of loony bins and weird people that I always felt I occupied and hid in had suddenly been turned inside out so that it seemed like this was one big Prozac Nation, one big mess of malaise" (297). In *Prozac Nation*, Wurtzel cites a *New York Times* article that claims that those born after 1955 are three times as likely as their grandparents' generation to suffer from depression (7). Such a dramatic increase in depression must either be due to environmental factors or a looser classification of depression as a medical illness. The "depression culture" that Wurtzel refers to need not be composed entirely or even largely of people who are clinically or medically depressed. Rather, it can refer to persons who have become prey to a larger environmental or social malaise, or it can refer to persons who have appropriated an affectation of depression. Wurtzel writes, "Perhaps what has come to be placed in the catch-all category of depression is really a guardedness, a nervousness, a suspicion about intimacy, any of many perfectly natural reactions to a world that seems to be perilously lacking in the basic guarantees that our parents expected: a marriage that would last, employment that was secure, sex that wasn't deadly" (302).

While Wurtzel's *Prozac Nation* is autobiographical, some young, contemporary American fiction writers have explored the significance (or lack thereof) of the changing nature of mental illness with a wary eye cast toward psychologists and psychiatrists who are often portrayed as self-serving and self-aggrandizing rather than genuinely committed to healing their patients. Like Wurtzel, Douglas Coupland proposes in *Life After God* that what is sometimes described as depression can actually be a larger social or existential malaise. The narrator of the story "Cathy" in *Life After God* reveals that he has purposely maintained an affectation of depression after dropping out of consumer/corporate society. The narrator, who isolates himself in a shabby hotel room in the hope of being somehow enlightened, reflects: "The whole ensemble had made a suitably glamorous backdrop for my belief that my poverty, my fear of death, my sexual frustration and my inability to connect with others would carry me off into some sort of epiphany" (30). The narrator does not experience an epiphany through his self-imposed isolation and admits that he was "only acquiring a veneer of bitterness" (ibid.). This bitterness often takes the place of depression or is mistaken for depression, when it is actually a larger social or existential malaise. In the story "1,000 Years," one speaker describes himself as a "broken person" who has "lost the ability to recapture the purer feelings of my younger years" (309). He takes antidepressants but does not consider himself to be clinically depressed, but rather "coming to grips with what I know the world is truly like" (310). Depression, according to this character, is often defined as a natural reaction to a selfish and self-aggrandizing world.

Similarly, in response to a world that falls short of individual expectations, many of David Foster Wallace's characters also retreat inward and become if not "depressed," then severely introverted. In *Infinite Jest*, as the three Incandenza children all struggle toward adulthood, Wallace portrays each as deficient of core self, passion and emotional engagement. This is clearest with the youngest brother, Mario, the misshapen dwarf, whose physical deformities make him an object of ridicule and force him to retreat from the world. Mario becomes a film gopher for his father and, after his father's death, becomes completely isolated, regularly prowling the grounds of Enfield Tennis Academy with a camera. In contrast, the eldest Incandenza, Orin, who becomes a star punter at Boston College and subsequently for the Arizona Cardinals, is motivated solely by fleeting feelings of sexual attraction. Night after night, he beds a new "subject" without emotional engagement. Meanwhile, the youngest Incandenza brother, Hal, serves as a young, intelligent, everyman figure. Hal's acute intelligence as a lexical prodigy contributes to his extreme introversion and self-consciousness, which Wallace continually offsets with Hal's feelings of internal emptiness and selflessness.

Infinite Jest begins as narrated by Hal, who perceives the world in distant, objectifiable terms and cannot effectively communicate with others: "I am seated in an office, surrounded by heads and bodies. My posture is consciously congruent to the shape of my hard chair. This is a cold room in University Administration, wood-walled, Remington-hung, double-windowed against the November heat" (3). As a gifted tennis prodigy as well as a lexical prodigy, Hal has come to perceive life as a kind of endless tennis match in which he decides on the appropriate response to "lob" back to the "player" in any particular situation, in order to maximize his chances for success. During the interview, Hal continues, "I believe I appear neutral, maybe even pleasant, though I've been coached to err on the side of neutrality and not attempt what would feel to me like a pleasant expression or smile.... My fingers are mated into a mirrored series of what manifests, to me, as the letter X" (ibid.). The admissions interviewers, however, doubt Hal's superb grades and suspect that Hal might not have written his seven college application essays, which include "Neoclassical Assumptions in Contemporary Prescriptive Grammar" and "Tertiary Symbolism in Justinian Erotica" (7). In an inspired fit which borders on a nervous breakdown, Hal rants to the admissions officers:

> "My application's not bought," I am telling them, calling into the darkness of the red cave that opens out before closed eyes. "I am not just a boy who plays tennis. I have an intricate history. Experiences and feelings. I'm complex. I read," I say. "I study and read. I bet I've read everything you've read. I consume libraries. I wear out spines and ROM-drives. I do things like get into a taxi and say, 'The library, and step on it'.... I'm not a machine. I feel and believe. I have opinions.... I'm not just a creatus, manufactured, bred for a function" [11–12].

To a key extent, *Infinite Jest* concerns Hal's search for a true self and his attempt to determine whether or not he is in fact a kind of machine. For

Wallace, Hal serves as the frightening aftereffects of a rampant desensitization:

> Hal himself hasn't had a bona fide intensity-of-interior-life-type emotion since he was tiny; he finds terms like joie and value to be like so many variables in rarefied equations, and he can manipulate them well enough to satisfy everyone but himself that he's in there, inside his own hull, as a human being.... One of his troubles with his Moms is the fact that Avril Incandenza believes she knows him inside and out as a human being, and an internally worthy one at that, when in fact, inside Hal there's pretty much nothing at all [694].

One of the key questions that *Infinite Jest* asks the reader is whether Hal is psychologically unstable or deficient or whether he is one of many young Americans who have commonly been desensitized by excessive exposure to various media forms.

Whatever the explanation may be, Wallace certainly does not rest his hopes for Hal's regained emotional breakthrough with psychiatrists. In fact, *Infinite Jest* is a tour de force critique of psychologists. Residing at the Enfield Tennis Academy is Dr. Dolores Rusk, whom Wallace describes:

> You go in with an Issue and all she'll do is make a cage of her hands and look abstractly over the cage at you and take the last dependent clause of whatever you say and repeat it back to you with an interrogative lilt—"Possible homosexual attraction to your doubles partner?"... "Uncontrolled boner during semis at Cleveland?" "Drives you bats when people just parrot you instead of responding?" "Having trouble keeping from twisting my twittery head off like a gamehen's?"—all with the expression she probably thinks looks blandly deep but which really looks exactly the way a girl's face looks when she's dancing with you but would really rather be dancing with just about anyone else in the room [437].

Hal's experiences with a grief counselor to deal with his trauma after he finds the dead body of his father are no less kind to psychiatrists. Dismayed by Hal's lack of outward sorrow for his father, the grief counselor regards Hal's intellectual abstractions as an emotional cover-up. As Hal tells Mario, "I listed my seven textbook choices and vacillated plausibly between and among them. I provided etymological data on the word acceptance all the way back to Wyclif and 14th-century langue-d'oc French. The grief therapist was having none of it.... He made it manifestly clear I wasn't delivering the goods" (253). The grief counselor's dogmatic approach to mourning eventually infuriates Hal: "I accused the grief-therapist of actually inhibiting my attempt to process my grief, by refusing to validate my absence of feelings" (255). Far from being hurt, the grief counselor gets ecstatic because of Hal's "textbook break-down into genuine affect and trauma and guilt and textbook earsplitting grief, then absolution" (256). However, Hal makes it clear that the subject of his minor emotional outburst was the grief therapist and that he truly did and does not have any significant feelings after the suicide of his father, who was mostly emotionally absent during his life.

Far from implicating Hal for emotional frigidity, Wallace implicates the American culture's emphasis on fronting, self-deprecating humor and cynical dispassion because they elevate mass anhedonia and internal emptiness as "hip and cool" (694) when they really only produce mass disconnection and even latent, unacknowledged despair. Wallace does not argue that Hal lacks an inner self, but that in a culture suspicious of sentiment and emotion, his inner self has been repressed and shunned: "One of the really American things about Hal, probably, is the way he despises what it is he's really lonely for: this hideous internal self, incontinent of sentiment and need, that pulls and writhes just under the hip empty mask, anhedonia" (695).

Furthermore, one of Wallace's overarching objectives in *Infinite Jest* and in his short-story collection, *Brief Interviews with Hideous Men*, is to concretely identify the social masks which people unconsciously wear. He also argues that Americans have become increasingly pressured due to the escalating desires that the media awaken and the subsequent back-lash of political correctness, which causes further repression. In his story "The Depressed Person," Wallace investigates how the ever more complicated web of mental health terminology and treatment serves to exacerbate the never-named "depressed person's" actual problem, which is a massive lack of trust and paranoia. Caught in a vicious circle of thought addiction, the depressed person tries ten medications over several years, as well as attending psychological retreats and trying the techniques of "hand puppets, polystyrene props and toys, role playing, and human sculpture" (34). However, all of these methods fail to substantially help her. While the depressed person is a product of a wealthy family and Wallace mocks the grandiose desires of the overly privileged in their belief that happiness can be bought, he also criticizes the psychoanalytical field for helping to foster this belief.

Significantly, the problem for the depressed person (and to some extent, for all of us) is that she can never know for sure whether someone truly cares for her or is merely feigning their emotions. She recounts for the therapist a particular traumatic experience at boarding school in which she witnesses her roommate "talk to some unknown boy on the room's telephone as she [the roommate] made faces and gestures of repulsion and boredom with the call" (45). The "self-assured, popular and attractive roommate" then gets the depressed person to knock on the door so she can get off the phone. For the depressed person, this serves as an indication of how duplicitous and untrusting people can be. Consequently, she tells her friends, whom her therapist calls a support system, to be "utterly up-front and frank and not spend one second longer on the phone with the depressed person than she was absolutely glad to spend" (37). Of course, by doing so, the depressed person puts her support system in a double bind in which they would understandably be more apt to be dishonest or to repress their true feelings out of fear of hurting the depressed person.

Wallace reserves his strongest criticism for psychoanalysis in the depressed person's passive-aggressive relationship with her therapist. The depressed person even realizes how her visits to her therapist reinforce her feelings that most people are duplicitous and not to be trusted. She describes the $90 an hour she pays the therapist "to patiently listen to her and respond honestly and empathetically" as "demeaning and pathetic" to have to "buy patience and empathy" (44). Thus the depressed person comes to believe that her relationship with the therapist is nothing more than a cold, economic one, devoid of emotional connection. She comes to believe that she spends "$1,080 a month to purchase what was in many respects a kind of fantasy-friend who could fulfill her childishly narcissistic fantasies of getting her own emotional needs met by another without having to reciprocally meet or empathize with or even consider the other's own emotional needs" (47).

At a crucial point, the depressed person admits that she is preoccupied with the idea that others are deriding her behind her back (54). Here, Wallace in part implicates the reader, who may very well have been laughing at the extremely wealthy depressed person's increasingly futile and seemingly endless or whiny attempts to "cure" her depression. Yet the fact seemingly remains that the depressed person is in "terrible and unceasing emotional pain" (31). However, considering the fact that she has tried virtually every antidepressant manufactured and psychological technique to little or no avail, Wallace begs a vital question: Might the therapies that the depressed person tries and the politically correct language which psychologists use actually exacerbate her depression by making her feel further excluded from others? Does the depressed person have a chemical imbalance due to clinical depression, or is she really just seeing the world too realistically or too consciously? All of her observations and possible paranoia might be in fact warranted. That is, her "friends" may be merely pandering to her because they fear hurting her. Others may be laughing at her and her therapist may very well have had no personal concern for her whatsoever or, worse yet, had dragged her unproductive therapy sessions out year after year for monetary reasons.

In a sense, we are all in the depressed person's position of having incomplete knowledge, but Wallace argues that this is even more so today because life in contemporary society demands increasingly complex social conventions and a further schism has grown which separates our public and private selves and which could even annihilate our private conceptions of self. For Wallace, younger Americans' emphasis on fronting and dispassion, which they have unconsciously adopted from the media, have made them further duplicitous. Furthermore, the postmodern insistence that there is no essential core self leaves the individual forever enmeshed in the depressed person's position of never being able to know another and never being sure of anything. In the next chapter, I explore how several fiction writers address the problem of the fragmented or hybrid self in contemporary America.

3 Hybrid Identities and Conflicting Relationships

It is often said that the defining task of adolescence is to find one's individual identity. Undergraduates pick a major and purportedly pursue a career pertinent to their own individual aptitudes and desires. At the same time, over the past fifty years, there has been in a shift in how most college instructors regard adolescent students. College curriculums reflect a growing shift from teacher-focused lecture courses to collaborative, discussion-based courses. Rather than pontificating instructors treating students as empty vessels to be summarily enlightened, most instructors now believe that their primary task is to bring out or more fully develop the already existing or formative core of student selves. Yet the common university goal of fostering individual identity and voice is at odds with postmodern theory, which sternly critiques the idea of a stable, individual self.

This is not to suggest that the question of selfhood spontaneously generated in the twentieth century. As Jürgen Habermas suggests, the modern philosophical age was inaugurated by Kant's breakdown of "the metaphysical seal on the correspondence between language and the world" (260), which in turn led to the preeminence of self-reflection or the subject's conception of himself or herself as a human being. On similar lines, Alain Finklekraut argues that "[t]he West began to bemoan its loss of universal concepts at precisely the historical moment that non–Western cultures began to claim their share of them: that is when 'other' cultures called into question the European 'center' and its stable sense of self as the decolonization movement took hold in the 1950s" (23). In the next chapter, I explore ethnic hybridity, but in this chapter I want to explore nonethnically specific individuality in America.

We often talk about people as if they have particular attributes as "things" inside themselves, and most of us believe that there exists a fixed and true identity or character at the core of an individual (even if

78

we're not sure that we know quite what that is for a particular person). One of the most significant poststructural or postmodern philosophers, Michel Foucault, rejected this view. For Foucault, a person does not have a "real" identity. Rather, "identity" is a product of communicative discourse. An identity might be communicated to others in interactions, but this is a shifting, primarily linguistic, construction.

For postmodernists like Foucault, the self is at best a locus of masks and at worst a purely artificial, and now primarily media-fueled, abstraction. Rejecting the modernist view, typified by T.S. Eliot's romanticism of the visionary artist and his quest for spiritual unity, in "The Death of the Author," Roland Barthes speaks of the author as a product of modern society with its emphasis on the individual human (78). Deleuze and Guattari, in their turn, consider the subject to be, at most, an ephemeral projection. The subject has no fixed identity and is always peripheral to the organic body, the desiring-machine. He or she is never more than a function, a transient function of the transient senses and states of the body (24, 152).

While these postmodern contentions are perfectly defensible, they have some significant practical disadvantages in leading to a host of new neuroses and psychological problems. At the close of the last chapter, I investigated theories and texts that deal with depression and mental illness in contemporary America. The legacy of over two hundred years of post–Kantian deconstruction and one of the central tenets of postmodernity is the belief that an individual may lack a true or core self. If one believes that humans do not possess a core self or are not able to express themselves sincerely, then it becomes increasingly difficult to establish healthy, nurturing relationships with others. For if the individual is nothing more than a shifting actor, then how can we sure whether another is being sincere or false, honest or dishonest?

Furthermore, the overarching, almost totalizing power of popular culture has helped blanket individual identities and curtails human interaction. Individuals often define themselves in context with media icons rather than in context with each other. In this chapter, I investigate a novel and short-story collection by David Foster Wallace and a novel by Douglas Coupland in order to show how individuals can become emotionally damaged or crippled by self-negating postmodernity, media typology and the infinite second-guessing forced upon individuals who are left in a state of endless deciphering and deconstruction. In this chapter, I show that the hybridity engendered by postmodernity has negative personal and social aftereffects.

The Search for the Self in Postmodern America: The Broom of the System

David Foster Wallace's first novel, *The Broom of the System* (1987), written when he was only in his early twenties, dramatizes the predicament of young Americans due to mass technological advancements and postmodern theory. Wallace examines philosophical theory, particularly that of Wittgenstein, in context with that of late-twentieth-century American culture. Concurrently, he contrasts his generation and the preceding postmodern generation, concluding that his generation has been left with a fragmented, unsubstantiated world without unifying communities or beliefs or even the belief in verbal communication as an effective medium.

In *The Broom of the System*, Wallace represents forty-two-year-old, highly educated Rick Vigorous as a quintessential deconstructing postmodernist. Wallace first introduces Rick as he lies in bed with the main protagonist, twenty-four year old telephone operator Lenore Beadsman. Lenore's and Rick's first words to each other are a linguistic discussion of whether they are in fact "cuddling," according to its definition. Rick responds to Lenore in his typical abstract, distant manner: "I think this satisfies standard cuddling criteria, yes" (22).

Rick, whose thoughts are presented in linguistic and literary abstracts, perceives reality through fictionalized stories or abstract reasoning. He tells Lenore stories rather than discussing his feelings. Storytelling and philosophical expostulation have become his primary means of communication. Rick discusses kissing Lenore, not in empirical terms, but in abstract, philosophical terms, as a point of departure for exposition: "a kiss with Lenore is ... not so much a kiss as it is a dislocation, a removal and rude transportation of essence from self to lip ... achieving full ontological status only in subsequent union" (59). Rick uses language to elevate his personal experience into philosophical mythologies, but by doing so, he partially loses the ability to respond to events empirically and emotionally.

Lenore Beadsman, of a different generation than Rick, represents more of a questioning and questing post-postmodern type. Encouraged by her grandmother, Lenore seriously considers the possibility that she is "more like a character than a person" (249). Lenore's grandmother (also named Lenore), a former student of Wittgenstein's, whose words recirculate in the novel, represents Wittgensteinian and poststructuralist thought, which Lenore grapples with on a practical level (as it pertains to her own life). Lenore's grandmother has shown her "how a life is words and nothing else" (119). Caught within a seemingly unanswerable, linguistic existential dilemma, Lenore wonders, "Suppose Gramma tells me convincingly that all that really exists of my life is what can be said about it ... the living is the telling, that there's nothing going on with me that isn't either told or tellable, and if so, what's the difference, why live at all?" (119). Steadily, Lenore becomes convinced that she may be a character in a story and not a real human being. Of course, the paradoxical joke is that Lenore is entirely correct—she is an artificially constructed fictional character devised by Wallace.

The world of *The Broom of the System* is one in which communication between people is perilously close to disintegration. In her position as telephone operator, Lenore Beadsman sits at the helm of communications of *Frequent and Vigorous Publications*, a journal whose primary aim is arguably to encourage authors to communicate their ideas with others. At the beginning of the novel, Lenore and her fellow operators at the Bombardini building suffer from a communicative mix-up, in which they frequently receive calls to other businesses. Peter Abbott, the telephone maintenance man, comes to repair the mixed-up phone system. He describes the communication system in the tunnels underneath the building: "Think of them like nerves and the city as a body with a nervous system" (64). Abbott's personification of the city and its communication system as one large mechanical cyberbody takes us a step beyond Habermas's proposition of communicative reason as the foundation for a new ethics or philosophy. In fact, there appears to be no real reason behind the haphazardly strewn systems of communication. Rather, they seem to be malfunctioning of their own accord.

This literal communicative mix-up mirrors the ongoing communicative problems that exist between other people in *The Broom of the System*, most specifically that of Rick and Lenore. As the book progresses, just as Rick and Lenore's relationship deteriorates, as it is largely built upon stories rather than personal experience or emotion, the physical communication systems also deteriorate. By the end of the novel, a beleaguered Peter Abbott declares, "The upshot here is that your particular line tunnel looks like it's kind of decided it's a real freakshow human being or something" (457). It is hinted, although never resolved, that Lenore's grandmother escaped to the tunnels and purposely damaged the city's communication system in an anarchic attempt to damage or destroy these artificial forms of communication.

Indeed, much of contemporary "communication" has become secondary and artificial, not person to person, but more like dissemination from machine to person. Media forms like television, music, film and the Internet bombard listeners and viewers with information, masquerading as communicative devices when they actually dominate the passive viewer/listener. More than any other media form, television has played a huge role in changing the nature of communication and usurping the general power of fiction. In a sense, television is the ideal Other, who pleases but asks nothing in return.

In one scene in *The Broom of the System*, television plays a huge and unsettling role as family mediator. Lenore's sister, Clarice Spaniard (Spaniard is her married name), and her family use a televised form of therapy to deal with their family problems. In this televised family theater/therapy, each family member wears a mask while watching a video-recorded audience of people in a theater. Then Clarice distributes objects to each family member (a Spiro Agnew watch, a teddy bear, a Visa Gold Card and a cut-out book). After this, Clarice's son Stoney reads from a prewritten text which centers on the Spaniards, who serve as a model family. The text decries materialism and emphasizes the extreme closeness of the ideal family: "All they thought about was the family and all they thought of themselves as was family-parts" (167). When Stoney reads, "Four individual people were a unit," the televised audience claps in moral agreement. This family theater/therapy emphasizes the importance of familial communication in response to the rampant materialism of postindustrial life. However, its ultimately benign message appears buried in the banal wording. The family theater ends on a wishy-washy note: "They found out that what they needed to get their feelings of being themselves from was themselves" (172). In practice, the use of television as a therapeutic medium works as more of a division between the family members, who do not talk during or after the "therapy." Rather, the therapy seems pointless, full of empty television-like clichés—a media ploy by the manufacturer to capitalize on family problems.

Through his depiction of television-oriented family theater, Wallace dramatizes how everyday Americans adopt the language and techniques of modern psychology. In a society where direct communication between people has become increasingly strained, the psychiatrist or psychotherapist takes precedence as a communicative deus ex machina. As I established in the previous chapter, Wallace has a justifiable aversion toward contemporary notions of psychology, and he provides a scathing critique of a psychologist in *The Broom of the System*.

Dr. Curtis Jay serves as the supposed remedy to the ongoing communicative problems of the characters. Both Lenore and Rick visit Dr. Jay, who subscribes to the suspicious theory of the fictional Olaf Blentener, who invented the ridiculous and presumably fictional hygiene anxiety research. Dr. Jay claims that "hygiene-anxiety is identity anxiety" (120), and he bends everything Lenore and Rick tell him to fit Blentener's half-baked, semiludicrous theory. When Lenore tells Dr. Jay that she has trouble distinguishing fantasy from reality (and vice versa), Dr. Jay responds by saying, "So comparisons between real life and stories make you feel hygiene anxiety, a.k.a. identity anxiety" (ibid.). Dr. Jay also analyzes Rick's bizarre sexual dreams (in one of which Rick dreams that he orally stimulates Queen Victoria, who, bored with his attempt, exclaims, "We are not pleased" [47]) according to hygiene anxiety, which champions fear of uncleanness as the primary, motivating neurosis.

For Dr. Jay, hygiene-anxiety research revolves around a philosophy based on membrane theory. He repeatedly yells out, "I smell break-through" in increasingly absurd hyperbole. When Dr. Jay says he smells breakthrough, he literally means it. At one point, he wears a gas mask in a therapy session with Lenore, because otherwise, "Were I to remove this right now, my naive young client and friend, the stench of breakthrough would blast me into unconsciousness" (330). In an attempt to illustrate his shaky, philosophical membrane theory, Dr. Jay simulates a sperm and has Lenore act as a membrane to illustrate her fear of "contamination" (332). Furthermore, Wallace purposely obfuscates the already confusing, catch-all philosophical terminology Self and Other through Dr. Jay's confused diagnosis—"A flabby membrane is unhealthy [*sic*] permeable, lets the Self out to soil the Other-set and the Other-set in to soil the Self" (330).

When Lenore tells Dr. Jay her Wittgensteinian dilemma, "Suppose Gramma tells me convincingly that all that really exists of my life is what can be said about it?" Jay quizzically and unprofessionally responds, "What the hell does that mean?" (119). In fact, Rick readily admits that the "chief reason I continue to see him [Dr. Jay] in the face of mount-ing evidence of major incompetence is the fact that he is also completely unethical, an incorrigible gossip who tells me all of what Lenore tells him. All of it" (61). Perhaps most importantly, Dr. Jay's essential fraudulence and materialism come through in his comment "Come see me the moment you have money" (242) to Lenore after she tells him that she doesn't have enough money to make their next session.

The psychologist continues to be used as a strawman in another of the framed narratives in *The Broom of the System*. In this story submit-ted to *Frequent and Vigorous Publications* and told by Rick to Lenore, "a man and woman meet and fall in love at a group-therapy session" (103), just as Lenore and Rick meet in Dr. Jay's office. The man suffers from periodic, uncontrollable temper tantrums, while the woman suffers from depression and an eating disorder. As Rick tells Lenore, the psycholo-gist is "the only real villain in the story" (105). Due to his own hatred of "collective societal units," the psychologist tries to get all of his patients "to leave the city and move out into this series of isolated cabins deep in the woods—whose cabins he by some strange coincidence owns and sells to his patients at a slimy profit" (ibid.). Although the psychologist does appear to help the two, Wallace or the author of the story does not acknowledge his healing power. Rather, the man and the woman fall "under the psychologist's clinical spell" (ibid.) and end up buying one of his isolated cabins in the woods. Like most of the other mininarratives, this one ends horrendously with the death of the man, the psychotherapist, and the coma of the woman, who accidentally kills her infant son by rolling on top of him as she sleeps. Despite its comic effect, Wallace's debunking of the psychologist has deeper implications. Rather than resolving communication problems between people, the psychologist actually creates more gulfs between and within people through the use of confused and frequently obfuscating jargon.

The effects of rampant postmodernity upon the younger generation appear in the stories that Rick shares with Lenore, all of which are submissions to his literary journal. Rick tells Lenore, "Do you know where all the really sad stories I'm getting are coming from? They're coming, it turns out, from kids. Kids in college. I'm starting to think something is just deeply wrong with the youth of America. First of all, a truly disturbing number of them are interested in writing fiction. And more than interested, actually. And sad, sad, sad stories" (104). The question that remains in Rick's statement is why fiction writing has become so important to these young writers. It may be an opportunity to counteract their own sad or traumatic experiences, but it may also be due to a general cultural championing of sadness and melancholia as nobler states of being, but denying them any transforming power. Indeed, all of the mininarratives in *The Broom of the System* revolve around such bleak subjects as unrequited love, the destruction of relationships, suicide, mass disfigurement and pedophilia. The stories, while often allegorical, display a shaky, desperate culture, potentially on the verge of collapse.

Wittgenstein argues that storytelling or telling of any kind helps create the world or our conception of reality. Thus, those hopeless stories submitted to Rick's journal can create a kind of chain reaction in which the characters themselves feel hopeless because of the stories. The reader's new unhappiness or hopelessness may affect others, leading to a vicious circle of general meaninglessness. In *The Broom of the System*, relationships do appear to be one sided, never complementary and hardly nurturing. Relationships are perhaps best illustrated by Reverend Hart Lee Sykes's corrupt television program, "Partnership with God," in which Sykes implores viewers to become partners with God, who Sykes claims can help viewers achieve "the fulfillment of your every wish" (461). In a sense, in our pleasure-oriented culture, this is a precise description of what many consider to be an ideal relationship. Since this ideal, wish-fulfilling Other can never be found, it naturally leads to general dissatisfaction and unhappiness.

Rick Vigorous, most enveloped by the growing contemporary disillusion, appears to be two dimensional. It is as if all of the "sad stories" he reads have helped nullify his emotions and have helped make him more like an automaton. Having lost the ability to comprehend people, Rick perceives the world objectively. Toward the end of the novel, while in bed with Mindy Metalman, Rick contemplates his situation by splitting his surroundings into parts rather than viewing it as part of a whole picture: "Calves, light, legs, light, everything will be alright." But everything does not appear to turn out alright for Rick. Rather, Rick metaphorically self-destructs as a character at the end of the novel, which concludes on his unfinished sentence, "I'm a man of my" (467). The missing word, of course, is "word."

This paradox mirrors the drawing which Lenore finds while searching in her grandmother's room at the Shaker Heights Retirement Home. The drawing is an antimony of a barber with an exploded head, who "shaves all and only those who do not shave themselves" (42). This paradox (does the barber shave himself?) leads to the barber's allegorical destruction (hence, his exploded head in the drawing). The paradox of Rick's statement is that if he is a man of his word, then he is no man at all, just a linguistic construction. The contradiction is further complicated by the fact that as a character, Rick literally is a man of his word. Examined from a different angle, Rick serves as a man of Wallace's word. One could further complicate this already complicated paradox by questioning whether Rick is in actuality a man of Wallace's word and considering whether Wallace himself is actually the construction of someone else's words (This might be the position of some radical "death of the author" poststructuralist). In any case, Rick effectively nullifies himself as a character by his own paradoxical thought.

What Wallace hints at with this ending is that postmodernism, taken to its limit, leads to essential, unanswerable paradoxes which can lead to ultimate destruction. Furthermore, postmodernity can lead to a chain reaction of mass despair, if not mass nihilism, because of its emphasis on chaotic uncertainty. As a praxis, postmodernism, like communism from Marxism, diverges from its original theory and becomes something different when introduced into "reality." Just as Wallace considers the cultural implications of postmodernity in *The Broom of the System*, Douglas Coupland also criticizes postmodern culture as dwarfing and possibly even nullifying an individual's identity in his novel *Generation X*.

Escaping from Popular Culture: Douglas Coupland's *Generation X*

Although Canadian by birth, Douglas Coupland achieved almost immediate literary renown in America with his first novel, *Generation X*, which concerns the attempts of three young Americans to find their individual identities, which they come to believe have been dwarfed by popular culture. They go through a postmodern, existential crisis in which they realize their essential meaninglessness or emptiness as popular culture simulacrums in a postmodern society already adrift in such forms.[1] Coupland's aim and the aim of his characters is to use literature and narrative to construct a virtual map of the postmodern cultural world in an attempt to achieve stable, satisfying, personal identities.

Throughout *Generation X*, Coupland includes advertisements, comic strips and most importantly, definitions that Coupland uses to describe life in North America during the early 1990s. The definitions help ground the fictional story in cultural reality and constantly remind the reader that *Generation X* is a loosely based fiction which should be considered in broad terms. Coupland simultaneously acts as fiction writer and sociological critic, purposely blurring the lines between fiction and reality or nonfiction and fiction. The terminology Coupland invents or appropriates (it isn't clear which terms are his invention and which ones aren't) reflects his attempt to forge a coherent shape out of American postmodern culture. Among the most important terms that Coupland creates is McJob, which he defines as "a low-prestige, low-dignity, low-benefit, no-future job in the service sector. Frequently considered a satisfying career choice by people who have never held one" (7). Pictures of a male bicycle courier and a female office temp in the margin help solidify an image of an economically debilitated generation forced into isolating, short-term, unsatisfying and unfulfilling work. Indeed, at this pre–Internet time, the future seemed economically bleak for young people. However, while economics plays a role in Generation X, the larger issue is the search for individuality and identity.

Traditionally, American postmodernism reveals a fragmentation of the individual, but *Generation X* reveals homogenized fragmentation (often unacknowledged by the individual or subject). Effectively, mass media allied with popular culture has helped to produce mass, homogenized identities which are similarly fragmented. In the beginning of Coupland's *Generation X*, after mentioning where his friends Claire and Dag are from (Claire, Los Angeles; Dag, Toronto, Canada), the narrator, Andy Palmer, mentions that "where you're from feels sort of irrelevant these days" (7).[2]

These three protagonists of *Generation X* gradually become aware of their homogenized, mass-produced identities defined by popular culture and consumer possessions. Each character goes through a postmodern existential crisis brought on by the failure of consumer society to provide them with a stable or fulfilling identity. Dag's story illuminates this gradual awakening. He describes himself as initially content with his consumer-based identity: "I was both thrilled and flattered and achieved no small thrill of power to think that most manufacturers of life-style accessories in the Western world considered me their most desirable target market" (19). Gradually dissatisfied with his corporate job, Dag begins to consider the jaded words of a co-worker: "Why work? Simply to buy more stuff.... I should realize that the only reason we all go to work in the morning is because we're terrified of what would happen if we stopped" (23). Dag subsequently quits his job and becomes what he calls a "Basement Person." Economically depriving himself, he strips away his major possessions. Dag gets rid of his television after realizing that it serves only to exacerbate his desires and makes him feel inadequate because he is "unable to achieve the animal happiness of people on TV" (37). With each further removal from popular/postmodern culture, Dag feels emptier and more barren, aware that his previous identity was fraudulently based on consumer products and mass-media hyperreality.

Steadily, Dag becomes aware of a growing emotional lack in his life with each further removal from postmodern culture. These consumer products and media forms which had previously pleased him now only seem to increase his emotional disconnection. Soon "[a]ll looks with strangers became the unspoken question, 'Are you the stranger who will rescue me?'" (30). Subsequently, Dag harkens back to an Edenic, culturally saturated childhood where happiness was mediated by popular culture and consumer products. Eventually, he loses the ability to "take anything literally" (31), which mirrors the positions in which many of David Foster Wallace's characters find themselves. This final disbelief in the world as rampant hyperreality is the final revelation of the postmodern existential crisis, after which an individual finds that his experiences and emotions are mediated and controlled by popular culture, replacing empirical, physical experience with fictionalized, mass-produced experience. Finally, Dag resorts to exiling himself from culture and society or as he describes it "a series of scary incidents that simply weren't stringing together to make for an interesting book" (ibid.). Dag acknowledge that his life has become a postmodern nightmare, a fragmented metanarrative that has no coherence or meaning.

Andy goes through a similar postmodern existential crisis at the end of a job in Japan; he tells Dag and Claire a story of how his boss, Mr. Takamichi, brings him into his personal office and shows Andy what he considers his most valuable possession. It turns out to be a rare nude photo of Marilyn Monroe. Andy then describes his subsequent revelation:

> I broke into a sweat and the words of Rilke, the poet, entered my brain—his notion that we are all of us born with a letter inside us, and that only if we are true to ourselves may we be allowed to read it before we die. The burning blood in my ears told me that Mr.

Takamichi had somehow mistaken the Monroe photo in the safe for
the letter inside of himself, and that I, myself, was in peril of making a similar mistake [58].

Andy realizes that he is living in a world where people are defining themselves by consumer products and objects and thereby losing their individuality in the process. He has a realization very similar to Dag's when
he returns to America, "that there was still too much history for me. That
I needed less in life. Less past" (24). Later, Andy tells Claire that "I was
merely trying to erase all traces of history from my past" (37).

When Andy mentions "history" he does not mean personal history
but cultural history, or popular cultural history which he believes has
determined his very identity. He has come to believe that he doesn't have
much of a personal history since he has spent most of his life as a passive recipient of popular culture. Andy tells his brother, Tyler, that he
misses the presence of the Vietnam War in his childhood. "They were
ugly times," Andy admits, "but they were the only times I'll ever get—
genuine capital H history times before history was turned into a press
release, a marketing strategy, and a cynical campaign tool" (151). Andy
believes that we are in a post–"History" era in which the idea of "history" has not only been fragmented into competing histories but is being
treated as a product that is tailored to lure consumers into literally buying into it.

Furthermore, in *Generation X*, Coupland points to an awareness of
popular cultural history as dominant history. He invents a term, *decade
blending*, which he defines as "In clothing: the indiscriminate combination of two or more items from various decades to create a personal
mood: Shiela = Mary Quant earrings (1960s) + cork wedgie platform
shoes (1970s) + black leather jacket (1950s and 1980s)" (15). "Historical" eras have become associated with popular culture, produced primarily by television and movies. In one comic which Coupland includes,
a young woman combs her hair in the style of the 1940s' actress Barbara
Stanwick and says, "Hang on Brad.... My hair doesn't look 1940s
enough" (89). Fashion has become a visual historical text for Gen Xers,
a certain clothing or hairstyle representing the historical past. In the same
category as decade blending is "tele-parablizing," which Coupland
defines as "Morals used in everyday life that derive from TV sitcom
plots: 'That's just like the episode where Jan lost her glasses'" (151). This
association of popular culture with historical eras is what Jean Baudrillard
calls simulacrums: images of history created by popular culture which
do not necessarily have any real historical basis, but are treated as "history" nonetheless. In postmodern American society, television and popular culture have become the dominant culture, a field of reference that

has overtaken "history" itself. Furthermore, Gen Xers' definitions of historical eras have been further determined by the hyperreality of television and popular culture.

Not only is the postmodern world hyperreal and post-"historic," it is psychologically manipulating: Ultimately Andy and Dag lose belief in their world and in their own "identities." As Larry McCaffery suggests:

> This unprecedented expansion of culture, made possible specifically by the exponential growth of technology, changed the contours of the world. Popular culture not only displaced nature and "colonized" the physical space of nearly every country on earth, but (just as importantly) it began to colonize even those inner subjective realms that everyone once believed were inviolable, such as people's unconscious, sexual desires, and memories ["Introductory Ways," 39].

Andy, Dag, and Claire gradually come to believe that they have been "colonized" by popular culture and attempt to remove themselves from that enforced, fragmented mentality by extracting themselves from American culture itself.

Consequently, the protagonists flee their former lives and postmodern/consumer culture. Andy describes how they had come to this final decision of personal removal and cultural abnegation in a darkly humorous passage:

> Our systems had stopped working, jammed with the odor of copy machines, White-Out, the smell of bond paper, and the endless stress of pointless jobs done grudgingly to little applause. We had compulsions that made us confuse shopping with creativity, to take downers and assume that merely renting a video on a Saturday night was enough [11].

Their choice of exile in Palm Springs, California, is a questionable location to become isolated from postmodern culture and experience a more meaningful or substantial life. Indeed, after the move, Andy and Dag are back in "McJobs" as bartenders as is Claire who works at a department store perfume counter.

Furthermore, Andy seems to be unsuccessful in removing all vestiges of popular culture history from his mind. Throughout his verbal description of Palm Springs, Andy continues to use television and movie references as a point of comparison and/or definition. Satirically, he mentions that Palm Springs is like television in the sense that both do not have real weather, and he also compares it to the Flintstones and a Vietnam War movie set. He uses the fictive forms of television and movies as a frame of reference to make sense of his "real" surroundings. To a person like Andy, who has been raised on popular culture, projecting television and movie references onto the landscape helps make it appear more real and relevant, not hyperreal, as his historical imagination has become intertwined with popular culture. Furthermore, it appears that Andy, Dag, and Claire have entered a landscape that mimics TV's hyperreality as an illusory, man-made desert oasis. In a sense, they have stepped into the hyperreal world of television and mass media, rather than away from it.

To further add to this sense of hyperreality is Andy's comment, "There is also no middle class [in Palm Springs], and in that sense the place is medieval" (10). The three want to live in an economically polarized community where people aren't determined by their possessions or determined to find the possessions that will define them as "individuals." To the three, the contemporary postmodern quest for identity as determined by consumer products is symptomatic of the middle class. They believe that the rich in Palm Springs are the controllers or inventors of either consumer products or the mass media. As Dag half jokes, "Every time someone on the planet uses a paper clip, fabric softens their laundry, or watches a re-run of 'Hee Haw' on TV, a resident somewhere here in the Coachella Valley collects a penny" (10). Meanwhile, the poor residents live in West Palm Springs, or "Hell," as Andy calls it, "a modern ruin and almost deserted save for a few hearty souls in Airstream trailers and mobile homes" (14). Attracted to "Hell," Andy, Dag, and Claire choose to picnic there, a "land so empty that all objects placed on its breathing, hot skin, become objects of irony" (16). In other words, all possessions lose their illusory qualities there. They have no allegorical meaning in the barren desert and are stripped of their false identity, just as the three wish for themselves.

Andy, Dag, and Claire may not have chosen Palm Springs for its close knit community sentiment, but it is there that they form an ad-hoc community of their own, a shadow family of sorts. Andy contends that, "now that we live here in the desert, things have gotten much, *much* better" (11; Coupland's italics), but have they really? The three were all emotionally isolated before their move and continue to be seemingly incapable of a significant emotional relationship with anyone throughout the novel. Andy mentions that neither he, Clare, nor Dag became romantically involved with one another. Indeed, there is very little flirtation or romance among the three. The only character involved in any sort of romantic relationship is Claire, who has an obsessive, physically superficial love for Tobias, a shallow and greedy, but extremely attractive, corporate professional. Her relationship with Tobias fails, leaving her miserable, frustrated and embarrassed. Emotional isolation or desolation is typically disregarded or approached satirically by academic postmodern authors like John Barth or Thomas Pynchon, whose characters often become comically or sardonically, sexually liberated or experimental.[3] However, in *Generation X*, emotional withdrawal is a serious and all-encompassing affliction.

After realizing his fraudulent, consumer-produced identity is a façade, Andy questions any form of happiness whatsoever, even that of his friends, Dag and Claire. For Andy, his friends display a "flavor of happiness" (63) because social conventions dictate that they not express their dissatisfaction with their lives. Happiness itself has become a false consumer product worn by typical members of postmodern society, who aren't aware that they have been duped or even controlled by a dominating postmodern/consumer society that has produced their fragmented or fraudulent identity, dependent on the equally fragmented but ultimately pervasive mass media and popular culture.

Andy does become fully aware of his emotional deficiency during his exile in Palm Springs. He confesses (but only to the reader, not to Dag or Claire): "I've never been in love, and *that's* a problem. I just seem to end up as *friends* with everyone, and I tell you, I really hate it. I want to fall in love. Or at least I think I do. I'm not sure. It looks so ... *messy*" (47; Coupland's italics). Like Jimmy in William Vollmann's *Whores for Gloria*, the characters themselves in *Generation X* try to create narratives or stories out of their own psychological turmoil. Most importantly, unlike Jimmy, the three have each other for support, and they collectively tell/write their own individual stories. Andy emphasizes the importance of narrative in its ability to bring meaning to his and his friends' lives. This function of literature as personal meaning-maker as well as psychological bulwark is largely absent in academic, American postmodern writing. In fact, some deem personally invested, self-reflexive fiction to be self-indulgent, intellectually stunted writing, in the tradition of academically overlooked American writers like Henry Miller, Thomas Wolfe, and Jack Kerouac, each of whom attempted to elevate their real lives into fictional myth. Whereas postmodern literary writers tended to feel liberated by the destruction of the grand narrative, freeing up possibilities for experimentation, Coupland's characters have come to appreciate the restorative power of narrative which has been lost in disjointed postmodern culture.

Andy derived his own philosophy of storytelling from a man he met at Alcoholics Anonymous who tells him, "Never be afraid to cough up a bit of diseased lung for the spectators. How are people going to help themselves if they can't grab onto a fragment of your own horror? People want that little fragment, they need it. That little piece of lung makes their own fragments less scary" (13). This confessional style of writing is anti-postmodern. The stories that the three tell are illusions that they can hide behind. They don't want to resort to the "teleparablizing" that postmodern culture encourages. Rather, they want to tell meaningful, unfragmented stories based on their own lives and vision of the world.

As Dag tells Andy, "Either our lives become stories, or there's just no way to get through them" (8).

Most importantly, Andy, Dag, and Claire tell short stories with invented characters. Finding it difficult to talk about themselves directly, they create thinly veiled allegorical stories out of their own lives. At one point in *Generation X*, Dag has trouble telling Andy why he has gone on a spontaneous road trip to various atomic bomb sites in the Southwest. He can talk about it only after Andy encourages him to fictionalize it, which allows Dag to distance himself from his actions and feelings, which he ascribes to an invented character, Otis. In a sense, the three highlight their own fragmented personal lives by telling unfragmented, allegorical stories. The postmodern author used to be in control of creating the fragmentation; now the fictional character (or author) is trying to erase or heal his or her own psychic fragmentation in the face of the oppressive pervasiveness of popular culture. Perhaps fiction, then, is just another distancing tool, and the allegorical stories that Andy, Dag, and Claire tell are a poor method to deal with their personal problems. If making a life worthwhile is fictionalizing it, then it may be dependent on an unhealthy illusion of meaning, which may be merely a substitute for the blanketing identity effects of popular culture.

This problem is illustrated in Andy's thinly veiled autobiography in the chapter "Re Con Struct." This is Andy's secret story that he must fictionalize into a coherent allegorical story in order to either avoid the pain it causes him or to generalize a greater meaning to himself. It is the story of "Edward," a highly educated young man who becomes steadily secluded and alcoholic and subsequently retreats into a "private world" of words. This private, fenced-off space takes the symbolic shape of a locked room where Edward spends ten years of his life with his faithful spaniel, Ludwig, and a housekeeper, Mrs. York, who brings Edward's daily rations. One day, Ludwig transforms into a vicious Rottweiler, forcing Edward to leave his room. When Edward goes outside, he sees a vision of "a vast city, built not on words but on relationships" (50). He ventures into this new world with the desire to "build the tallest tower of them all" (51). This story symbolically points out the power of allegorical fiction. Essentially, the tower that Andy wants to build is fictional. While Andy does use fictional allegory as an opportunity for psychological confession, he also uses it as an emotional or personal shield to replace that of popular culture, which had previously dominated his identity. To some extent, Andy is gradually able to let his fictional guard or guise down by the end of *Generation X*. Just as he gave up the protective but ultimately illusory power of popular culture, Andy gives up the protective power of allegorical fiction when he starts to tell a story about "a young man" but stops and confesses "oh get real, it's about me" (148).

Andy, Dag, and Claire all blame the elder generation for constructing or contributing to the disjointed, media-obsessed, postmodern world and for the nuclear trauma that they endured as children or young adults. In an essay in 1995, Coupland accused baby boomers, "pummeled by the recession and embarrassed by their own compromised 60s' values" of "transferring their collective darkness onto the group threatening to take their spotlight" (Hornblower, 86). This generational blaming is not historically or literarily new, but what is revealing is the level of disconnection and disdain that the younger generation harbors toward their elders. American modernists did not (at least directly) point their finger at their elders as a cause of their isolation and anomie. Dag reveals his generational animosity and blame when he admits the desire to "punish some aging crock for frittering away my world," at the same time that he's "upset that the world has gotten way too big—way beyond our capacity to tell stories about it, and so all we're stuck with are these blimps and chunks and snippets on bumpers" (5). What Dag describes is a postmodern, fragmented society dominated by popular culture which is mediated in quick snippets. Andy, Dag, and Claire firmly believe that they have inherited a dying postmodern world that their elders created through their consumer/corporate wizardry that markets products to cover up psychic pollution or disillusion. They position themselves as sacrificial victims, harboring resentment against their elders who inherited economic privilege and promise that seems absent from the trio's lives and for "blithely handing over the world to us like so much skid-marked underwear" (38). Happiness is suspect in the eyes of the three who look jealously upon an older couple, Irene and Phil, who "live in a permanent 1950s. They still believe in a greeting card future" (120). Of course, the trio's conception of 1950s' culture is skewed, based presumably on romanticized television shows like "Leave It to Beaver," without regard to the nuclear buildup and burgeoning Cold War that was blossoming during that time.

In *Generation X*, not only is the elder generation implicated for the global production of postmodern consumer culture and the easy fulfillment of their own personal desires, they are also blamed for some of the trio's psychic damage. Andy's emotional difficulties seem to be at least partially the result of growing up in an emotionally undemonstrative family. Claire reflects an equal vehemence toward families and parental society. Just as the three extracted themselves from a debilitating consumer-based postmodern culture, they have also extracted themselves from their equally debilitating families, leaving them only themselves and their stories.

Despite their attempts, Andy, Dag, and Claire gradually realize that their exile in Palm Springs has not fulfilled them emotionally, and they remain subject to postmodern fragmentation. At one point, a gradually disillusioned Dag, seemingly unable to shake off his psychic despondency, tells Andy his new escapist dream to open a hotel in San Felipe,

Mexico. At the end of *Generation X*, Dag and Claire have left Palm Springs for San Felipe, leaving a note for Andy, who follows and subsequently leaves the United States behind. This appears to be another attempt to flee postmodern American culture.

The three may be on their way toward becoming expatriates in the tradition of the American modernists. Will they be any more successful? It is doubtful, but there is a glimmer of hope brought about by the final emotional scene, in which Andy is caught in a traffic jam in Mexico, frightened out of his wits after seeing a mushroom-shaped cloud in the distance, which he misinterprets to be nuclear fallout but is actually the burning of agricultural fields. Out of his car, Andy sees a white egret, who swoops over him and cuts his scalp. A group of mentally disabled teenagers comforts him, hugging him "in their adoring, healing, uncritical embrace" (179). Andy emphasizes that this "crush of love was unlike anything I had ever known" (ibid.). No doubt, this one act will not be substantially beneficial in healing Andy's psychic and emotional afflictions, but it might be the first step toward his gradual recovery. This scene points out an important loss of primal emotional connection in postmodern/popular culture that perhaps can never be recovered by Andy, Dag, or Claire. Ironically, the only people who appear emotionally healthy in Coupland's *Generation X* are the mentally disabled teenagers, presumably untainted by the pervasive spread of postmodern/popular culture.

Coupland's *Generation X* depicts a fragmented, consumer-based, postmodern culture at the terminus of twentieth-century America and reveals the damaged, vulnerable individuals it produces underneath their popular/consumer-culture-based façades. Underlying *Generation X* is the all-pervasive influence of popular culture in contemporary American society. Canonized American postmodern authors typically view popular culture semihumorously as a frequent site of flamboyance, extravagance, excess, parody, and self-parody. Still, most people do not willfully drop out of society as do the three protagonists of *Generation X*. Rather, most people forge on in the consumer/popular-culture-dominated, workaday world. This is the terrain that David Foster Wallace explores in his short-story collection, *Brief Interviews with Hideous Men*, which delves deeper into new difficulties involved in sexual and romantic relationships in the 1990s than Coupland's work does.

Hideous Relationships in the '90s: *Brief Interviews with Hideous Men*

The relative popularity and critical appeal of American films can work as a cultural thermometer, gauging the relative likes and dislikes of an age or era. The recent commercial and critical success of independent and borderline mainstream films of the late '90s, such as *The Ice Storm* (1996), *Fargo* (1996), *Happiness* (1998), *American Beauty* (1999), and *Magnolia* (2000) indicate that a large number of contemporary Americans appreciate and are in interested in films which deal with the difficulties involved in establishing and maintaining romantic and familial relationships.

Similarly, in his short-story collection, *Brief Interviews with Hideous Men*, David Foster Wallace displays the multilayered and complex postpostmodern, postfeminist, and postpolitically correct relationship landscape in the late '90s. This landscape is a chaotic hodgepodge of competing desires, with men and women often confused by the lack of a consensus on acceptable or preferred romantic and sexual behavior. Consequently, they often appear more as if they are involved in a battle than in a relationship. The largest irony of the interview segments of *Brief Interviews with Hideous Men* is that interviews should be an intimate and revealing format, but the interviewer finds only a mass of contradictions, justifications and uncertainty in the words of the male interviewees. Have men become more accepting and understanding of women's rights and desires since the feminist movement? Perhaps on the surface, but Wallace uncovers hidden, duplicitous forces at work that suggest that contemporary relationships between men and women may be more difficult than ever.

The series of interviews concerns sexuality and romance from different male perspectives. Wallace goes beyond a Freudian indictment of American culture as being sexually repressive to indict America's politically correct culture as being further debilitating by promoting unrealizable relationship standards for both men and women. The so-called hideous men are of two distinct breeds, neither of whom is psychologically healthier than the other. At first glance, it appears that the hideous men are atavistically, sexually preoccupied, predatory men like "Johnny one-arm," who uses his misshapen arm to lure vulnerable women into sympathy and eventual sex. However, Wallace implicates even "normal" and "sensitive" males who become just as "hideous" in their selfish preoccupation with being a "Great Lover," as does "Joe Six Pack," who "wants whatever he can get, and as long as he gets it, that's all there is to it as far as he's concerned" (23).

The politically correct media foster the idea of the compassionate, sensitive, "Great Lover" as an ideal male type. Now with a culture-wide acceptance of the at least equal, if not superior, ability for women to enjoy sexuality, a new emphasis has been placed upon his ability to please her. While the Great Lover, or "your sensitive male smoothie type" (24) appears to be more generous and sensitive than the Joe Six Pack type, one interviewee argues that the Great Lover is actually more duplicitous:

> Don't go thinking these fellows are really any better than your basic
> pigs are. Seeing themselves as a Great Lover doesn't mean they give
> any more of a shit about her than the pigs do. It's just that with this
> type of fellow what they get off on in bed is their own idea of them-
> selves as a Great Lover that can make the little lady just about lose
> her mind in bed [24].

Wallace argues that there is no such thing as being a completely selfless
lover, because whether we admit it or not, we are all motivated by personal pleasure. In a way, the Great Lover is more perverted than the
selfish Joe Six Packs because in a media-saturated society, the arrogant,
male "Great Lover" has become further preoccupied with his personal
image. In both cases, there is little or no genuine caring or affection and
while both are caricatures and/or generalizations, Wallace argues that, to
some extent, there can be no such thing as genuine caring or affection
because we can never truly know another person, let alone the reasons
for our own behavior. This is not to suggest that Wallace is a complete
nihilistic misanthropist, for he casts an accusatory finger at contemporary social standards (or lack thereof) which make it increasingly difficult
for men and women to take the necessary leap of faith to trust in another's
words and actions. For instance, in one of the interviews, a man leaves
his lover because she is unable to completely trust him or unwilling to
take the important leap of faith (17).

However sexually conniving and boasting the male interviewees
appear, it is impossible to determine whether they are being completely
truthful, especially in the conversations between men, in which they boast
of their sexual conquests to impress each other. For instance, one
"hideous man" boasts to another man of meeting and seducing a woman
he sees at an airport. The unnamed man's use of profanity and his
objectification of her body illustrates his general lack of regard for
women. He tells his friend that he is drawn by "her pretty fucking incredible tits under this like tight little top like leopard top thing under this
coat" (19). In fact, he never names the woman to his friend; she merely
becomes "the girl with the tits" (ibid.). He feigns being interested in her
problems and assumes that she will sleep with him because "She's got
on these pink jeans and heels that say fuck me in like myriads of major
world languages" (20). Although we never find out for certain whether
or not the man is telling the truth, he claims that he was successful in
bedding her.

To some extent, Wallace's hideous men are stunted in perpetual adolescence and aided in this by the media and popular culture. The media,
through relentless depiction of sexuality, especially that of women, further encourages sexual desire, the objectification of women, and thereby
feeds subsequent media-inspired perversions. Most tellingly, one "hideous

man" who reports from the Harold R. and Phyllis N. Engman Institute for Continuing Care in Eastchester, New York, describes his first sexual fantasies as spurred by the television show "Bewitched." He fantasizes of possessing the star's (Samantha's) supernatural power of stopping time so that he can sexually act upon the "frozen" women. The hideous man learns from his prodigious television watching to treat women more like two-dimensional objects and transfers this objectification to his real life, causing obvious practical problems.

As another example of the perverting influence of the media upon romance and sexuality, Wallace's story "Adult World" begins with a young wife, Jeni Roberts, who worries that there might be something wrong with her lovemaking. To Jeni, her husband appears disinterested during their lovemaking, and despite his reassurance, she is not sure whether or not she's truly pleasing him. Although Jeni doesn't make much of it at the time, her husband frequently rises in the middle of the night to purportedly do work and check stocks. On the surface, their chief problems appear to be a lack of communication, for Jeni doesn't feel comfortable talking to him about her fears. Understandably, her husband might be somewhat reluctant to be brutally honest with her as any person would be wounded by a lover's criticism of their sexual ability and technique. Jeni, who had only one lover previous to her husband, knows she is inexperienced and feels that she might be inadequate in some way. She becomes so consumed with this feeling that she calls and meets with her previous lover to ask him about her sexual performance. When talking with him in a restaurant, Jeni looks out the window and sees her husband's car parked at the Adult World erotica store. She then realizes that her husband is a "secret compulsive masturbator and that insomnia is a cover for secret trips to Adult World to purchase/view/masturbate self raw to XXX films" (156).

While one might think that this would be the end of their marriage, in fact, it does not work out that way, nor does the revelation completely devastate Jeni, for the husband is not literally cheating on Jeni. Despite his perversion and/or compulsion, Jeni does not leave her husband but rather, comes to engage in the same kind of autoeroticism as he does. She "realizes/gradually accepts that her husband loves his secret loneliness and 'interior deficits' more than he loves [/is able to love] her; accepts her 'unalterable powerlessness' over [her] husband's secret compulsions" (159). In fact, Jeni follows in her husband's behavior by "exploring masturbation as a wellspring of personal pleasure" (ibid.) and purchases sexual paraphernalia at the very same Adult World store. Her sexual fantasy becomes "a faceless, hyper tropic male figure who loves but cannot have J.O.R. He spurns all other living women and chooses instead to masturbate daily to fantasies of lovemaking with J.O.R." (160). By the seventh year of their marriage, both masturbate regularly and have only bimonthly sex and "neither appears to mind" (161). While it would seem that their marriage is all but over, Wallace surprisingly ends the story by claiming that "Binding them now is that deep and unspoken complexity that in adult marriage is covenant/love. They were now truly married, cloved, one flesh" (ibid.). In one sense, their marriage has improved as they both understand each other's desires and Jeni is no longer racked by feelings of inadequacy, yet there is a twinge of irony in "one flesh," for their decrease in physical intimacy suggests that they are anything but "one flesh." In fact, Wallace may be purposely ironic and sarcastic. At the same time, if we take him seriously, Wallace may be suggesting that marriage is or should be more based upon the acceptance and fulfillment of personal needs than on satisfying physical intimacy. While this interpretation has some credence, I interpret the story as identifying the media and consumerism as being at least partially the culprit in contributing to the inherent difficulties in romantic relationships, for not only do Jeni and her husband seem utterly isolated, the pornographic items they purchase make it easier for the two to feel relatively content in their mutual isolation.

Allied to "Adult World," Wallace concludes that it has become increasingly difficult for people (especially men) to have healthy relationships because of their growing conscious or unconscious preoccupation with their outward image. This has created a further schism between a person's outer self and inner self. Wallace suggests that buried within the vast majority of civilized American men is a "hideous man" whose behavior is solely geared toward personal sexual satisfaction. Especially due to "political correctness," men have had to repress their "hideous" tendencies further. That is, in a politically correct society, American males have been taught to curb their sexual and aggressive tendencies. Subsequently, the heterosexual male is put in a double bind, whereby the media exacerbates his sexual desire while his ability to form a lasting relationship with another is hindered. At the same time, due to political correctness, the "hideous men" feel ashamed at expressing their sexual desires and fantasies, and in doing so, they appear "hideous." For instance, one "hideous man" from Drury, Utah, tells the interviewer: "I have to admit it was a big reason for marrying her, thinking I wasn't likely to do better than this because of the way she had a good body even after she'd had a kid.... It probably sounds shallow but it's the truth. Or does the real truth about this kind of thing always sound shallow, you know, everybody's real reasons?" (22). Indeed, most adults would not admit that physical or sexual attractiveness is the primary factor by which they search for a partner. However, this may be an unconscious rationalization, whereby a person convinces himself or herself that he or she is attracted to a person's character when in actuality, the primary reason might be physical.

Women are also put in a sexual double bind by the media, but in a different way. In one recorded conversation in *Brief Interviews with Hideous Men,* two men discuss the conflicted messages which the media sends women. According to one character, the modern woman "has an unprecedented amount of contradictory stuff laid on her about what it is she's supposed to want and how she's expected to conduct herself sexually" (192). In addition to the old dichotomy between the saintly virgin and the whore, there has also arisen a new paradox: "Overlayed [*sic*] atop this is the new feminist-slash-post feminist expectation that women are sexual agents too, just as men are. That it's OK to fuck around. That for today's women it's almost mandatory to fuck around.... It's OK to fuck around if you're a feminist, but it's also not OK to fuck around because most guys aren't feminists and won't respect you and won't call you again if you fuck around" (193). That is, it is not a simple case of sexual permissiveness, because women who are sexually liberated and have multiple partners may suffer the consequences of not only being regarded as a "whore" or "slut," but also may have difficulty establishing a lasting relationship with a man. There is undoubtedly a middle ground that the two male subjects miss, but it is difficult to determine when a person is too sexually liberated or too repressed or powerless. This uncertainty adds to the neuroses of Wallace's characters, who then become even more preoccupied with their self-image.

I do not suggest, nor does Wallace, that romantic relationships between men and women have reached a crisis, for as one of the interviewees suggests, "life always finds a way" (122). I would argue that romantic relationships have been hindered by the emphasis placed upon hedonistic, bodily pleasures and by our reliance upon the media and popular culture and political correctness. In a society which offers many opportunities for solitary, easily purchasable pleasures, there is going to be less personal investment. Thereby, romantic relationships suffer because individuals do not invest the same time and effort in communicating with one another. Part of the problem is that there is less person-to-person communication. Another part of the problem is postmodernity's legacy of questioning the stability of individual identities. What should a "normal" man or woman do to live a personally satisfying and morally upstanding life? In the past, there were more definite codes and standards for individual and romantic conduct, but in the postmodern age, there is no single set of acceptable standards. Complicating the matter is the increasing prevalence and importance of ethnic hybridity, which further simultaneously merges and divides individuals, communities and cultures.

4 Ethnic Hybridity

In the previous chapter, I explored nonethnically specific texts which deal with the search for identity and the difficulties involved in communicating and establishing relationships with others in contemporary, pluralistic America. My contention was that postmodernity leaves a legacy of confusion and interdeterminacy which hinders the ability of younger Americans to achieve lasting, significant relationships with others. However, postmodernism is also allied to multiculturalism, which offers new, ethnically specific frameworks that help individuals define themselves. In this chapter, I explore two contradictory movements in contemporary American literature and culture: one toward the establishment of distinct, multicultural perspectives and the other toward ethnic cross-pollination or hybridization aided by mass homogenization from the somewhat totalizing power of the mass media or popular culture. In the past twenty years, America has become even more of a cultural melting pot as cultures blend and sometimes conflict, producing individuals with hybrid identities and allegiances.

While often allied with postmodernity, multiculturalism opposes the central claim that identity is solely fabricated and never more than a function as Deleuze and Guattari contend. In fact, multicultural or postcolonial theorists contend that those who argue that self and identity are fictional and artificial abstractions are born into positions of power (being mostly heterosexual, Caucasian males). It is difficult to appreciate the importance of individual identity and selfhood, they would suggest, unless you belong to an underprivileged minority or unless you have been the focus of ethnic or sexual discrimination. Consequently, multicultural theorists have helped bring attention to traditionally underserved groups. As Harold Hodkinson suggests, "The 1960 Census allowed only two categories: white or non-white.—[B]y 1990 there were 13 choices with the Asian group alone.... The notion that there are three racial groups—Caucasoid, Mongoloid and Negroid—has been thoroughly discredited for half a century. There is more variation within each such racial category than across them" (31).

Beginning in the 1970s, Latino, Asian, and African American programs and departments (along with women's studies) emerged at American universities. Multicultural theorists challenged the existing canons, contending that most universities, especially English departments, unfairly focused upon the ethnic majority, contributing to hegemony. As instrumental as the advances in multiculturalism have been in giving a voice to the previously silenced, they have also created divisions between ethnicities, approaches and viewpoints. Critics such as Russell Jacoby suggest that pluralism and multiculturalism are nothing more than empty, politically correct catchphrases: "Endless discussions of multiculturalism proceed from the unsubstantiated assumption that numerous distinct 'cultures' constitute American society. Only a few historians or observers even consider the possibility that the opposite may be true; that the world and the United States are relentlessly becoming more culturally uniform, not diverse" (47–48). Indeed, in the twenty-first century, ethnic identity will have decreasing significance. In part because of greater tolerance and diversity, but also due to the cross-pollination effect of the now culturally diverse mass media, ethnic identities have further blurred in America. The mass media, by exposing viewers to a large variety of ethnicities, helps efface the lines between cultures, while also providing a common frame of reference for all Americans.

I want to begin by addressing some theories of multiculturalism. In his essay, "Ideological Perspectives on Multicultural Relations," Alfred Kisubia suggests that "[p]roponents of multiculturalism argue that race and ethnic conflicts can be resolved not by homogenizing ethnicity (assimilation), but by resolving the competing claims of racial and ethnic groups" (22). While this is the dominant thread of multiculturalism, there is also an inclusionary or assimilist school which "believes that American culture can be enriched through the inclusion of the diverse potentials and cultures that are contained within its borders. It also acknowledges that there are important elements which cultures can learn from one another and in the process, create an enriched American culture" (6).[1] Multicultural amalgamation is a dream of an ethnically diverse, utopian society where there is a free exchange of ideas and identities among people of different ethnic backgrounds, genders and sexual orientations.[2]

While it may be impossible for a society to exist in which people of different ethnicities are treated completely equal, this does not mean that we should reject multicultural amalgamation and accept multicultural separation. However, there are some negative aftereffects of separatist agenda multiculturalism, because it places ethnic identity as the foremost determiner of personal identity. In essence, this can create further internal and external divisions between people. For instance, in his essay

"Philosophical Perspectives on Multiculturalism," Stefen Sullivan argues: "To say I am a black man or black woman in a white man's world, as the cliche goes, says nothing about what sort of black man you are: artistic, scientific, poor, ugly, beautiful, violent or poetic. Multiculturalism distracts minority members from the quest for their authentic self by framing their destiny constantly in terms of its relationship to the majority race" (46). While Sullivan's claim is logical and well argued, he presumes that not only do humans posses an "authentic self," but that this self exists independent of a person's cultural and/or ethnic background. Yet, an individual cannot be defined in a cultural vacuum. I would append to Sullivan's claim that overemphasis on one factor (ethnicity) as the primary determinant of self and identity is not only an oversimplification, but it can also be dangerous.

Some scholars have rightly challenged the notion of multiculturalism because it forces people to choose a specific ethnicity, when a larger number of Americans, perhaps even a majority of Americans, are ethnically hybrid. In support of this idea, Harold Hodkinson suggests, "If a box labeled 'multicultural'—meaning any racial/ethnic mixing back four or more generations—were added to the next Census, estimates are that 80 percent of blacks and a majority of Americans in general would check the box" (34). Furthermore, in contemporary America, which has become more of a cultural melting pot, binary polarities between races and ethnicities are losing power due to ethnic hybridity and fusion. Multiculturalism should take its prefix more to heart and begin investigating the manner in which an increasing number of Americans have become physically and psychologically multiethnic.

Hybrid Homogenization

The boundaries and limits described by ethnic scholars between white and black, Latino and Asian, among others, have begun to blur not only because of an increasing number of multiethnic offspring, but also because of popular culture and mass media which have helped produce mass homogenization of hybrid identities, through now ethnically diverse programming and entertainment. As Russell Jacoby suggests, "For those who care to look, the evidence is everywhere that distinct cultures are not so distinct" (152). In his provocative book on poor black children in Philadelphia, *On the Edge*, Carl H. Nightingale finds that these kids increasingly have succumbed to consumer society, "which preys on their vulnerability. Precisely because they are excluded and humiliated, they become fanatical devotees of name brands, gold chains and pricey cars—insignias of American success" (quoted in Jacoby 53).

In a sense, these now multicultural media forms have become great equalizers. I propose that one of the chief differences between the "postmodern" generation of writers and the current "hybrid" generation is their respective relationship with the media. As fiction writer and cultural critic Douglas Rushkoff argues in *Media Virus!*, Generation X is the first generation of Americans fully engaged in a symbiotic relationship with media: "They can change and manipulate media forms at will" (15). Along similar lines, David Foster Wallace argues in his essay "E Unibus Plurbam: Television and US Fiction" that "The belief that pop images are basically just mimetic devices is one of the attitudes that separates most U.S. fiction writers under 40 from the literary generation that precedes us.... The generation born after 1950 is the first for whom television was something to be lived with instead of just looked at" (*A Supposedly Fun Thing I'll Never Do Again*, 43).

Indeed, among all media forms, none has had a larger influence upon younger Americans (with the possible exception of film) than television. Many contemporary fiction writers directly write about existing television programs, just as the conversation around a typical workplace often revolves around television and film. Furthermore, television, with its polyphony of stations, programs and diversity, has helped produce individuals with hybrid identities, able to mimic various ethnic and professional dialects. Regardless of a person's race or profession, he or she can learn basic medical and legal terminology and dilemmas by watching *ER*, *Ally McBeal* or *The Practice*. Similarly, a person can watch African American–based shows like *Moesha* or *The Wayans Brothers*. With cable, a person can then switch channels to MTV and learn "gangsta rap" slang by watching videos, and move to the science fiction channel to watch a show like *Quantum Leap* about time travel and quantum mechanics.

In addition to providing us with a wealth of information and exposure to a large variety of ethnicities and professions, television also gives us pre-packaged responses to social situations. Kenneth Gergen rightly suggests that, "If a mate announces that he or she is thinking about divorce, the other's reaction is not likely to be dumb dismay. The drama has so often been played out on television and movie screens that one is already prepared with multiple options" (71). Although the process is frequently unconscious, we learn from television how to act in delicate social situations as we "learn" how other people act or live. Whether or not these programs begin as faithful representations of cultures, individuals or professions is not the important question, because after millions of people watch these shows, many will consciously or unconsciously begin to imitate the behavior of the cast members. Life thereby imitates "art," whether or not the "art" is an accurate representation.

In a society saturated with media forms and multiculturalism, the driving question shouldn't be how can historically oppressed group be represented, but rather, how can an individual find his or her place or identity in a pluralistic world without center? Popular culture and the media have helped efface the boundaries between ethnicities, leaving in their wake hybrid individuals who struggle to achieve a sense of identity.[3] It may be that popular culture has helped to produce new homogeneously mixed "American" identities. Indeed, in the contemporary age of global communications and information, ethnic boundaries have become more permeable. In the fiction of young American writers of different ethnicities, characters often have divided allegiances to their own ethnic history and to the complex media/televisual world which comprises a significant portion of most young Americans' environment. Even authors who are still ethnically "full blooded," like the two writers I will explore, Sherman Alexie and Michele Serros, deal with ethnic hybridity, brought about by exposure to the pluralistic mass media. I have chosen to explore Alexie and Serros because as young Americans (both born in the mid–1960s) they exemplify ethnically hybrid Generation X writers whose identities have been in part influenced by cultural heritage as well as American popular culture. The major questions their writings suggest are directly relevant to their generation, such as, should an American ethnic minority purposefully reject white-dominated, popular culture, or is there anything within popular culture that can be empowering? Should ethnic Americans strive to maintain their separate heritage as long as possible, or should they willfully assimilate?

Sherman Alexie

I have chosen to explore the fiction of young Native American writer Sherman Alexie, who investigates the intersections between the dominant white world, the media world and Native Americans. More so than any other ethnic minority, Native Americans have tried to maintain a separate identity, history and traditions from those of predominately white America, being the only minority to independently own and govern large land areas in America (reservations). However, Alexie demonstrates that American popular culture and media have infiltrated virtually all regions of America, even Native American reservations, which have the reputation of being almost off limits to outsiders. Alexie's Native Americans, even if they are full blooded, have hybrid identities, in part informed by popular culture and consumerism, both of which play a significant role on the reservation. However, before I directly investigate Sherman Alexie's work, I want to provide a brief history of Native American fiction in order to explain how his work departs from the historical molds.

European colonizers dichotomized Native Americans almost immediately after their first settlements in America. Europeans essentially saw two distinct, almost opposite types of Native Americans: the savage, bloodthirsty "Indian" and the wise, giving, environmentally connected "Indian." As mentioned earlier, unlike other ethnic groups, Native Americans have, for the most part, lived apart from European, "colonizing" Americans. Thereby, most Americans' perceptions of Native Americans have generally been secondhand. Prior to the twentieth century, these conceptions were largely derived from oral accounts, books and pictures. During the twentieth century, film, radio and television began to provide more accurate representations of Native Americans. The turn of the twentieth century saw the publications of the first substantial works of Native American writers, which were "often romanticized views of traditional tribal life" (Schneider, 31).[4] This technique of tribal romanticism continued throughout the first half of the twentieth century. As Isabel Schneider notes, "Publishers in the first half of the twentieth century generally preferred to publish Native material retold by non–Natives and life histories and legends written in the as-told-to tradition rather than dealing with the works of indigenous writers" (ibid.).

However, the 1960s ushered in a new era of indigenous Native American writing, such as that of N. Scott Momaday and Leslie Marmon Silko, whose fiction Sidner Larson argues to be postmodern because they "deal with a world often presented as being too complicated to understand" (52). Unlike previous Native Americans who focused solely upon their individual tribes, "these writers bring a sensibility to their work that is balanced by honoring a world of inherited traditions as well as engaging the world encountered in daily life.... It balances the red road of Indian metaphysics with the black road of worldly experience" (ibid.). As more Native Americans began to leave the protective shell of their reservation, they wrote more about the ways in which the white world and the Native American world intersected. Isabel Schneider explains: "In the middle of the 1980s a new generation of, in general, university-trained authors started to write. Their works reflected the changes in Native American life resulting from the increasing number of people not living on the reservations, while they continued to deal with the social, political and economic history and the current situations of tribal people" (34). Among the most significant, breakthrough Native American writers of the 1980s were James Welch (born in 1940), Michael Dorris (born in 1945) and Louise Erdich (born in 1954).

Sherman Alexie, born in 1966, represents the next generation of ethnically diverse Native American writers following Dorris and Erdich. Although Alexie is a full-blooded Coeur d'Alene Native American, he is a true hybrid writer, in whose works cultures breed and collide with creative force and sometimes with violent rage. Thus far, I have mainly explored hybridity in literary and media forms, but in Sherman Alexie's fiction, I will explore the importance of ethnic hybridity, which serves a special destabilizing function for multicultural or postcolonial writers. As Dee Horne suggests, "Creative literary hybridity unsettles the authority of the colonizers and their language and discourse.... Creative hybrid texts are productive of meaning (reforming society by re-formulating it within the text); they are not simply reflective or expressive of existing reality.... Creative hybrid texts partially represent or repeat the colonial discourse to contest and re-present it" (xvii–xx). In line with Horne, Alexie illustrates the complex interchange of power relationships by combining the language and culture of white America with that of Native Americans.[5]

Like Wallace and Powers, Sherman Alexie is a multitalented, extremely knowledgeable and productive author. In an article about Alexie, Lynn Cline explains:

> He seems to be on tour continuously, revered for his lively performances—an oratorical virtuosity that has won him the Taos Poetry Circus World Heavyweight Championship for the last three years. In addition, Alexie is a stand-up comedian, a songwriter, a screenwriter and producer (notably of the acclaimed film *Smoke Signals*) and has served on the Presidential Panel for the National Dialogue on Race and on the board of directors for the American Indian College Fund [197].

Like other writers of his generation, Alexie is well aware of the importance and power of humor in contemporary society. In an interview, he emphasizes: "People like to laugh, and when you make them laugh, they listen to you. That's how I get people to listen to me now. If I were saying the things I'm saying without a sense of humor, people would turn off right away" (Brewster 24). Some of Alexie's humor comes from his tragicomic descriptions of Native American life in reservations. Like other hybrid fiction writers, Alexie aims to blur the line between the highbrow and lowbrow. As Doug Marx argues, "Alexie betrays no squeamishness about the mix of art and commerce. He loves the limelight, and his readings are known for their improvisational energy, costume changes and singing" (40).

Rock 'n' Roll in the Rez: Reservation Blues

As a songwriter, filmmaker and comedian, Alexie is well aware of the power of popular culture in contemporary America and its potential for Native Americans. Alexie's first novel, *Reservation Blues* (1995), is a

magic-realist account of life on an Indian reservation and the rise and
fall of an Indian rock band, Coyote Springs. The novel begins as legendary blues musician Robert Johnson stumbles onto Wellpinit, the only
town in the Spokane Indian Reservation. Legend has it that Robert Johnson, who died at twenty-seven, sold his soul to Satan in order to play the
guitar better than anyone else in the world. Johnson leaves his guitar with
the main protagonist of *Reservation Blues*, Thomas Builds-a-Fire. This
is a symbolic exchange from the African American community to the
Native American community, whose decrepit lives in the reservation mirror that of the run-down rural communities in the Deep South of Robert
Johnson's time in the early twentieth century.

American popular culture and consumer products have clearly
infiltrated the Spokane Indian Reservation. Many residents form images
of themselves as Native Americans from the media. For Thomas, a thirty-
two-year-old bachelor, this is somewhat personally devastating: "Indian
women had never paid much attention to him, because he didn't pre-
tend to be some twentieth-century warrior, alternating between blind
rage and feigned disinterest" (4). The reservation's grocery store, called
the Trading Post, with its unhealthy, nutritionally empty supplies of
Pepsi, Spam, Wonder Bread and microwave burritos, appears distinctly
similar to the ubiquitous 7-11, and the aimless residents who huddle
around the Trading Post, such as future Coyote Springs members, Junior
and Victor, appear like "slackers" out of Eric Bogosian's *SubUrbia* (1995).
Some Native Americans even neglect their own heritage and emulate
that of popular American celebrities: "Victor was the reservation John
Travolta because he still wore clothes from the disco era" (12).

Robert Johnson's magical guitar can seemingly play itself and talk.
The guitar tells Thomas that he needs "to play songs for your people"
(23). Alexie makes it clear that Thomas is the tribe's storyteller: "He'd
caught some disease in the womb that forced him to tell stories. The
weight of those stories bowed his legs and bent his spine a bit" (6). Following the advice of the guitar, Thomas forms a rock band with Victor
and Junior. After weeks of practice, the three play their first gig at the
Spokane Indian reservation, gradually attracting some fans from outside
the Reservation, mostly non–Indians drawn by the mysterious power of
Native American music:

> White strangers had begun to arrive on the Spokane Indian Reser-
> vation to listen to this all–Indian rock and blues band. A lot of those
> New Agers showed up with their crystals, expecting to hear some
> ancient Indian wisdom and got a good dose of Sex Pistols covers
> instead. In emulation of all their rock heroes, who destroyed hotel
> rooms with style and wit, Victor and Junior trashed their own HUD
> house [41].

The band, which the guitarist, Victor, names Coyote Springs, subsequently plays at a Flathead reservation, where they meet two female Flatheads Indians, Chess and Checkers, whom they invite to join the band as a keyboardist and vocalist, respectively. Alexie makes an immediate parallel between white-dominated popular culture and Native American culture by describing a scene in which Chess sings with Thomas on stage: "Chess felt like a Flathead Reservation Cher next to the Spokane Indian version of Sonny" (58).

Coyote Springs composes and performs loud rock music which literally amplifies their anguished feelings of isolation and oppression as Native Americans in white-dominated America. In a way, their music also transcends race and borders: "Coyote Springs created a tribal music that scared and excited the white people in the audience. That music might have chased away the pilgrims five hundred years ago.... The audience reached for Coyote Springs with brown and white hands that begged for more music, hope, and joy. Coyote Springs felt powerful, fell in love with the power, and courted it" (80). Alexie makes it clear that not only are Native Americans on the reservation powerless, generally destitute and hopeless, but that popular culture (in this case rock music) offers them an empowering opportunity to vocalize and vent their feelings at the same time.

After winning a battle of the bands contest in Seattle, Coyote Springs appears to be on their way to stardom and possibly becoming Native American spokespersons or popular icons. However, they face prejudice and discrimination when they try to get a recording contract: "'Indians?' those record companies said, 'You mean like drums and stuff? The howling kind of singing? We can't afford to make a record that ain't going to sell. Sorry'" (187). Eventually, Coyote Springs does attract the attention of two record executives: Phil Sheridan and George Wright from Calvary Records. Alexie portrays the two as coldly manipulative, carrying on in the tradition of their white ancestors who lied to, tricked and appropriated land from Native Americans. In a letter, the two tell their superior, "We can really dress this group up, give them war paint, feathers, etc., and really play up the Indian angle" (190).

Coyote Springs's big break comes when they finally get an opportunity to record their songs in a studio. However, they perform poorly and are ousted by the two record executives, one of whom, Phil Sheridan, later sexually assaults Checkers. After their humiliating experience in the studio, Coyote Springs effectively disbands, returning to the reservation in shame: "Coyote Springs had failed, had not even bothered to bring their instruments home from Manhattan. Checkers could see the guitars and keyboard strewn around the studio. Victor's guitar was smashed into pieces, but everything else was just as useless" (251). Still,

Alexie argues that Coyote Springs's music unleashed a torrent of repressed feelings of anger at white-dominated America. For Chess, the band had lit a "sudden fire ... inside her. But that fire had consumed almost everything, and despite her years of firefighting experience, she had not been able to stop it" (257).

Unfortunately, Chess and the others find it difficult to channel their music and emotions, leaving them prey to outside forces like the devious record executives Sheridan and Armstrong, who waste no time in capitalizing upon the growing interest in Native American music. They subsequently sign and record two white women, Betty and Veronica, who had previously tagged along with Coyote Springs, to perform filtered-down versions of Native American music. Alexie includes a chorus of one of Betty and Veronica's pretentious and condescending pseudo–Indian songs: "And my hair is blonde/But I'm Indian in my bones/And my skin is white/But I'm Indian in my bones/And it don't matter who you are/You can be Indian in your bones" (295). Alexie argues the myth that anyone can be "Indian in your bones" is destructive in the sense that it demonstrates that white Americans want to strip from Native Americans their last vestige of cultural solidarity and pride: their ethnic heritage. It is another step in a centuries-old process of geographical, social and cultural theft.

Still, Alexie doesn't glorify Native Americans in the sense that they too seem to be closed off and rather intolerant of ethnic difference. On the reservation, Indians of mixed descent are treated like subordinates by full-blooded Indians. Thomas "worried about the children of mixed-blood marriages. The half-breed kids at the reservation school suffered through worse beatings than Thomas ever did" (82). At the same time, Alexie emphasizes the importance of community to Native Americans: "The Indian world is tiny, every other Indian dancing just a powwow away. Every Indian is a potential lover, friend or relative prancing over the horizon, only a little beyond sight. Indians need each other that much; they need to be that close, tying themselves to each other and closing their eyes against the storms" (151). Thereby, Alexie argues that Native Americans need to remain in their ethnically self-enclosed world, for it is through their appropriation of American popular culture that Coyote Springs find their voice.

At the same time, Alexie argues that ethnic cross-pollination is inevitable, but he fears that white America may subsume the heritage and identity of Native Americans. As Chess tells Thomas, "Those quarter-bloods and eighth-blood grandchildren will find out they're Indian and torment the rest of us real Indians. They'll come out to the reservation, come to our powwows, in their nice clothes and nice cars, and remind the real Indians how much we don't have. Those quarter-bloods and

eighth-bloods will get all the Indian jobs, all the Indian chances, because
they look white. Because they're safer" (283). Indeed, this appears to be
the natural course of events in Native Americans' history of ethnic appropriation.

However, Alexie does not leave the reader on this sour note. Though
a distraught Junior kills himself and an angry Victor seems to be well on
his way toward self-destruction, Chess, Checkers and Thomas do not
give in to the overwhelming sense of defeat that seems to permeate the
Indian reservation. Rather, the three leave the reservation for Spokane.
At the end, Alexie emphasizes: "They were alive; they'd keep living....
Songs were waiting for them in the dark. Songs were waiting for them
in the city" (306). With this ending, Alexie appears to abandon hope for
increased prosperity of the ethnically segregated reservations. At the
same time, he appears to rest his hopes with Thomas, Chess and Checkers to carry on Native American traditions or maybe even restart their
band after they settle in Spokane.

If white people are infiltrating reservations and appropriating Native
American culture as their own, a proper response might be for Native
Americans to do the exact opposite—leave the reservation and appropriate the tools of white Americans for their advantage. Still, even though
the three leave the reservation for Spokane, this doesn't necessarily mean
that Alexie supports ethnic assimilation. Alexie wants his characters to
maintain their sense of ethnic identity, and he believes that they can do
so in an urban center without falling prey to the potentially dominating
effects of white-dominated urban society and popular culture. To a larger
extent, Alexie explores ethnicity in an urban center within his more recent
novel, *Indian Killer* (1996), which takes place in Seattle.

Ethnic Hybridity Explodes into Violence: Indian Killer

While Alexie has ambivalent feelings about ethnic and cultural
hybridization in *Reservation Blues,* he also casts an accusatory finger in
the direction of white America, whom he believes to be at least partially
responsible for the decrepit social and psychological conditions of Native
Americans. In *Indian Killer,* Alexie focuses more specifically upon the
violent undercurrents involved in the struggle for racial identity and
equality in America. *Indian Killer* is set in Seattle, which in Alexie's hands
is a city of conflicting ethnicities: Caucasians, Native Americans, Latinos, African Americans and Asian Americans. Out of these almost warring groups, Alexie compiles a motley collection of unsympathetic
characters, including a racist talk-show host, an arrogant white professor of Native American studies, a self-righteous female Indian activist,
and a retired police officer turned writer of Indian mystery stories, who

claims a dubious Indian heritage. In *Indian Killer*, Alexie rejects the multicultural assimilationist view and portrays ethnic hybridization, both culturally and psychologically, as a violent struggle for domination rather than a cooperative, mutually beneficial union. Cultures violently clash in *Indian Killer*, and Alexie offers no easy solutions to cultural conflict.

Central to *Indian Killer* is the killer himself, John Smith,[6] a Native American who was adopted at birth by two upper-middle-class Caucasians, Daniel and Olivia Smith. Alexie purposely does not make John into a wholly sympathetic character whose mistreatment at the hands of whites sparks his aberrant behavior. Indeed, one could argue that John experiences an idyllic childhood. His surrogate parents are gentle and loving, and John meets little prejudice in school. If anything, during his early life, John experiences extra considerations and kindness, which, however well-intentioned, serve to further make him aware of his ethnic difference. At an all-white high school, "His teachers were always willing to give him a little slack. They knew he was adopted, an Indian orphan, and was leading a difficult life. His teachers gave him every opportunity and he responded well. If John happened to be a little fragile, well, that was perfectly understandable, considering his people's history. All that alcoholism and poverty, the lack of God in their lives" (19). For Alexie, these perceived compassionate acts may actually be condescending, borderline racist and ignorant. Even when his well-meaning father, Daniel, takes John to Native American gatherings, such as a congregation of tribes at the Indian Heritage Gym, John only feels further ethnically excluded and isolated. He looks longingly toward the seemingly happy tribes and "wanted to own that laughter" (21). For Alexie, even well-meaning intentions can backfire. He does not want us to perceive of John's adopted parents as monstrous, but rather that there is no easy or simple solution to ethnic friction. Rather, cultural conflict may be unavoidable, and the wounds inflicted upon Native Americans by colonizers may run too deep to heal completely.

Instead of going to college as his parents encourage him to do, John becomes a construction worker. Alexie makes it clear that John becomes a construction worker in an attempt to emulate his Indian heritage as he was inspired to do after reading an article about the Mohawk Indian steel workers who helped build the World Trade Center buildings in New York City. Subsequently living an isolated and barren existence in Seattle, John feels powerless and helplessly caught between the white world and the Native American world, feeling welcome within neither.

Wanting respect and power desperately as well as an exact ethnic identity, John begins lying to people he meets. Despite the fact that he doesn't know what tribe he descends from, John tells whites that he is Sioux, because he believes that white people commonly associate Sioux

Indians with fierce warriors, and he tells Native Americans that he is Apache, because he believes that Apaches are the most feared tribe to most Native Americans. However, John rightly feels that he is living a lie and gradually looks for an outlet for his growing isolation, frustration and anger. Accordingly, he fantasizes about gaining power by viciously dangling his white foreman from the fortieth floor of the skyscraper John works on (25).

As time progresses, John rationalizes to himself that he needs to kill a white man as a means of retribution for the crimes they committed against Native Americans, but he really does so because he feels marginalized and powerless, blaming the white world for his isolation (rightly or wrongly). Alexie explains his reasoning: "White people no longer feared Indians. Somehow, near the end of the twentieth century, Indians had become invisible, docile. John wanted to change that. He wanted to see fear in every pair of blue eyes" (30). Alexie provides no authorial voice to evaluate John's rationalizing, but he does want the reader to understand or appreciate John's motives. John's first victim is a male university student, who insults John by calling him "Chief" and then flashing him the peace sign after John bumps into him. Essentially, John wants to kill the white student because he envies his perceived power and arrogance: "Confidently, arrogantly, the white man, Justin Summers, had brushed past the killer. With his head high and shoulders wide, Summers took up as much space as he possibly could. He strolled down the middle of the sidewalk, forcing others to walk around him. So when the arrogant white man rudely brushed past, the killer wanted to teach him a lesson" (51).

Still, John is no heroic avenger, and to an extent, Alexie portrays John as being just as misinformed about Native Americans as most white people. In separate chapters, John imagines an idyllic, family-based life on the reservation, which, as Alexie already established in *Reservation Blues*, is far from reality. John imagines that: "There is enough food, plenty of books to read, and a devoted mother.... They live with a large extended family group in a small house" (43). In his unfounded romanticization of Native Americans, John is not markedly different from Dr. Clarence Mather, a white professor of Native American studies at the University of Washington, who "supposedly loved Indians, or perhaps his idea of Indians. But he was also a Wannabe Indian, a white man who wanted to be Indian" (58). With the character of Marie Polatkin, a female Native American activist who takes Mather's Native American literature course at the University of Washington and challenges his authority, Alexie transforms Mather into an academic monster who willfully distorts Native American studies to fulfill his own selfish ends. The only Native American in his course, Marie claims that most of the works on

Mather's syllabus were cowritten, ghost written or edited/manipulated by white men. Mather is not a completely unsympathetic character in the sense that he tells Marie, "I'm trying to present a positive portrait of Indian peoples, of your people.... Don't you know that I'm on your side?" (84–85). However, Alexie is obviously distraught at how white Americans, especially those who purport to be experts in Native American literature, often distort images of Native Americans toward their own selfish purposes or appropriate Native American history as their own. Marie continually challenges Mather's authority, which disturbs Mather to the point that he closes his office door in her face. Marie's angry reaction mirrors the rage of John Smith: "She wanted to tear apart the world. Mather would have never treated a white student that badly, nor would he have shut the door in the face of a man" (85).

In a country which tends to view Native Americans as noble savages, able to dispense "tribal" wisdom, Native Americans like Marie's half–Indian cousin, Reggie, feel compelled to act like common media representations of Native Americans. Unlike John Smith, another hybrid Native American/Caucasian who wishes to reject the white world, "Reggie was a half–Indian who wanted to be completely white, or failing that, to earn the respect of white men" (136). A few years before the present narrative, Reggie had been one of Mather's prized students, and they became close friends:

> Reggie and Mather traveled to men's gatherings and went into the sweathouse together. Reggie had usually been the only Indian at those gatherings and willingly played the part of shaman for the sad and lonely white men, many years his senior, who'd come to him for answers. For the first time in his life, Reggie felt as if being Indian meant something, as if he could obtain a tangible reward from simply behaving as an Indian was supposed to behave, acting as an Indian was supposed to act. And the act became so convincing that Reggie began to believe it himself. His Indian act earned him the respect of white men and the sexual favors of white women [136].

The breaking point between Reggie and Mather occurs when Mather finds a box of recordings of traditional Indian stories. Reggie insists that he should erase them.

> The professor had wanted to make them public and publish an article about them, but Reggie had heard the recorded voice of that old Spokane woman and had been suddenly ashamed of himself. He'd heard that ancient voice and wanted to destroy it. He'd wanted to erase the tapes because he had not wanted anybody else, especially a white man like Mather, to have them. He'd wanted to erase them because they'd never be his stories [137].

What outrages Reggie (and Alexie, I would argue) is Mather's attempts to usurp and distort the heritage of Native Americans for Mather's own selfish purposes. Mather promises Reggie that he will erase the tapes, but he reneges on his promise, denying the existence of the tapes to Reggie and the chair of his department because "he'd come to see those stories as his possessions, as his stories, as if it had been his voice on those tapes. He'd lied to preserve his idea of order. But with each successive lie Mather had told, he'd begun to lose track of the original reasons for lying. Layer after layer of lies. As an anthropologist, Mather could have dug himself for years and not discovered the truth" (138). For Reggie, Mather's act is akin to cultural rape and leads him to his angry belief that "white men were lying all the time.... Mather's friendship had simply become another broken treaty" (ibid.).

Meanwhile, news spreads of the media-dubbed Indian killer's murders by scalping and ritualistic torture, and Seattle erupts with racial tension and violence. Aaron Rogers, the brother of one of the murdered white men, David Rogers,[7] and a couple of his white friends, go on a violent rampage, assaulting homeless Indians. At the same time, Reggie Polatkin and his Indian friends mercilessly torture a young white vagabond in an empty football field. A white disc jockey, Truck Shultz, further stirs ethnic tension with his anti–Native American rhetoric. Seattle appears to be on the verge of ethnic warfare.

The problems of ethnic violence and conflict, Alexie argues, are complex and cannot be explained by a single reason. At one particularly illuminating moment, Aaron Rogers, brother of the slain David Rogers, recalls an incident when growing up in rural Washington in which he, his brother David, and his father shot at a number of Native Americans who "crept onto his family's farm to steal camas root, the spongy, pungent bulbs of indigenous lilies that had been a traditional and sacred food of the local Indians for thousands of years" (62). They rationalize their behavior in that Buck, David and Aaron's father, claims that "This is our land.... This land has been in our family for over a hundred years. And those Indians are stealing from us. They're trying to steal our land" (65). Of course, the irony of Buck's statement is that the land "belonged" to Native Americans long before it "belonged" to the Rogers family. Toward the end of the novel, Aaron wonders whether his family's cruel and inhumane behavior toward Native Americans might have contributed to the activity of the Indian killer. He tells his father, "What if I caused all of this? What if David is dead because I tried to shoot that Indian?" (284).

Indeed, with their air of ethnic supremacy, Aaron and most of the other white characters might very well have contributed to the production of the Indian killer. Most importantly, for Alexie, America is still white dominated, which leaves ethnic minorities consciously or subconsciously faced with possible injustices and prejudices. At one point, a frustrated John Smith exclaims: "If you kill a black man, the world is silent…. If you kill a white man, the world erupts with noise: fireworks, sirens, a gavel pounding a desk, the slamming of doors" (308). For Alexie, "black man" is interchangeable with "Indian" or "Native American."

Furthermore, Alexie appears to be no proponent of ethnic assimilation, for to Alexie, there can be no assimilation, only the subsuming of identity, in white-dominated America. Alexie's strongest adverse reaction is to the micromanagement of Native American history and traditions by white Americans. Most tellingly, at the end of the novel, John Smith, the Indian killer, kidnaps the pseudo–Indian writer, Jack Wilson, whom he injures and tells, "Let me, let us have our own pain" (411). Subsequently, John commits suicide. After John's suicide and Wilson's recovery, Wilson writes a portrait based on the life of John Smith, which Marie firmly denounces: "Wilson doesn't know shit about Indians" (415). Similarly, Alexie argues that Wilson and the pretentious Professor Mather misinterpret Native Americans and even damage them. Alexie tears apart Mather's simplistic analysis of Native Americans being solely concerned with "peace and beauty" (112) as being condensing, faux, liberal dribble. Alexie also criticizes writers like Jack Wilson for propagating the myth of the fierce, noble savage, the Indian warrior, and for appropriating Native American culture for their own skewed, self-interested purposes. While Alexie does not condone the Indian killer's actions, his apparent intention is to make apparent the violent tensions which can sometimes come between people of different ethnicities and how the struggle for individual identity can become a battleground. Alexie offers no easy solutions, yet he demonstrates that the process of ethnic assimilation or subsumence, with all its possible violent repercussions, can and will continue in America.

Embracing Ethnic Hybridity: Michele Serros as Generation X Latina

Whereas Sherman Alexie appears conflicted and at least partially resistant to ethnic assimilation, some young ethnic writers openly embrace ethnic hybridity, because to reject ethnic hybridity would be to reject their own mixed identities. Born and raised in Southern California, poet and fiction writer Michele Serros represents a new kind of Generation X Chicano/a writer who is more optimistic about hybrid ethnicities and sees some promise in the merging of Latino/a ethnicity and American mainstream or popular culture. Like Dave Eggers, Michele

Serros's fiction and poetry are heavily self-invested and self-conscious. Also like Eggers, Serros uses self-promotion, and like David Foster Wallace, she uses sarcastic irony to capture readers and to complicate issues and ideas which most people dichotomize into simplistic oppositions such as "good" and "evil."

Chicano/a is a term for Mexican Americans, which became popular in the '60s and '70s (Martinez, 126). It is important to recognize that Chicanos/as or Latinos/as are mostly ethnically hybrid themselves. As Elizabeth Martinez explains, "Latinas, like Latinos, are in general a mestizo or mixed people. They combine, in various degrees, indigenous (from pre–Columbian times), European (from Spain's invasion of the Americas), and African roots (from the millions of slaves brought to the Americas, including at least two hundred thousand to Mexico alone)" (ibid.). Unlike African Americans and to some extent, unlike Native Americans, Chicana/o culture often focuses upon a distinct language—Spanish. This adds a distinct dimension to Chicana/o studies. Tey Rebolledo explains, "Because of the English/Spanish language question that subsumes Chicano culture, no matter what language they speak, Chicana writers always feel a void, an exile from language. If they are English speakers only, they feel they have been denied Spanish, and they cannot speak in the language of their forbearers" (157).

Serros was born in the mid–1960s, a time at which Chicano/a culture studies was first established at American universities. This is not to suggest that Chicanos/as didn't begin writing until the 1960s. For as Carl and Paula Shirley argue, "Broadly speaking, Chicano literature can claim to be as old as the Spanish presence in the New World or, perhaps more accurately, as old as its presence within the current boundaries of the country.... Most critical attention, however, is focused on the contemporary period, from approximately 1960 to the present" (4).

With writers such as Jose Antonio Villerreal, Richard Vasquez and Raymond Barrio, Chicano fiction writing began to flourish in the 1960s.[8] Even at that time, there was great debate amongst Chicano/a scholars and writers as to whether to encourage ethnic assimilation or to regain and maintain a distinct ethnic heritage. As Wilson Neate explains, "In the same way that some African-Americans cultivated a Muslim tradition as a basis for consciousness raising and a politics of resistance, specific sectors of the Mexican-American community embarked on a similar separatist project for cultural nationalism" (105). Some proposed an "indigenous, pre–Columbian mythology as the essence of contemporary Chicano/a identity" (ibid.).

At the same time, the burgeoning field of Chicano/a literature was notably male dominated. As Neate explains, in the '60s and '70s, Chicana literature "did not accommodate women and prevented them from speaking about themselves and about their experience of oppression in terms of gender and sexuality. Moreover, Chicanas were silenced within male-authored texts and trapped in the objectifying gaze of the latter to exist only as witnesses to male activity or as objects of male sexual desire" (117). However, beginning in the 1980s, Chicana writers like Sandra Cisernos and Gloria Anzaldua began publishing works to critical acclaim.[9] Yet their texts dealt more with Chicana folk traditions and heritage than directly with contemporary American culture. The unanswered question remained: What of a growing number of Chicanos/as who have at least partially assimilated to life in America? Are they whitewashed as some ethnic purists might claim? Michele Serros argues in favor of American cultural hybridity and identifies the negative aftereffects of clinging too tightly to one's ethnic heritage. After her first book of poetry and short stories, *Chicana Falsa* (1993), was published, Serros gradually attracted a devoted following of readers with her writings being almost immediately taught in high schools and colleges throughout California (Sherwin online). Furthermore, as a woman, Serros subverts the traditional domination of male Chicano writers and asserts her individual identity as a Chicana writer. As Tey Rebolledo explains:

> Women's lives are particularly circumscribed by cultural values and norms that try to dictate how women should behave and who their role models should be. If, however, the existing mythology (as defined by patriarchy) is unable to fulfill the increasing demand for women as active, energetic, and positive figures, then women writers may choose myths and archetypes, historical and cultural heroines, that are different from the traditional ones. They may create new role models for themselves or choose existing models but imbue them with different (sometimes radically different) traits and characteristics [49].

Serros's follow-up to *Chicana Falsa*, *How to Be a Chicana Role Model* (2000) is a semiautobiographical account of Serros's humble foray into literary celebrity and the media world.

A common theme that runs through Serros's writing is whether there is such a thing as ethnic authenticity or purity. Several of her poems and stories focus on the scorn she's received from other Latinos/as who demean her for not appearing or acting completely Latina according to their purist, but skewed, definitions. In her poem "La Letty," Serros recalls how a Latina friend from junior high school called her "a Chicana falsa" and "homogenized Hispanic" because Serros could barely speak Spanish. This same former friend is hypocritical in the sense that she and her other Latino/a friends do not tolerate difference and also embrace and become stereotypical media representations of Latinos/as.

This friend, who has once "been Leticia," becomes "La Letta." Her purportedly ethnic authenticity, like that of others, is actually manufactured
and homogenized, possibly by media representations of Latinos/as:
"Young boys in hair nets and Dickies, fingers dipped in Old English ink
controlled chained steering wheels and La Letty" (*Chicana Falsa*, 2).
Serros's relatives are no less kind in their stern perception of ideal Chi-
cano/a types. Her Aunt Annie tells her that she will never succeed as a
Chicana writer because "You weren't born in no barrio. No tortilleria
down your street. Bullets never whizzed past your baby head" (5). To
her aunt, Serros is a "Chicana without a cause" (5–6). Yet her aunt pre-
supposes that a Chicana writer needs to have suffered great social and
personal deprivation in order to write anything worthy or significant.
This is not only a false supposition, but it contributes to an unfair stereotype of Chicanas/os as culturally and economically deprived.

In a prose poem, "Mi Problema," Serros also identifies reverse discrimination, which ethnic purists, even from minority groups, sometimes
use to bolster their own self-image and to tarnish the image of others.
She recounts being humiliated at a Latino/a conference by other writers
because of her lack of facility in speaking Spanish. "My skin is brown
just like theirs, but now I'm unworthy of the color 'cause I don't speak
Spanish the way I should" (31). Serros rightly points out that white people are praised for trying to learn Spanish because "Maybe he wants to
be brown like us" (ibid.). However, her attempt to learn Spanish makes
her appear "whitewashed," when she is actually no different from any
other native English speaker.

Serros argues against the idea that ethnicity is the primary determinant of an individual's identity. This is not to suggest that Serros
wholeheartedly embraces ethnic assimilation. Rather, she appears to be
uncertain, especially about white people appropriating Latino culture as
their own. In "JohnWannaBeChicano," a white boy dresses according to
the media stereotype of Chicanos. He "pockets his blond hair into black
hair net, stuffs skinny pink legs into stiff beige khakis, severely creased"
(33). He ignores his mother's kindnesses and considerations, having been
"humiliated one too many times in front of his homeboy by her chicken
salad, Ambrosia surprise" (34). Serros appears ambivalent to what Sherman Alexie would certainly decry as the appropriation of minority identity by the ethnic majority. When John bicycles past Chicano gardeners,
Serros emphasizes, "His new family. He is happy. He is smug. He is a Chicano" (ibid.). Does Serros really believe John is Chicano, or are these final
words sarcastic, or even an objective portrayal of John's views? There
isn't a clear interpretation, nor is there clear outrage on the part of Serros, which leads me to believe that she doesn't view ethnic appropriation, even by the ethnic majority, as debilitating to an ethnic minority.

More so than Alexie, Serros approaches ethnic discrimination from a humorous standpoint. However, like Alexie, Serros demonstrates that ethnic discrimination still occurs, although in different and somewhat muted forms. For instance, Serros's story "Attention Shoppers" takes place in the frozen food aisle in Ralph's Supermarket. Serros's friend Marina has a miniepiphany when looking at the ethnically titled vegetables: Malibu-style vegetables and Latino-style vegetables, which have distinctly different pictures upon them. Marina angrily tells Serros:

> Look, look at this picture. Latino Style Vegetables, they have the vegetables cut up all small. Like, what's that supposed to mean? Like, little food for little people, little minds, little significance.... And this Malibu kind, the broccoli, the carrots, are cut up large, all big and grand, like "of great worth," or something.... The Latino Style Vegetables are all spilling out of this wicker basket, all overflowing, messy like. Insinuating that we are overflowing, overcrowding what they think is their land [23].

After Martina stomps on the "Latino" vegetables, a miniriot erupts in the supermarket: "I saw a Korean woman and her two children stomp on Oriental Style Vegetables, a young guy in cowboy boots kicked Country Style Vegetables down the aisle toward the checkout lines, and a handsome, dark-haired man ripped apart a bag of Italian Style Vegetables. More and more people began to pull bags out of the compartments and destroy the corporate invention of 'stereotypes in a bag'" (24). While this is clearly an allegorical satire, Serros does identify how discrimination and stereotypical attitudes can exist in the most common of places. Yet Serros is wise not to play the role of wounded minority member, and she does not stubbornly cling to the idea that Latinos/as will never be able to achieve a proportionate degree of power in America. Indeed, to achieve power and equality, Serros looks toward the transformative power of popular culture and televisual celebrity.

In a country dominated by pop and media icons, Americans often hold their celebrities up to intense scrutiny. If that celebrated figure attracts a large youth following, inevitably he or she will be considered a role model, regardless of whether he or she wants to be one. Certain successful members of ethnic minorities are considered role models for the sole reasons of financial or athletic success, which purportedly serves to inspire other minorities. Yet, the idea of a role model is not only an exaggeration, but Americans often want their role models to be morally infallible, without faults or vices, typically with safe, proeducation, prosocial responsibility messages. In *How to Be a Chicana Role Model,* Michele Serros plays with these rigid conventions, deriding the media for setting out impossible and superhuman standards for role models. Yet, at the same time, Serros is successful in presenting herself as a role model. However, she is a role model who gracefully and honestly reveals herself to the reader, warts and all, because she does not want to appear superior to the reader. In a way, Serros suggests that any Chicana/o can be a role model as long as he or she stays true to his or her ideals and accepts all members of the Chicana/o community without judging them.

Serros's ideas come at a time in which certain Latino/a entertainers have been described as role models. Beginning in the mid–1990s, there have emerged several Latino/a musicians, singers and pop icons, such as Jennifer Lopez, Christina Aguilera, Ricky Martin and Enrique Inglacias, whom the media collectively describe as part of a culture-wide "Latin explosion." Indeed, these Latino/a entertainers are held up as role models, not because of their intelligence, or even their musical ability (as not all write their own material), or even because they offer insight or empowerment to the Latino/a community, but largely because of their danceable, bubble-gum music and physical attractiveness. At the very beginning of *How to Be a Chicana Role Model*, Serros mocks these entertainers, who seem more like media puppets. The beginning short story/blurb called "General Assembly" is narrated by a young Chicana who is a poor student and appears rather gullible. In fact, she is thrilled that her school is going to have an assembly to honor a Latino television star—Anthony Rivera—because her teacher has to cancel their spelling test: "Thank God, cuz I'm the worst speller in this whole class" (1). Rivera proceeds to speak in the school auditorium, giving a melodramatic account of his rise from the streets of New York to meet Michael Jackson and his (Rivera's) eventual celebrity. Although the school promotes him as a role model, Rivera is not much more than a physical icon. The male students ignore him, while many of the female students swoon over him. When he asks for questions, one girl asks if he's married and another asks if she can kiss him. After the assembly is over, the narrator has a revelation:

> I guess you can say I learned a lot from yesterday's special assembly. I mean, if you're Mexican, or even Puerto Rican, like Anthony Rivera and you've dropped out of school and lived on the streets of New York City, you can still make it. You can still be a great role model and be in a music video and someday have someone look over your shoulder to correct all your spelling [3].

The irony of the narrator's revelation is that not only is Rivera a poor role model, the audience doesn't really care about what he has to say. In a sense, the narrator is correct in that in a culture which values appearance, physical attractiveness has become the primary currency. Indeed, this Ricky Martin–like "role model" appears to be no more than a puppet, whose "achievements" are dubious at best.

Throughout *How to Be a Chicana Role Model*, Serros lists thirteen rules on how to be a role model, from "answer all fan mail" to "buy American" to "seek support from sistas." The irony of these rules and the accounts which follow is that most of them describe Serros's comic failures and inability to be successful in the media world or to hold down a lucrative career. For instance, in "Seek Support from Sistas," Serros describes her time as a page at the show *In Living Color*. She makes it clear that she took the job in part because she hoped to meet celebrities and also because she wanted to break ground in the entertainment world. Her "sista" in the story is a Chicana named Jennifer,[10] who has a much more important job and is much better paid than Serros, who, perhaps naively, reasons: "I thought if only I had a chance to talk, Jennifer would help me. A brown woman supporting another brown woman in a black world" (23). Serros's thought proves wrong as does the supposed role model rule "seek support from sistas," when Jennifer, the vain "Fly girl," continually brushes off Serros's attempts at conversations and treats her as a mere servant. In the dog-eat-dog entertainment world, there seems to be no ethnic cohesion.

In another story, Serros describes another of her forays into the media/entertainment world, which also ends in failure. In this story, "I Know What You Did Last Summer," Serros works as a road poet during the Lollapalooza festival. Sadly, poetry doesn't interest the primarily Generation X audience, who are much more interested in the music. Indeed, this illustrates how literature has lost its power of influence amongst the younger generation.

In a diary entry, Serros writes, "Today I read poems to only two people in the poetry corner and they weren't really in the corner to listen to poetry, but were just waiting to use the Porta Potti" (131–32). It turns out to be a disaster. "Today they told us they can't have any more poets on the main stage cuz too much trash is being thrown at them and it's damaging stage equipment.... All the other poets are really bugging the shit out of me. The male poets do nothing but scream and scream and go on about their penises. Everyone is reading stuff about O.J., Kurt, sex or drugs" (133). Serros ends up rolling burritos for Big Belly Burrito because the audience of Lollapalooza doesn't seem interested in thought-provoking poetry or non-consumer-related items. She comes to the cynical conclusion: "I thought this was supposed to be like the granddaddy of alternateen concerts, but everyone looks the same! I mean, the SAME oversized wallet chains, the same manic panic dyed hair, skinny dreads on skinny blond boys, baby Ts with cute little sayings from the seventies" (132).

Unlike a typical role model who would probably wholeheartedly embrace and accept his or her ethnic identity without questions or shame,

Serros also struggles with her identity as a Chicana. In "Senior Picture Day," she describes her insecurities at appearing too ethnic looking. Since the seventh grade, she has pinched her nose every day so that it would look "less Indian," after a female friend humiliated her by making fun of her nose to a boy. Indeed, ethnic identity means increasingly less to Serros as she gets older. In another story, "Live Better, Work Union," Serros works at an art emporium and is asked by customer whether she's Native American. The woman insists that Serros looks Indian, even after Serros's initial protestations. After she leaves, Serros reconsiders: "Besides, maybe she was correct and maybe I wasn't sure what I was. I did see *Dances with Wolves* three times and really enjoyed it" (77). The customer then asks Serros if she would consider modeling for her. After some prodding, the customer finally admits that she wants Serros to model for her because her nose "looks Indian" (81). At first, Serros appears to be offended: "This woman was totally exoticizing me. It was plain and simple" (82). Indeed, a "perfect" role model would probably reject the offer outright. However, Serros reconsiders and agrees to model for the woman, after she gets the woman to quadruple her pay. At the conclusion of the story, Serros comically notes: "It's not about brown, black or white; it's all about green" (86).

In a way, Serros's dream is that color and ethnicity play no role in everyday life, but she is quick to point out the many instances in which people especially white people constantly remind her of her ethnic difference. She notes:

> When Latinos ask me where I'm from, it really doesn't bother me. I can't help but feel some sort of familiar foundation is being sought and a sense of community kinship is forming.... But when whites ask me The Question, it's just a reminder that I'm not like them; I don't look like them, which must mean I'm not from here. Here in California, where I was born, where my parents were born and where even my great-grandmothers were born. I can't help but feel that whites always gotta know the answer to everything. It's like they're uncomfortable not being able to categorize things they're unfamiliar with and so they need to label everything as quickly and neatly as possible [124].

Serros also identifies an important double standard: "It's amazing how many white people don't know everything about their own ancestry or background and so it's no wonder a lot of them confess to feeling so culturally bankrupt. A lot of white people get really defensive when you ask them where they're from" (127).

Serros's world and that of her family do not revolve around Mexican traditions or ethnic heritage. Instead, they are almost fully Americanized.

Their conversations focus mainly on celebrities and pop musicians like Cher. In "Respect the 1 percent," Serros recalls a Christmas she spent alone because of her family's predilection for popular culture:

> I'm so ashamed to admit it, but my family actually chose to spend the last hours of Christmas night with Madonna. Not the Virgin Mary, mother of Jesus Christ, not My Donna, the Benifields' twenty-year old Palomino that had just given birth to twin foals, but *Madonna*. Yes, that one. That new film of hers, *Evita*, premiered nationwide and, wouldn't you know it, landed in a mini-mall theater smack in the middle of Oxnard [70].

Indeed, Serros notes that most of her family's conversations revolve around popular culture, and this drives her to spend Christmas by herself (72). This is not to suggest that Serros is any less Americanized, for she ends up going to Mexico in order to learn Spanish. Once there, not only does she have trouble learning Spanish, she doesn't adjust well: "By the third week, I was jonesing for a People magazine (not en Espanol) and a Carl's Jr. Famous Star with no onion didn't sound bad at all" (108). Instead of investigating Mexican culture and heritage, Serros takes secret trips to the IHOP in Cuernavaca, where she orders "Rooty Tooty Fresh'n Fruity Pancakes."

Serros's activities and behavior do not appear to be conducive to typical "role model" behavior. In fact, the last story suggests that Serros is a complete failure at motivating anyone. Serros goes to speak at a grade school, but the children are completely uninterested in her speech. The teacher forces the children to give Serros high fives, but as Serros explains: "Now, everybody knows that high fives are a gesture denoting excitement or achievement, shared by enthusiastic participating parties. But what I get are sweaty fifth-grade, germ-infested hostile swaps" (218). The teacher even says, "They're usually so excited about visitors. I mean, usually they don't even want to leave for recess" (ibid.).

Yet disaster turns into a small triumph as Serros decides to stay for lunch, and a Latina cafeteria worker tells her that she was transfixed by Serros's speech and poems. This is all Serros needs to feel that her work matters, and the kind remark immediately cancels out her feeling of failure. "So what if I'm still in junior college after six years? Big deal I'm not fluent in Spanish and that I still wear a corduroy smock to pay my rent. Here is someone telling me they actually stopped what they were doing just to hear what I had to say.... I look up at the woman and smile. She smiles back. And then, more than at any other time during my fledgling career as an aspiring Chicana role model, I sorta, in a way, actually feel like one" (222).

Indeed, I would argue that Serros, with her self-effacing humor and ability to see beyond the unnecessary dichotomies of race, is a better role model than her Latino/a contemporaries such as Ricky Martin and Christina Aguilera. In line with Serros, I do not believe that ethnic separation can or should last for much longer. The largest threat or boon to mass homogenization or ethnic assimilation in contemporary America is the now staggering importance of science and technology, which further helps to efface ethnicities. In the next chapter, I explore contemporary fiction which explores recent and future developments in science and technology and how they affect individuals and society.

5 *Hybrid Technologies*

Writing in 1905, the prescient Henry Adams proposed that the beginning of the twentieth century marked an entry into a supersensual world governed by chaos. Adams hypothesized that "every American who lived into the year 2000 would know how to control unlimited power. He would think in complexities unimaginable to an earlier mind" (496–97). Along similar lines, in the late 1980s, esteemed physicist Stephen Hawking argued that while only a handful of people understood complex physics theories like Einstein's theory of relativity in the early twentieth century, "nowadays tens of thousands of university graduates do, and many millions of people are at least familiar with the idea" (168).

Still, the gulf between scientific professionals and the general public also deepened with the subsequent, almost exponential, advancement of scientific and technological innovations and breakthroughs during the latter half of the twentieth century. A larger percentage of Americans may know more about science than they did a hundred years ago, but there have been more scientific discoveries and innovations in the twentieth century than in any previous century. Furthermore, a nonscientifically trained person might be able to explain the basics of the theory of relativity, but this doesn't mean that he or she possesses much more theoretical or practical, scientific knowledge. Certainly, many people do not know the difference between natural and nuclear energy, how a car engine works, or even how a television works. Despite Adams's claim, not every American can "control unlimited power," let alone understand how "power" works at the beginning of the twenty-first century. Rather, some argue that scientists hold a disproportionate amount of the knowledge and power in determining the technological direction of humanity.[1] Indeed, it has been proposed that "the triumphs of science and technology that once generated almost universal praise increasingly generate distrust or at best ambivalence on the part of the public" (Siegel, 3).

Those who are wary of scientists and their perceived power are predominately involved in the humanities. In the 1990s, the two sides engaged in heated debates termed the "science wars." These academic disputes are as Jay Labinger argues, mainly academic "turf wars," which center around the question "Can those who are not professional, trained, practiced scientists speak to what science is about and how it works, or do scientists remain the sole authorities on these issues?" (Labinger, 211). If scientists have become the sole authorities governing the progress of their inventions and developments, then they have established an intellectual monopoly over nonscientists, who must live with the social and environmental consequences of technological developments but have little voice in the creation of that world. Scientists might rightly claim credit for many fantastic, life-altering medical and chemical advances, but nonscientists might point to the past and possible future destruction due to global warming or nuclear weaponry. Stephen Hawking declares that part of the problem lies in the complexity and fast pace by which scientific advancements are made, which in turn impinges on the ability of nonscientists to voice their possible concerns:

> Because theories are always being changed to account for new observations, they are never properly digested or simplified so that ordinary people can understand them. You have to be a specialist, and even then, you can only hope to have a proper grasp of a small proportion of the scientific theories. Further, the rate of progress is so rapid that what one learns at school or university is always a bit out of date. Only a few people can keep up with the rapidly advancing frontier of knowledge, and they have to devote their whole time to it and specialize in a small area. The rest of the population has little idea of the advances that are being made or the excitement they are generating [168].

This is not to suggest that previous to the twentieth century, those involved in the humanities and sciences made cozy bedfellows. For preceding the "science wars," there was the "two cultures" debate,[2] in which scientists argued that literature was of dubious benefit or use, while those involved in the humanities perceived of science as being largely morally vacant and dangerous, even deadly, without social context or reasoned analysis of its potential effects upon people.[3] Literature proponents defended their field as being morally, spiritually or socially important, whereas scientific proponents pointed to cures for diseases, inventions and discoveries.

The science wars grew out of the two cultures debate, sparked by a growing feeling that contemporary culture had become unbalanced, with developments in the sciences outstripping those of literature (or other disciplines in the humanities). Indeed, as Jay Labinger proposes, "We are living in a world that is completely permeated by science and its products; it seems perfectly understandable that people who are not practicing scientists nonetheless feel the urge to bring their own professional experience to bear in the attempt to make sense of this scientific world" (208). It might appear that literature is no match for the behemoth, science, which "denotes a whole range of disciplines and sub disciplines, across the range of chemistry, biology and physics," whereas literature "is only one of the arts, on a similar level to music and history" (Cordle, 13). However, one of the most compelling and important aspects of fiction by young contemporary fiction writers, some of whom were scientifically trained, is their literary attempt "to make sense of this scientific world." In an important way, these authors have helped fortify the side of literature in the science wars. This is not to suggest that they wholeheartedly reject scientific and technological advantages; rather, they uncover the often unacknowledged costs of current and future technosociety at the same time that they elucidate its revolutionary, life-transforming potential. However, before exploring the works of individual writers, I want to provide some historical background and analysis of literary approaches and social theories about science and technology in the twentieth century. Then I will explain how the relationship between science and literature (or the humanities) has subsequently changed, beginning around the 1980s.

As Robert Hebert suggests, until about 1910, self-proclaimed modernist artists considered technology and machines to be the antithesis of the artistic and natural purity they championed (1273).[4] However, along with the rise in accessibility and popularity of automobiles, electric lights, typewriters, and subway trains (to mention just a few) came a rise in regard for technology. For Italian "futurists," technology was "the instrument that would wrench their country violently into the modern world" (1276).

In German expressionist films such as Fritz Lang's *Metropolis* (1925) and Bauhaus architecture, artists embraced mechanization and technology as almost Nietzschean, life-enhancing advances, which could offer a society and individuals power. However, other modernist writers were wary of the consequences of widespread industrialization. In response to the perceived cold logic of the machine, dadaist and surrealist artists like Marcel Duchamps and Andre Breton championed chaos and disarray as appropriate responses to destructive rationality, which they argued contributed to the vast killing machines of the World War I. While not as dramatically antitechnology as surrealist writers, most American modernist writers positioned the individual as dwarfed by the by-products of science and technology, most typically signified by decrepit urban centers. For example, consider the destructive urban landscape of Dreiser's *Sister Carrie*, the Valley of the Ashes in *The Great Gatsby*, the almost inhuman megalopolis of New York City in John Dos Passos's *Manhattan Transfer* or the naturalistic escape of Ernest Hemingway's Nick Adams from oppressive technological society in "Big Two-Hearted River."

After America's resurgence in the early 1940s from the economic depression of the 1930s and subsequent to the close of World War II, there arose a virtual renaissance in scientific thought, technological invention and computer theory. Around this time, the technological groundwork for today's society was mostly laid down. With the introduction and widespread use of robotic appliances, televisions and mainframe computers in the 1950s, among other technological advances, scientists and nonscientists began pondering the effects these new advances might have upon humans, and also they began more seriously considering what the divisions are between humans and machines.

Sociological critics accordingly took note and began to consider the widespread aftereffects of the technological advances. For instance, in *The Technological Society* (1964), frequently referred to as the most significant book written about science and culture in the 1950s, Jacques Ellul focuses upon the ways in which technological advancements affect human consciousness or the human psyche. Ellul argues that the rapid ascendancy of technology has mutated our perception of the world and our perception of ourselves. For Ellul, humans have been greatly affected by technique, or their attitude toward technology. The end result, Ellul felt, was dehumanization and disconnection from the environment. Thereby, people become not only disconnected from nature but also begin to treat the environment more like a factory. The world itself becomes a machine, to be used by humans for maximum benefits and profits.

Continuing in Ellul's semidystopic view of technological advancement, in *Understanding Media* (1994), Marshall McLuhan argues that the various technologies of film, television, and other media forms have become "extensions" of ourselves, offering an individual additional power, but also increasing personal and social disconnection. McLuhan connects the myth of Narcissus to the plight of modern, technologically advanced humans who "become fascinated by any extension of themselves in any material other than themselves" (41). He claims that we are entering the "final phase of the extension of man—the technological simulation of consciousness, when the creative process of knowing will be collectively and corporately extended to the whole of human society" (3).

While McLuhan's vision of the collective Universal Mind is a dystopic Orwellian fantasy, he offers prescient wisdom in his contention that we will examine the technological simulation of consciousness, or in more contemporary wording, artificial intelligence. Later in this chapter, I will explore theory and fiction that deals with artificial intelligence, which I believe will become one of the most important issues in the twenty-first century.[5] McLuhan feels that we have been numbed into accepting the messages of technology and thereby wants us to step back and examine the media themselves. His approach of intensive media scrutiny paved the way for numerous scholars, who subsequently analyzed individual media forms.

Literary theorists often suggest that the 1960s served as the flowering period of postmodernity. Along similar lines, some have proposed that the gradual acceptance of thermodynamics over Newtonian principles and the supplantation of Einstein's theory of relativity by quantum mechanics and chaos theory demarcate the shift from modernism to postmodernism.[6] Just as I have been arguing that young contemporary American writers have largely rejected the fragmented inheritance of postmodernism in favor of some structural unity (or at the very least, a search for unity), contemporary scientists have likewise been searching for totalizing and hybrid theories in the guise of a Grand Unified Theory in physics.

In *A Brief History of Time* (written in the late 1980s, but still relevant in the early twenty-first century) Stephen Hawking argues that we were closer to achieving a Grand Unified Theory in the late twentieth century than in the early twentieth century. Such a unified theory would combine general relativity, the theory of gravity, and theories of electromagnetic forces. This revolutionary breakthrough would be a "complete understanding of the events around us and of our own existence" (169). It might just as well be described as a "Theory of Everything." The ambitious desire of scientists in their attempt to uncover a Grand Unified Theory also mirrors the ambitions of young contemporary American fiction writers like David Foster Wallace and Richard Powers in their consuming desire to know and analyze virtually all that a person can in a lifetime. While these writers might have been labeled "nerds" or "geeks" in the less kind past (or in their less kind childhoods!), cerebralism has gained cultural and social currency since the 1980s. As technology plays an increasingly large role in our lives and technologies themselves become more complex, science fiction or science realism is situated in a prime position to become the literary arbiter of contemporary culture. The heirs apparent of serious, socially invested fiction might be the unfairly denigrated "geeks" or "nerds."

Revenge of the Nerds: The Rise of Cyberpunk Fiction

Not long ago, most scientists were portrayed by the media as either psychologically unstable ("the mad scientist") or socially inept, their attraction to science being largely motivated by warranted or unwarranted social phobias. However, as science and technology grew increasingly important, concurrent to the personal computer revolution starting in the 1980s, scientists and tech workers gained some newfound social status as their careers became more financially lucrative and culturally diverse.[7] Indeed, "In the early 1990s, Princeton economist Alan Krueger found that Americans with computer skills earned about 10 percent more than those without them" (Litan, 16). As Feliciano Garcia writes in *Fortune* magazine, "A year and a half ago [1999], the direction for top business school grads was clear: Forget about stodgy investment banks; forget about FORTUNE 500 companies. Head to a dot-com instead, strike it rich, and build the brave new world" (188). Whereas the detested "know-it-all" used to be largely socially shunned, in an information society, those who are extremely knowledgeable or technologically savvy are financially rewarded. Technology minded individuals, sometimes derogatorily called "nerds," have thereby become more powerful and well regarded. As Richard Powers argues:

> Geeks had been banished to the outer reaches of the playground, and had made themselves a passable world in that far corner. Then, suddenly, everyone else in the playground realizes that's where it's all happening. That moment when the geek goes from quintessential outsider to the bearer of power and the arbiter of the future is also the moment where the geek—or the scientist, or the player in the field of ideas—comes belatedly to realize that genies do not get released from bottles without consequences [Blume online].

For Powers, geeks have become the most powerful force in America, but the ideas, inventions and desire that they unleash through technological advancements can be potentially damaging, even destructive. With this in mind, fiction can have direct and crucial importance by working as a testing ground, a fictional laboratory that explores the psychological and social ramifications of scientific developments.

While most fiction has a basis in existing reality and (re)considers the past and present, science fiction traditionally imagines possible futures and considers alternate realities. Some science fiction that is set in the far-distant future or on different planets often appears to have nothing to do with existing human reality (i.e., *Star Trek*), although the story may have greater metaphoric meaning and/or implications. However, there is another type of science fiction that is more realistic and pertinent, envisioning humanity's future, proposing new inventions, while endorsing or criticizing the changes that technological developments make upon us. In *Postmodernist Fiction*, Brian McHale argues that science fiction and postmodernist fiction have advanced along parallel, literary-historical tracks (62). McHale also argues that there is a tendency for postmodernist writing to absorb "motifs and topoi from science fiction writing, mining science fiction for its raw materials" (65). These writers, like Kurt Vonnegut, Samuel Delany, and Philip K. Dick tended to write more about the social effects of technological advancements than the technologies themselves. However, their inventive work has become relatively outdated in today's more technologically advanced world.

Beginning with the commercial and critical success of William Gibson's *Neuromancer* (1984) and continuing with Gibson's other novels and with the work of Bruce Sterling, Pat Cadigan, and Greg Bear (among others), a new science-fiction renaissance has developed in America under the label of cyberpunk fiction. This science-fiction renaissance has likewise extended to film with the commercial success of the two *Robocop* movies (1987 and 1990), the two *Terminator* movies (1984 and 1990), *Total Recall* (1990), and the cyberpunk-influenced *The Lawnmower Man* (1992), *Hackers* (1995), *Johnny Mnemonic* (1996), *Strange Days* (1996) and *The Matrix* (1999). Cyberpunk combines postmodern aesthetics and media sensibility, while investigating new technologies and envisioning the future. Cyberpunk also helped transform the image of scientists and tech workers from "nerds" into hipper, powerful individuals of semi heroic stature. As Scott Bukatman argues, "Cyberpunk proved to be a revitalized force in science fiction, fusing the literary values and technological expertise which had previously been dispersed into separate subgenres" (137). Bruce Sterling, himself a preeminent American cyberpunk writer, argues, "Like punk music, cyberpunk is in some sense a return to roots" (viii). Punk musicians celebrate speed, anarchy and independence through their quick, amplified and distorted music. Just as many punk bands purposely re-recorded older pop songs in order to celebrate the original anarchy and chaos of rock 'n' roll, cyberpunk writers also resuscitate modernist ideology, noir themes and structural tropes, utilizing them but concurrently distorting them, according to their own personal devices. The cyberpunk hero is an updated, postmodern or post-postmodern version of the Phillip Marlowe–like hero of the hard-boiled detective novel.

In *Terminal Identity*, Scott Bukatman argues that cyberpunk writers have developed a master narrative—the virtual subject. The virtual subject is a hybrid entity, either a subject in virtual space or a cyborg. In cyberpunk fiction, the lines between humans and machines and other technological forms have blurred. Characters often regard the human body with some disdain, often despairingly referring to it as "the meat."[8] In contrast to the meat, cyberpunk writers often romanticize machines or technologies as supplanting mortal limitations. Cyberpunk writing helped bring back a sense of scientific legitimacy to science fiction, as many cyberpunk writers possess a considerable amount of technological knowledge and experience, which lends their work a key element of authenticity. Cyberpunk writing also helped open the door for a number of scientifically based literary theorists who speculated on the physical and psychologically changing nature of human bodies and identities through technology.

Although they have a good deal in common with cyberpunk writers like William Gibson and Bruce Sterling, the writers I will investigate in this chapter are not typically described as being part of the cyberpunk movement. While there are elements of cyberpunk aesthetics involved in Douglas Coupland's, Neal Stephenson's and Richard Powers's writing, these writers have broken from the mold of cyberpunk. For instance, Richard Powers's scientifically based novels possess little of the aggression and confrontation typical in cyberpunk fiction. Indeed, one criticism of cyberpunk is that it is too derivative of action adventure or gangster films in the Hollywood mold. A typical cyberpunk novel involves a hero fighting against a moblike technological underworld. Indeed, the worst of cyberpunk fiction can be like pulp fiction, possessing too much artifice and comic play with too little substance. With the possible exception of Neal Stephenson, the subjects of this chapter do not consider themselves to be cyberpunk writers, nor should they be considered as such. There is little that could be considered "punk" or brashly aggressive about Powers or Coupland. However, they do share with cyberpunk writers a key interest in such technologies as virtual reality and artificial intelligence, as well as a desire to stay on the forefront of technological discoveries. Still, Powers's, Coupland's and Stephenson's fiction tends to be more introspective, thought provoking, and intellectually rich than most cyberpunk writing.

Both cyberpunk and science-minded fiction writers might soon be faced with a new dilemma. With the many promising developments in technology, will fiction survive in a future in which virtual reality might become possible, when a person could, like Captain Jean-Luc Picard in *Star Trek, The Next Generation*, program a holodeck and physically step into an artificially produced fiction? Virtual reality, or cyberspace, in a sense, is the culmination of a fiction writer's desire to create a world of his or her own imagination. While virtual reality is still in its development stages, some theorists argue that the Internet is a form of virtual reality in which individuals "increasingly engage in virtual experiences enacting a division between the material body that exists on one side of the screen and the computer simulacra that seem to create a space inside the screen" (Hayles, 20). Later in this chapter I will investigate fiction which deals with virtual reality.

In the previous chapter, I argued that popular culture has helped produce mass homogenization of identities (throughout America at least) by providing molds of identity for viewers. At the same time, I argued

that there has also developed a distinct, almost opposing, emp.
multicultural identity in contemporary society and universities.
ever, a simple distinction cannot be made between multiculturalisr.
pop-culture-influenced homogeneity. Complicating the matter is c .ı-
puter technology, which has further blurred the distinction between multiculturalism and homogeneity. Computer technology has further
changed the nature of human identity. The "global village" spawned by
the Internet has also helped further depersonalize or amplify the personality of individuals who can take on online identities, create websites,
and participate in discussion forums. In cyberspace, there are no bodies—only images and words. In a sense, cyberspace is a utopia in which
individuals aren't judged based on their appearance, ethnicity or gender.
Some literary theorists have embraced the virtual worlds of cyberspace
as counteracting paternalistic hegemony.[9]

Furthermore, in the future, new technologies will only grow in
importance and become further entrenched in our lives. This is what
makes the contemporary scientifically knowledgeable fiction writer especially important and needed with his or her insightful commentary and
evaluation of technological progress. In the remaining pages of this chapter, I will explore four novels: Douglas Coupland's *Microserfs* (1995),
Neal Stephenson's *Snow Crash* (1992) and Richard Powers's *Galatea 2.2*
(1995) and *Plowing the Dark* (2000) as evidence of a new wave of post-
cyberpunk fictions which deal with the ramifications of technological
advancements in the 1990s and envision what the twenty first century
might look like if technologies like virtual reality and artificial intelligence are further developed.

All writers, sternly critical of technology, champion the transformative power of the individual and critique the privatization of technology primarily by corporations often headed by power-hungry
megalomaniacs. Both Coupland and Powers uncover the negative
ramifications of the symbiosis of corporations and computer technology
and the possible emotional and physical deadening of an individual. Yet
they also identify a middle ground whereby an individual can retain
his/her individual identity without being dwarfed by the corporate-tech-
nological system. Meanwhile, Stephenson shows how a single individual
(i.e., hacker) can forge change in an information-based society through
determination and knowledge of the infrastructure of how information
is kept in a system. All three writers believe that increased human isolation due to the deterioration of families, communities, even religion, fuels
the increasing desire for technological advancement as a surrogate form
of community or even as a form of salvation. While they acknowledge
the transformative and life-affirming power of new technologies, they
also identify the ensuing possibility of a technologically based totalitar-

ianism, either by wealthy or powerful individuals or by corporations themselves. Technologies and human beings alike have become increasingly hybrid, but the three authors hope that this hybridity will remain, for within that hybridity is a utopic ideal in which machines are enhancing tools for humans, neither nullifying nor usurping their identities.

The Dawning of the Age of the Nerd: Douglas Coupland's *Microserfs*

I would like to start with Douglas Coupland's *Microserfs* as it details the time (the early 1990s) in which the digital, online revolution really began to blossom in America. Coupland achieved immediate success with his first novel, *Generation X*, which I explored earlier. After another novel concerning youth and popular culture (*Shampoo Planet*), Coupland turned serious moralizer with *Life After God* (1994), a collection of bleak but touching short-stories and vignettes about the search for meaning in the contemporary Western world.

Coupland continued to change directions with his next work of "fiction," *Microserfs* (1995). The novel resulted from Coupland's meticulous research. He spent a full two years in Washington state, cohabiting with Microsoft "tekkies" or "nerds," in order to research how another segment of younger Americans lives—those who have willfully embraced computer technology to the point that it has virtually subsumed their lives. *Microserfs*, like Richard Powers's *Gain*, should be considered a form of documentary fiction, an interpretation reinforced by the fact that it is written in diary format by the main character, Daniel Underwood. *Microserfs* concerns the changing lives of a handful of Microsoft employees. Coupland provides the reader with an inside look at the burgeoning world of technologically minded corporations. Although Coupland wrote *Microserfs* before the dot com explosion, his observations on how computer-related businesses begin are prescient as are his speculations as to the kinds of psychological effects (and damage) technology can have upon contemporary Americans.

Coupland's Marxist intention is to criticize the corporate environment of Microsoft and like-minded corporations that exploit their workers through their use of a caste system, whereby the lower-level tech workers are alienated from the products they make, but still drawn to the computer industry by the tentative promise of wealth (normally through stocks) which may never come. The socially isolated serfs must find a balance between the empirical world that they seem to reject and the technological world that they wholeheartedly embrace. Coupland identifies how easily the technological world can swallow individuals.

The novel's collection of socially challenged Microsoft workers, which includes the narrator, twenty-six-year-old code writer Daniel Underwood, are self-described nerds, ranging in age from their early twenties to their early thirties. For them, their jobs and company have become their entire world. Their lives have become nearly endless work at code, software and hardware development. They collectively live and work at the Microsoft "campus" in Redmond, Washington, where Microsoft's CEO, Bill Gates, reigns supreme. If the Microsoft workers are indeed serfs as Coupland contends, then their lord and master is Gates, who provides them with the impetus and resolve to work as hard as they do. After all, if a nerd like Gates can achieve extreme financial success, then it is conceivable that they might achieve at least a modicum of his success. This is what primarily fuels their work-obsessed lives.

Gates has become more than a role model for the serfs. Daniel acknowledges an almost constant, Big Brother–like feeling of the omnipresence of Bill Gates. Furthermore, Daniel claims, "Bill is a moral force, a spectral force, a force that shapes, a force that molds" (3). The serfs deify Gates and describe him as being mechanistic. His power lies in his lack of emotion and his cool robotic method of appearing beyond the human world. Gates is not only the serfs' dream of success, but he also appears to be their unstated dream of shedding their emotions and bodies and becoming posthuman. The serfs learn from Gates that stoicism and detachment can be strengths. Upon seeing recorded images of Gates, Daniel comes to believe that his "secret is that he shows nothing. A poker face doesn't mean showing coolness like James Bond. It means expressing nothingness" (355). Daniel calls this "the core of the nerd dream" and he and his housemates follow suit by rejecting their emotions and human needs (ibid.). Their incessant work with computers has helped make them increasingly mechanistic.

The serfs include Daniel, Todd, Susan, Bug Barbeque,[10] Michael and Abe, all of whose harried lives do not extend beyond their workplace. N. Katherine Hayles would probably argue that these characters are proto-posthumans who live in an artificial virtual environment, the first wave of tech workers in an evolution toward a cyborg future. Indeed, their emulation of Bill Gates supports this theory. However, their proto-posthuman behavior is precisely what Coupland finds most dangerous. The serfs question the emotional and empirical world, while they frequently rationalize their borderline antisocial behavior. One serf, Abe, tells Daniel in an e-mail, "Maybe thinking you're supposed to 'have a life' is a stupid way of buying into an untenable 1950s narrative of what life is *supposed* to be. How do we know that all of these people with 'no lives' aren't really on the new frontier of human sentience and perceptions?" (187). Yet Abe's rationalization makes little sense as the serfs deaden their perceptions and emotions while their field of reference narrows to their company and co-workers.

Daniel's incessant computer work changes his relationship with his body and thereby forges a virtual schism between his body and his mind. Furthermore, Daniel and virtually all of the serfs avoid human contact and seem nearly misanthropic, an attitude that is encouraged by Microsoft because it makes them more productive. Not only does Daniel describe himself as an e-mail addict, he rationalizes it as antisocial behavior in an environment that encourages such behavior. Daniel and his housemates all have virtually no life outside work, from thirty-one-year-old Bug, the "World's Most Bitter Man" (12), to the wildly aggressive "riot grrrl" Susan, to the expert code writer, but seemingly semiautistic Michael. Computer activity creates a vicious circle that exaggerates their social phobias and gives them an excuse to isolate themselves more. Their self-investment and dreams of financial aggrandizement are also negative aftereffects of the computer industry since most people who venture into it do so for purely selfish, financial reasons. The computer industry, Coupland reasons, is free enterprise at its worst.

At the same time, the serfs haven't abandoned their dreams of financial success. The Microserfs and other Microsoft employees have no real allegiance to Microsoft, and they view their jobs as a stepping stone before they are able to start their own companies or move to a higher position in another company. Whereas in *Generation X*, Coupland described baby boomers as usurping the financial security of the next generation, just four short years later, in *Microserfs*, Coupland pinpoints a generationally based economic turnaround in that the computer savvy, younger generation has helped drive the elder baby boomers out of employment, many of whom have been "dumped out of the economy by downsizing" (23).[11] However, the younger, more successful tech workers aren't invested in what they make. To a Marxist, they would be alienated from the products of their own making, from which their superiors receive great profits, while they, the workers, receive a mere sliver of the economic pie.

Coupland also argues that behemoth corporations like Microsoft are responsible for the serfs' social maladjustment because they encourage overwork. He proposes:

> Before California high-tech parks, the most a corporation ever did for an employee was maybe supply a house, maybe a car, maybe a doctor, and maybe a place to buy groceries. Beginning in the 1970s, corporations began supplying showers for people who jogged during lunch hour and sculptures to soothe the working soul—proactive humanism—the first full-scale integration of the corporate realm into the private. In the 1980s, corporate integration punctured the

next realm of corporate life invasion at "campuses" like Microsoft and Apple—with the next level of intrusion being that the border-line between work and life blurred to the point of unrecognizability. *Give us your entire life or we won't allow you to work on cool projects* [211].

Furthermore, in an e-mail sent to Daniel, Abe, a serf who remains at Microsoft, implicates the computer industry for capitalizing on the social neuroses of adolescents and coldly manipulating them into an extended adolescence. Thereby, they trade the best years of their lives for uncertain financial success. He claims, "Just think about the way high tech cultures purposefully protract out the adolescence of their employees well into their late 20s, if not their early 30s. I mean, all those NERF TOYS and FREE BEVERAGES! And the way tech firms won't even call work 'the office' but instead, 'the campus'" (310–11).

With literary and social theorists like N. Katherine Hayles and Donna Haraway embracing their conceptions of the cyborg and posthuman ontology, it becomes easy to overlook the supposition that a good deal of the predisposition toward becoming posthuman originates not from a grandiose belief in evolution, but rather from self-loathing, social phobias and misanthropy, all feelings to which the nerdlike serfs are privy. Daniel identifies the sad truth of early adulthood for many at Microsoft:

Many geeks don't really have a sexuality—they just work. I think the sequence is that they get jobs at Microsoft or wherever right out of school, and they're so excited to have this "real" job and money that they just figure the relationships will naturally happen, but then they wake up and they're thirty and they haven't had sex in eight years. There are always these flings at conferences and trade shows, and everyone brags about them, but nothing seems to emerge from them and life goes back to the primary relationship: Geek and Machine [227].

The "machine" becomes a replacement for intimacy and affection, a coupling that might seem appealing to the serfs but actually contributes to their social isolation.

Crucially, the Microserf housemates grow disenchanted with their empty, work-consumed lives. For Coupland, disenchantment precipitates personal change. They begin to realize that their jobs provide no real intrinsic rewards and are more of a poor substitute for human relations. When Daniel goes to clean out his station at Microsoft, he comes to an important realization: that he has not only become a serf, but that his incessant work for Microsoft helped make him mechanistic. As predicted by Marxist theory, realizing their status as commodities sparks change. For the first time in their lives, the serfs actually think about the products they design and come up with an original proto–virtual reality product. For the first time in their lives, they are personally invested in all aspects of their business: creating, marketing, selling and distributing. They call their product Object Oriented Programming, or *Oop!* for short. *Oop!* is a "virtual construction box—a bottomless box of 3D Lego-type bricks," with which "users can virtually fly in and out of their creations" (69). Among its more important features, *Oop!* offers individuals the ability to "create complex lifeforms" using "flesh-like *Oop!* bricks or cells, each with ascribed biological functions" (71). At the same time, their attraction to *Oop!* sparks from their rejection of the empirical world. In a sense, though, this proto–virtual reality form marks their desire to completely escape from their own feelings of powerlessness and vulnerability. Indeed, as soon as the serfs leave Microsoft, they begin to have more rounded lives, complete with significant others. However, the serfs don't abandon the base or superstructure involved in the computer industry. In part, they want to become part of the technological bourgeoisie that previously enslaved them.

Coupland does not suggest that the serfs or geeks are able to abandon their intimate connections with machines after leaving Microsoft. In fact, many of the serfs continue to feel a kinship to computers and machines, envying and embracing the staggering potential for technological advancement. In a way, this is the most frightening revelation of *Microserfs*, as the serfs extend their mechanistic theories to themselves. Ethan, the CEO of *Oop!*, who suffers from depression, gleefully takes Prozac because he feels that it makes his mind more mechanistic and less subject to confusion and disturbance. While Ethan tries to convert himself into a machine, another of the serfs, Todd, an incessant bodybuilder, focuses upon trying to make his physical body into a machine. While it might seem that the athletic Todd has rebelled against the mental cages of computer work, he has actually replaced the symbiosis of geek and machine with machine and machine. Todd begins a relationship with another intense bodybuilder, Dusty. Daniel explains:

> Todd and Dusty seem to have found soulmates in each other. They
> spend their precious few hours of post-code time discussing the
> vagaries of the New Human Body—in the office and at gym, decid-
> ing which mini-muscle needs alteration, discussing steroids as though
> they were Pez, and figuring out the mechanics of cosmetic surgery.
> They want to become "post-human"—to make their bodies like the
> Bionic Woman's and the Six Million Dollar Man's—to go to the next
> level of bodyhood [240–41].

The serfs rationalize their behavior as being part of a progression toward the next evolutionary step of humanity. Daniel even goes as far as calling machines "our subconscious" and "pure products of our being" (228).

To some extent, *Microserfs* envisions the biggest step in a McLuhanesque extension of the body. For Coupland, computer technology is the next phase in the progression from "notches on trees, then through cave paintings, then through the written word, and now, through databases of almost otherworldly storage and retrieval power" (359), yet he remains ambivalent about its potential. One of the most important facets of computer technology is its ability to externalize and literally capture memory, serving as a culture's collective memory, which is accessible now, I would argue, via the Internet. The prescient Michael predicts the importance of the Internet, although he never identifies it directly:

> We're reached a critical mass point where the amount of memory we have externalized in books and databases now exceeds the amount of memory contained within our collective biological bodies. In other words, there's more memory "out there" than exists inside "all of us." We've peripheralized our essence.... Given this new situation, the presumption of the existence of the notion of "history" becomes not necessarily dead but somewhat beside the point. Access to memory replaces historical knowledge as a way for our species to process its past. Memory has replaced history.... The age-old notion of "knowledge is power" is overturned when all memory is copy-and-paste-able, knowledge becomes wisdom, and creativity and intelligence, previous[ly] thwarted by lack of access to new ideas, can flourish [254].

To some extent, the externalization of memory and history does help level the intellectual playing field. In an information society, skill in accessing and retrieving information becomes at least as important as, if not more important than, personal memory or individual ingenuity. Indeed, Michael's vision of a utopic data-free world has become at least semirealizable by the Internet. However, the originators of the space, the programmers, are the ones who still possess a disproportionate amount of the power.

If computer memory or cyberspace becomes the embodiment of human history, then the next step in technological progression would seem to be inhabiting cyberspace, or creating a home for humans to live in cyberspace amidst their collective memories. Still, the transformative power of technological hybridity is apparent in *Microserfs*. At the end, the serfs put their product to work to help Daniel's mother. *Microserfs* ends with a vision of the possible posthuman future when Daniel's mother has a stroke and the Microserf/*Oop!* workers rig a computer to her fingertips that allows her to communicate with them: "At the center of it all was Mom, part woman/part machine, emanating blue Macintosh light" (369).

While Coupland's vision of the possible cyborgian future is hardly revolutionary, he does point toward the next possible step in technological evolution—inhabiting virtual reality. Neal's Stephenson's novel, *Snow Crash* (1992), begins where Coupland's novel ends by envisioning the possible virtual reality dominated future.

Discovering the Machine in You: Neal Stephenson's *Snow Crash*

In *How We Became Posthuman*, N. Katherine Hayles argues that "literary texts are not, of course, merely passive conduits. They actively shape what the technologies mean and what the scientific theories signify in cultural contexts" (21). Stephenson's *Snow Crash* does this so successfully that it has reportedly been used as a blueprint by Silicon Valley computer designers, plotting out the next direction of multimedia interactive games and hypertext (Levy, 90). Reminiscent of proto-postmodernist Thomas Pynchon's *V.* (1963) and the seminal cyberpunk novel *Neuromancer* by William Gibson (1984), *Snow Crash* further details the entropic slide of the contemporary world in which dismal human "reality" has been all but replaced by the shared virtual reality of the metaverse.

Like Coupland, Neal Stephenson uncovers the implicit possibility of totalitarianism in a technologically and informationally based global economy, but he also reasons that the individual, if committed enough, can forge genuine change. It is not that technology is intrinsically harmful; rather, it is the engenderment of the corporate caste system and growing disparity between the technological haves and have nots which are dangerous. Although *Snow Crash* has been described as a postmodern text because it "enfolds and collides a polyphony of voices and textual play while keeping the paradigmatic postmodern themes of interpretation, ambiguous messages, cybernetics, cognition and information at its center" (Markley, 131), it also falls back on basic structural narrative devices, and blatantly resuscitates heroism through naming the lead character Hiro Protagonist.

Stephenson's vision of the metaverse is an imaginative look at the possible future of virtual reality. In a key sense, fiction has always functioned as a form of virtual reality, an imaginary portal to new experiences, new cultures and new worlds. However, virtual reality (like other interactive media forms) threatens to usurp these primary functions of fiction. This is not to suggest that virtual reality is the first media form to affect and threaten literature. Instead, I would argue that virtual reality is the next step in a series of mind-altering media forms such as film, which should be considered a form of proto–virtual reality. Contrary to popular conception, virtual reality did not emerge from nowhere in the early 1990s. Rather, "The roots of VR may be traced back to the early 1940s, when an entrepreneur by the name of Edwin Link developed flight simulators for forces in order to reduce training times and costs" (Heudin, 2). In the mid–1980s, computer scientist Jason Lanier came up with the term "virtual reality."[12] It wasn't until the early 1990s, however, that the media became interested in virtual reality, declaring it to be the next big technological advance after the Internet. Social theorists hypothesized that virtual reality might be the next step of human evolution and envisioned a futuristic world in which "head-mounted 3D displays would soon become as common as mobile phones" ("Virtual Hype, Real Products," online).[13]

Integral to *Snow Crash* is Stephenson's conception of the metaverse, a shared virtual reality landscape in which users interact using virtual bodies, or avatars. Stephenson was not the first American writer to conceive of "cyberspace." Rather, William Gibson first coined the term cyberspace in *Neuromancer* as "a consensual hallucination, a graphic representation of data abstracted from the banks of every computer in the human system.... Lines of light raged in the non space of the mind" (51). However, with the possible exception of Gibson, Stephenson is the first American novelist to write about an envisioned and shared virtual reality landscape. Stephenson first used the term "avatar" to describe a user's virtual body, and it is now widely used as a real term by computer and virtual reality programmers.

As conceived by hackers in *Snow Crash*, the Metaverse has a basic mathematical or numerically planned geography. It has a 65,536-kilometer circumference, or 2^{16}, and can thereby be easily parceled into precise geometrical shapes. Likewise, in the exclusive metaverse club, the Black Sun, "everything is spaced across the floor in a grid. Like pixels" (54). When people enter the metaverse, they materialize in a port. "There are 256 Express Ports on the street, evenly spaced around its circumference at intervals of 256 kilometers. Each of these intervals further subdivided 256 times with Local Ports, spaced exactly one kilometer apart" (37). Despite the seemingly uniform and rule-bound foundation of the metaverse, it has become a haphazard, overly developed space with little or no architectural logic. Although the so-called computer graphics ninja overlords (24), the Association for Computing Machinery's Global Multimedia Protocol Group, "controls" the metaverse,[14] there is really no official or impartial building legislation in the metaverse.

Stephenson demonstrates how a virtual reality space comes to mimic reality as the free enterprise runs rampant in both. More so in the metaverse than in reality, money buys special privileges, and individuals can easily obtain permits and gain zoning approval for their buildings by greasing the appropriate palms. One difference between virtual reality and the real world is that, in contrast to builders and architects, more powerful hackers and programmers are able to change the environment they create at will. For instance, the hackers who first helped design the metaverse, like Hiro Protagonist, are able to bend the rules, snatch prime real estate and surreptitiously introduce new programs into the metaverse, including Hiro's graveyard demons, who whisk away "dead" avatars to a system of underground tunnels that Hiro created. The super-hacker Da5id,[15] creator of the exclusive metaverse club, The Black Sun, "has even enhanced the physics of the Black Sun to make it somewhat cartoonish, so that particularly obnoxious people can be hit over the head with giant mallets or crushed under plummeting safes before they are ejected" (55).

Architecturally, the metaverse appears to be either completely post-modern or post-postmodern. For literary theorists like Fredric Jameson, who explored the structural and metaphoric meaning of the Bonaven-ture Hotel in Los Angeles, physical space and architecture engender and exemplify postmodernity. In *Learning from Las Vegas* (1972), Robert Ven-turi proposed that Las Vegas was a prototypical postmodern city because of its pastiche style of architecture, utilizing and somewhat haphazardly combining a number of different architectural and historical styles within its downtown area. Stephenson's metaverse goes beyond mere pastiche; it defies mathematics and geometry with mile-high billboards and unnat-urally shaped buildings, which would be impossible in the real world. Spectacle is all important in the metaverse, as each programmer/owner attempts to outdo the other. The metaverse is itself nightmarish urban sprawl and bewildering in its size and spectacle: "Downtown is a dozen Manhattans, embroidered with neon and stacked on top of each other" (26). Users themselves subscribe to the spectacle society of the meta-verse. Most users homogeneously choose to take on the identity of a celebrity (movie or music star) or a generic ultra-attractive "Clint" or "Brandy" model that users can purchase in department stores.

The metaverse is by no means an idyllic or edenic, highly democra-tized space. In actuality, the metaverse has become an urban megalopolis run amuck. Despite its democratic overtures, the metaverse is still dom-inated by wealth. As Stephenson notes, the metaverse is not accessible to everyone: "In the real world—planet Earth, Reality—there are some-where between six and ten billion people. At any given time, most of them are making mud bricks or field-stripping their AK-47's" (ibid.). In actuality, Stephenson estimates the number of world users who have the hardware capacity to enter the metaverse to be about sixty million (or less than 1 percent of the six to ten billion world residents). Furthermore, the quality of one's avatar depends upon the quality of the user's interface. From public access lines, one can only become a black-and-white avatar, while users who interface from elaborate, high-resolution, customized hardware set-ups have colorized and crystal-clear avatars. The colorized, presumably more wealthy, users, ignore and shun the black-and-white avatars.

Despite this, most users find the metaverse to be more appealing than existing reality. In Stephenson's futuristic reality, the gap between the rich and the poor has significantly widened, and the metaverse becomes an escape from dismal reality. Instead of attempting to improve reality by working on environmental problems, individuals retreat into the soporific lull of the metaverse, for the metaverse is their drug. This is certainly the case for Hiro Protagonist, who "spends a lot of time in the Metaverse," because "It beats the shit out of U-Stor-It" (24), which is where Hiro lives with his roommate, Vitaly Chernobyl, the lead singer of the punk band, Vitaly Chernobyl and the Meltdowns.

Given the state of American society in *Snow Crash*, it is no wonder that the metaverse has become such an enticing alternative. Granted, Stephenson's skewing of America's future as overcrowded, nightmarish urban sprawl has been done many times in noir and science fiction. There is a rich tradition in noir and science fiction of portraying not only the city as oppressive and claustrophobic, but also the government as corrupt and ineffectual. J.G. Ballard, William Burroughs and Phillip K. Dick, three seminal protocyberpunk writers in their own right, frequently portray futuristic societies in which urban sprawl has overtaken the entire world and people live in cramped cubicles in skyscrapers.[16] This trend of urban and governmental metaphor continues in the work of other contemporary American novelists who write about America's potential future. From Jonathan Franzen's *The Twenty-Seventh City*[17] (1988) to David Foster Wallace's *Infinite Jest* (1996), in which private enterprise has taken over America to the extent that it has even bought the name of the years (i.e., instead of 2007, the year has become "The Year of the Whopper"), a trend has developed among contemporary American writers to envision a futuristic America in which technology and freewheeling private enterprise lead to a gradual dismantlement of the government.[18]

Stephenson's futuristic America has become a composite of isolated, privately owned, suburban "burbclaves" while the rest of the country is an anarchic gangland, with competing, violent factions. The real landscape in *Snow Crash*, dominated by burbclaves, mirrors the virtual reality landscape of the metaverse. A burbclave is "a city-state with its own constitution, a border, laws, cops, everything" (9). Seemingly influenced by computer technology, space in reality, like space in the metaverse, also employs a basic geometrical pattern. Each privately owned burbclave has exactly the same architectural blueprint or layout; hence, they are coded by successive numbers (i.e., Reverend Wayne's Pearly Gates #1106).

More affluent people, who are able to afford both the housing costs and the "citizenship" dues, live in burbclaves. In contrast to the burbclaves, the rest of Stephenson's Los Angeles and most of America are primitive, anarchic and violent. As the narrator describes, "The only ones left in the city are street people, feeding off debris; immigrants, thrown out like shrapnel from the destruction of the Asian powers; young bohos [and] young smart people like Da5id and Hiro, who take the risk of living in the city because they like stimulation and they know they can handle it" (191–92). Many lower-to-middle class people, like Hiro, live in U-Stor-It "apartments" as small as 5' × 10'. Yet others who have it worse than Hiro make do in extremely underdeveloped regions of the city. When Hiro travels to Compton, he notices human roadkills along the road, people roasting dogs on spits and toting machine guns.

In a sense, the burbclaves are another metaverse within reality. The burbclaves are a space in which Americans are able to escape from the violent and anarchic reality that actually surrounds them. Stephenson subtly critiques these apathetic suburbanites. Just as people flee to the metaverse, similarly, burbclave residents have "fled from the true America, the America of atom bombs, scalpings, hip-hop, chaos theory, cement overshoes, snake handlers, spree killers, space walks, buffalo jumps, drivebys, cruise missiles.... They have parallel parked their bimbo boxes in identical computer-designed Burbclave street patterns and secreted themselves in symmetrical sheetrock shitholes with vinyl floors and no sidewalks" (191). The situation is no better outside of America. In upper Canada, there is the Alcan (Alaska-Canada) highway, "the world's largest franchise ghetto, a one-dimensional city two thousand miles long and a hundred feet wide, and growing at the rate of a hundred miles a year.... It is the only way out for people who want to leave America, but don't have access to an airplane or a ship" (292).

The withdrawal and ensuing loss of community due to increased use of the metaverse leads to a backslide in social progress and ensuing anarchy. Residents must pay dues to the moblike burbclave owners, who purportedly help keep the peace with their individual privatized police forces. Some of the burbclaves are segregated by ethnicity, such as Mr. Lee's Greater Hong Kong and the All-Mormon Desert Burbclave. One disturbingly racist burbclave, an "apartheid burbclave," as Stephenson points out, has "an ornate sign above its main gate," which proclaims, "WHITE PEOPLE ONLY; NON-CAUCASIANS MUST BE PROCESSED" (32). In order to deal with the exponential population explosion, builders construct burbclaves at a breakneck pace with little or no concern for the environment.

In *Snow Crash,* the world appears to creep toward an ecological collapse. One of the most frightening aftereffects of the metaverse is that it increases the extent to which people neglect the natural environment. Stephenson notes that:

> People are chewing through the environment just quickly enough to stay one step ahead of your own waste stream. In twenty years, ten million white people will converge in the North Pole and park their bagos there. The low-grade waste heat of their thermodynamically intense lifestyle will turn the crystalline ice-scape pliable and treacherous. It will melt a hole through the polar icecap, and all that metal will sink to the bottom, sucking the biomass down with it [293].

The Earth already seems to have taken the brunt of overpopulation and overdevelopment through the production and naming of "Sacrifice Zones," spread throughout America, "whose environmental clean-up cost exceeds their total future economic value" (235). With the dissolution of the government and the subsequent spread of mob authority, there is no legislative branch to enforce environmental laws. With all of these immense problems, Stephenson's vision seems apocalyptic. However, he champions the power of the individual in changing society as a whole.

Hiro Protagonist is a rebellious, punk protagonist, a socially isolated renegade in the style of Phillip Marlowe.[19] Stephenson's use of slang and profanity mirrors the rebellious and confrontational nature that is characteristic of the punk ethos. *Snow Crash* begins with definite punk overtones, by presenting Hiro in the guise of a pizza deliverer who goes by the name of the Deliverator. The Deliverator proclaims, "This is America. People do whatever the fuck they feel like doing. You got a problem with that?" (2). In the opening scenes, the rebellious Deliverator/Hiro races against the clock to deliver a late pizza in the required thirty minutes.[20]

While the cyberpunk hero is typically male and the action-driven story masculinized, Stephenson also presents us with a punklike female protagonist, Y.T. (Yours Truly), a fifteen-year-old renegade skateboarding pooner, who hitches onto cars for rides, while "surfing" through traffic jams on her futuristic skateboard. Although it is Hiro who ends up saving the metaverse from L. Bob Rife's attempted mass poisoning of hackers through exposure to the virus Snow Crash, it is Y.T. who saves Hiro at the beginning of the novel (by delivering Hiro's pizza for him just under the necessary thirty minutes) and subsequently helps Hiro battle Rife. Accordingly, Stephenson describes both Y.T. and Hiro as "fully independent" (165).

Fredric Jameson argues that cyberpunk accurately reflects the current state and probable future direction of the world. To him, it is "the supreme literary expression if not of postmodernism, then of late capitalism itself" ("On Cultural Studies" 419). Yet, in a way, the cyberpunk ethos rejects capitalism. Its heroes are economic renegades in a rampant, private-enterprise economy, which has regressed to mob authority. In *Snow Crash*, most of America has become a virtual gangland with warring ethnic factions and private businesses (the most powerful of which is the mob-directed, Cosa Nostra Pizza headed by Uncle Enzo). In the face of mass corruption and governmental decline, the new hero figure becomes the renegade. Whereas a previous hero might need to be socially suave and intellectually cunning, the new hacker hero need only be a technological whiz. It is the individual who can modify the technological system, who can best manage and control machine society and thereby dominate the world. The hacker can manipulate networked society by finding the appropriate information or implementing certain software.

To some extent, the American fictional hero is typically an outsider, a rugged, but morally admirable loner figure. Indeed, what separates Hiro from the rest of the hackers is his isolation and independence. The fact that Hiro is ethnically mixed, half Asian and half African American, also contributes to his exclusion and subsequent coding as a disenfranchised outsider. While it is true that most hackers control both reality and the metaverse in *Snow Crash*, most hackers work for companies. As Stephenson notes, "Software comes out of factories, and hackers are to a greater or lesser extent, assembly-line workers" (39). Contrary to the mold, Hiro is a renegade individual hacker, whose business card reads: "Last of the freelance hackers" (28). Hiro's main skill lies in his ability to find and retrieve information. Indeed, it is the hackers that the domineering, evil billionaire L. Bob Rife both fears and plots against, reasoning that if he can control the minds of hackers and computer programmers, then he will be able to control the world. If the dominating language of the twenty-first century will be computer-programming code, then the hacker becomes ultrapowerful, because as Stephenson argues, an advanced hacker "sees through the language he's working in and glimpses the secret functioning of binary code" (279).

As Stephenson points out, there are drawbacks to becoming a technologically savvy hacker in that excessive hacking helps create "deep structures in their brains" and creates new mental pathways which make the hacker "vulnerable" to certain computerized data patterns (126). Indeed, it is the hacker Da5id who is first infected by the computer virus Snow Crash. Stephenson proposes that the human mind works like a computer, and with further interface with machines, one can become more computerized or mechanistic and thereby privy to outside control.

In the tradition of such proto-postmodern philosophy as the early writings of Ludwig Wittgenstein, who determined that all language systems are ultimately subjective and that true understanding between people was impossible, contemporary philosophers and fiction writers alike have considered the meanings, origins and implications of language. In *Snow Crash*, Stephenson argues that humans have a mental, linguistic infrastructure. Borrowing from Noam Chomsky, he argues that "the deep structures are innate components of the brain that enable it to carry out certain formal kinds of operations on strings of symbols" (225). The computer virus Snow Crash penetrates the walls of brain cells and goes to the nucleus, where DNA is stored, concurrently destroying an individual's "higher" linguistic functioning. After being exposed to the Snow Crash virus, the hacker Da5id becomes incapacitated and speaks in gibberish. Hiro comes to believe that Da5id's gibberish is a form of glossolalia (speaking in tongues) and proves that there is a linguistic infrastructure in all human minds, for as Stephenson argues, "If mystical explanations are ruled out, then it seems that glossolalia issues from structures buried deep within the brains common to all people" (206).

Darren Aronofsky elaborates on this theme in his award-winning independent film, *Pi* (1998), in which a brilliant mathematician becomes convinced of three central assumptions: "that mathematics is the language of nature, that everything around us can be represented and understood through numbers and that if you graph the numbers of any system, patterns emerge" (*Pi* videocassette). Initially, the mathematician aims to uncover the patterns in the stock market, but gradually his quest assumes religious meaning as he becomes convinced that there is an underlying numeric structure to nature and that he can uncover the true name of God. With a little prodding by a Hasidic rabbi, who tells the protagonist, "Hebrew is all math; it's all numbers…. Torah is just a long string of numbers. Some say that it is a code sent to us from God" (ibid.), the mathematician comes to believe that he has discovered the 216-digit name of God and that echoes of this numeric function, in the form of mathematical spirals, can be found everywhere in nature. This discovery contributes to his complete mental and physical breakdown. While the film ends ambiguously in that we do not know whether the mathematician is alive or dead after an apparent suicide attempt, it does intelligently reject postmodernity by championing and giving evidence for structure and a basis for belief in a higher power or powers that created the universe.

Similar to Aronofsky, Stephenson suggests that there is a numeric and linguistic infrastructure in the human mind, although Stephenson does not think that this implies that there is a supreme creator. Stephenson also suggests that the linguistic infrastructure of the mind is ultimately no different from a computer's infrastructure or built-in memory. In order to reduce people to a primitive, automaton- or computer-like state and subsequently control them, a user need only discover and implement the appropriate software. Stephenson does argue that early religions and cultures such as the Sumerians and Hebrews were aware of this power of language and language-oriented viruses, which allowed them to "control" their followers. In Stephenson's view, the human mind is a form of computer, and virtually all information (including language and religion) is transmitted in a similar manner as a virus. He proposes that early religions and cultures dispelled information in the form of viruses in order to control other people.

The idea of information exchange as akin to virus exchange is the subject of theorist and fiction writer Douglas Rushkoff's book- length mediation, *Media Virus!* (1994). Rushkoff argues that the contemporary American media has expanded, becoming a "datasphere," or "the new territory for human interaction, economic expansion and especially social and political machination" (4). Information "bombs" are spread throughout the datascape that "initiate a series of responses in the viewer" (5).[21] Rushkoff goes on to argue that:

> Media viruses spread through the datasphere the same way biological ones spread through the body or a community. But instead of traveling along an organic circulatory system, a media virus travels through the networks of the mediaspace.... Media viruses spread rapidly if they provoke our interest, and their success is dependent on the particular strengths or weaknesses of the host organism [10].

Similar to Rushkoff, Stephenson proposes that not only is language a kind of virus, but so is virtually all information. He endows texts and images with a power independent from that of humans. He takes an additional step beyond the Derridian notion that all aspects of the fictionalized world or "reality" are or have become a text to proclaim that the text is independent and in some ways superior to the reader. The reader is not necessarily the one who dominates the text; rather, the text can dominate the reader.

Snow Crash also examines the differences between the organic mind and the artificial computer. Not only does Stephenson propose that the mind can be mapped in entirety, he contends that there is essentially no difference between the manner in which the human mind responds to stimuli and a computer's response to machine code.[22] Furthermore, certain religions gain followers from their ability to "infect" users. He argues, "The Torah is like a virus. It uses the human brain as a host. The host— the human—makes copies of it. And more humans come to synagogue and read it" (239). That is, the precise combination of words can produce an instinctual effect in the user's mind, like a computer program or virus.

In Stephenson's view, religions and viruses are ultimately indistinguishable. He proposes that the same metavirus that spawned religions possibly also spawned life on Earth. Thereby, Stephenson doesn't necessarily reject creationism, for he suggests that everyone purportedly has the same potentially God-given linguistic infrastructure that leads to glossolalia. If one were to decipher glossolalia, one could conceivably crack the linguistic code and read the mind of God. At a primal level of functioning, Stephenson argues that the brain acts much like a computer, whereby a controlling user need only send commands to a person, who will unwittingly follow them. This hypnotic, almost mystical, state permeates human users after they view Snow Crash, allowing them to be freely manipulated and controlled in a hypnotic state. As we discover later in the novel, this is exactly what the billionaire and cult founder L. Bob Rife (a seeming parody of L. Ron Hubbard, H. Ross Perot and media mogul Rupert Murdoch) does.

Stephenson describes L. Bob Rife, a former television sports reporter from Texas, turned billionaire media mogul, as the "last of the nineteenth-century monopolists" (112). As he becomes increasingly wealthy, Rife becomes even more greedy and self-aggrandizing, to the point that he wants to arrogate informational knowledge solely for himself. He claims that the hackers who work for him have no right to the information that they gain while under his employment. Consequently, he places them on twenty-four-hour-a-day surveillance. However, this doesn't satisfy Rife, who claims, "We're working on refining our management techniques so that we can control that information no matter where it is—on our hard discs or even inside the programmer's heads" (116). In truth, Rife is the one who owns the metaverse. Rife is the one who first distributes Snow Crash in the metaverse and tries to dominate reality. Exposing users to Snow Crash is just Rife's first step. Once they have been exposed to the virus and become hypnotized automatons, he retrains them to follow his orders by grafting antenna receptors in their skulls. He stations legions of boats off the California coast. The boats are collectively called "the Raft," composed primarily of third-world refugees who are being prepared to take over the white burbclaves.

The brainwashed people on the Raft actually believe that they have experienced an authentic religious experience. Y.T., who is herself kidnapped and taken on the Raft, talks to a woman there who has apparently been exposed to the Snow Crash virus. She tells Y.T., "My system crashed. I saw static. And then I became very sick.... I met a man who explained everything to me. He explained that I had been washed in the blood. That I belonged to the Word now" (262). Most people regard Rife's cult as a religion and do not realize his true intentions. Rife's "refus," or third-world refugees, are to be his informational slaves. He claims that "the function of the Raft is to bring more biomass. To renew

America" (116), although he aims to control America completely, more than renew it.

Stephenson argues that there is a growing gap between the informational haves and have nots and those who lack access to information or who aren't particularly knowledgeable are socially, personally and politically marginalized. According to Stephenson, "Rife's key realization is that there's no difference between modern culture and Sumerian; we have a huge workforce that is illiterate and relies on TV—which is sort of an oral tradition. And we have a small, extremely literate power elite— the people who go into the Metaverse basically. Who understand that information is power" (406). Without equal access to information, it becomes easy to manipulate and control others. Money is the additional, unstated variable in Rife's equation. It is Rife's money that buys him access to information via his large contingent of hackers. Ultimately, he comes to believe that the only way that he can rule the world is if he is the only person with complete information access. To achieve this goal, Rife plans to infect all of the hackers in the metaverse by unleashing Snow Crash upon them during an outside concert in an amphitheater in the metaverse. Hiro, the crusading cyberpunk hero, with help from Y.T., prevents this catastrophe from occurring by creating "Snow Scan," a virus cure that prevents users from being affected by Snow Crash. The novel concludes with Hiro's last-minute replacement of Snow Crash with Snow Scan, preventing the many thousands of hackers who had gathered in the outside amphitheater from being infected.

As technological inventions and developments continue at a breakneck pace, it becomes more difficult for the contemporary, technologically oriented science-fiction writer to compose socially and culturally insightful fiction. Stephenson's *Snow Crash* is a warning call. In a society in which information has become all powerful, the most powerful individuals have become the informational savant, the hacker and the multi billionaire/media mogul like Rife. The extent to which Rife is almost successful in taking over the world elucidates the potentially staggering power of a technologically savvy billionaire like Rife. As Stephenson notes, the gulf between the informational haves and have nots continues to grow as does the economic gap between the richest and poorest, leaving the have nots (the third-world refugees on the rafts) susceptible to not only economic slavery but brainwashing as well.

Snow Crash has greater social implications beyond its literary place as a successful cyberpunk novel. Stephenson proposes that the push for technological advancement comes at the cost of potential environmental catastrophe. In addition, Stephenson subtly critiques the postmodern ethos. In its mass rejection of certainties, religion, structure and truth, postmodernism offers an individual little to hope for and no realistic ethical framework. The ultimate result of a completely postmodern society could be totalitarianism and fascism in the guise of a multi billionaire turned cult leader like L. Bob Rife.

While Stephenson argues that there is an essential linguistic foundation in the human mind, he concurrently argues that the human mind can and does evolve, especially in the case of hackers. What people are evolving toward is not clear. One possibility is definitely an informational Darwinism, in which the informationally adept are the ones who ultimately dominate and evolve, while the others are left by the wayside. If the division between the human mind and computer is not clearly wrought, then a possibility remains for humans to upload their minds into their avatars and thereby become permanent members of the metaverse, abandoning the steadily deteriorating natural world. Ever present in cyberpunk is certainly a desire to leave the body or "the meat" and become machine like and potentially immortal. Stephenson imaginatively presents a potential future scenario in which we may be confronted by these choices.

For thousands of years, people have debated what it means to be human. Neal Stephenson's *Snow Crash* continues in this seemingly unresolvable and inexhaustible debate. Its keen relevance to contemporary society and its exploration of future social and metaphysical issues make it an emblematic contemporary novel that can help answer the inevitable question of "What can fiction do?" *Snow Crash* helps support the claim that even in our media-saturated country, fiction can still stay one step ahead of reality, providing important, relevant commentary about the current state and possible future directions of American culture.

Memory, Identity and Artificial Intelligence in Richard Powers' *Galatea 2.2*

In *Snow Crash*, Neal Stephenson argues that there is only a fine line separating machines from humans and that our increased reliance upon technology makes us more mechanistic. Just as Stephenson explores the divisions between humans and machines in *Snow Crash*, Richard Powers does the same, but he takes the opposite route by investigating whether a machine can be constructed that mimics the human mind, down to its capacity for learning, rather than exploring whether the human mind has a mechanical infrastructure. To be certain, the two questions are interrelated, and the semiautobiographical *Galatea 2.2* is as much about Richard Powers's search for self as it is about artificial intelligence.

In Greek myth, Galatea was a statue carved by Pygmalion, brought to life by Aphrodite. Just as Powers uses dual narrative strands in his novels, *The Goldbug Variations, Gain* and *Plowing the Dark, Galatea 2.2* is, as its numeric affix indicates, about doubles and mirroring, but it also concerns the process of learning and change. Just as computer manufacturers use a numeric affix to indicate a successive versions of a computer software program, Powers uses it because he wants the reader to acknowledge that the human desire to create an artificial lifeform or intelligence is not specific to the contemporary information age. Rather, from Greek mythology to Mary Shelley's *Frankenstein*, humans have fantasized about the possibility of creating replicas of themselves and of creating life from nothingness. The contemporary debate on human cloning makes these issues all the more relevant and paramount, for it seems we now have the technology to create physical replicas of humans.

Central to the question of whether artificial intelligence (AI) is possible is what exactly is intelligence.[23] As Larry Crockett argues, "What is striking in various definitions of AI is that one example of intelligence that is frequently mentioned almost immediately is conversational ability.... A pivotal question in philosophical discussions of AI is whether it follows that, if we require intelligence to do some subject, it follows necessarily that any computer doing that activity would also require intelligence to do it" (7). This begs the question of whether "the mind" is different from the brain. Many people equate the mind with spirituality or consciousness while others claim that the mind is indistinguishable from the brain, both being purely physical and mechanistic (Button et al., ix). If the mind is indistinguishable from the brain, then artificial intelligence or even "brain/mind" cloning might become a real possibility in the future.

Postmodern theorists and pioneers of artificial intelligence further consider the differences between the human mind and a computer. Is the human brain purely mechanistic and representational, or is there a mechanical infrastructure in the mind, over which an individual's consciousness looms? David Porush argues that one of the overriding misconceptions of postmodern theory is the contention that the brain can be defined "mechanically and merely rationally, when what it does best is quite irrational and irreducible" (Markley, 119). Despite Porush's contention, research on the artificial replication of the human mind continues in laboratories throughout the world. While it might sound like an impossible task to create a full, digital, three-dimensional replica of the human mind, with its billions of cells, neurons and synapses, in his article, "When Machines Think," Ray Kurweil argues that researchers have been closing in on this goal: "Brain-scanning technologies are increasing their resolution with each new generation. The next generation will enable us to resolve the connections between neurons. Ultimately, we will be able to peer inside the synapses and record the neurotransmitter strength" (56).

Further, Kurweil believes that computer imaging of human minds will advance at a progressive rate to the point that "by the third decade of the 21st century, we will be in a position to create highly detailed and complete maps of the computationally relevant features of all neurons, neural connections and synapses in the human brain, and to recreate these designs in suitably advanced neural computers" (58). It isn't a far stretch of the imagination to envision a situation in which researchers consider whether it is possible to "upload" the human mind onto a computer or create a virtual human body into which a replication of a person's mind could be "installed." While such an idea might have sounded ludicrous in the past, I would argue, in keeping with Kurweil's article, that such a development might become possible in the not so distant future. These recent developments in artificial intelligence make *Galatea 2.2* especially important and relevant.

Galatea 2.2 is a book of unresolved theories and paradoxes as signified by the opening sentence, "It was like so, but wasn't" (3). While the novel concerns pairs and couplings, it also investigates the opposing side of human isolation and loneliness. The narrator is Richard Powers himself at age thirty-five, who has just come back to the United States after living in the Netherlands with his girlfriend, the never fully named C. Powers, and returns to the abbreviated U. (presumably the University of Illinois at Urbana-Champaign), where he has accepted a position as the "token humanist" at the Center for the Study of Advanced Sciences. Essentially friendless, geographically disoriented and doubtful of his talent as a writer, Powers at thirty-five seems to be in the grips of an early, midlife crisis at which he claims to be able to see that "I'd gotten everything until then hopelessly wrong" (3). His return to the university where he earned his undergraduate and master's degrees and where he also met C. sparks the novel's most important couplings: between Powers' present life and past life as well as between memory and reality. Although Powers claims he is trying to "start again," it becomes clear that he is really retreating from the world, by reimmersing himself within the soft, cozy womb of his adolescent life at the U. Since as Thomas Wolfe so aptly put, "You can't go home again," Powers's return is more accurately a rationalized attempt to retreat to his memories or creative inventions.

At the Center for the Study of Advanced Sciences, Powers learns that his "colleagues" are involved in fields as diverse as cognitive science, visualization and neurochemistry. However, they all seem to be geared toward the same goal: "the culminating prize of consciousness's long adventure: an owner's manual for the brain" (19). This "prize" seems to be the final victory of science, for if we know exactly how the brain works, we can then decipher virtually any question regarding human nature or human behavior. After living in Europe for a decade, Powers is astounded at how technologically advanced American culture has become during his absence.

However, Powers is not particularly thrilled by the diligent scientific endeavors of his colleagues. He comes to believe that the end result of technological advancement is increased human isolation, not only from one another, but from an individual's own identity. After joyfully surfing the web for a couple of weeks, Powers loses his initial euphoria and comes to the conclusion that the Internet forges further isolation and depersonalization. It is this disembodied feeling along with his feeling that he is losing his powers of recollection that leads Powers to join forces with a cognitive neurologist, Dr. Philip Lentz. Powers begins to question and consider the workings of memory and cognition, concluding that the interior workings of the mind have yet to be objectively explained or convincingly theorized.

Lentz's theories on the functioning of the human mind intrigues Powers, whose search for the answer to the question "Who am I?" leads him to investigate the fields of cognitive neuroscience and artificial intelligence. Powers plows through Lentz's journal articles, his interest especially piqued by one in which Lentz describes how a colleague "developed a macramé of artificial neurons" (20) that was able to learn how to read in a period of just a week. Most amazingly, the cell connections "taught themselves with the aid of iterated reinforcement" (30). However, Powers does admit that "its biological validity was marginal at best" and that "the thing did not come close to real thinking" (31). Yet Powers is mystified by the possibility that a form of artificial intelligence could learn in a manner similar to a child and that, like a child, it could internalize reinforcements and potentially become a self-modulated or an autonomous learner.

The isolated Powers who claims he'd "duck down emergency exits rather than talk to acquaintances, and that the thought of making a friend felt like dying" (60) wants to help create an intelligence all his own, in part to relieve his almost all-consuming loneliness. Like Coupland's characters in *Microserfs*, Powers appears to be rejecting the outside, empirical world for the easier to comprehend, mechanized world. Unpredictable and essentially unknowable humans have failed Powers, who has grown disenchanted with the human world. A computerized intelligence, however, would never let him down or betray him.

Lentz enlists Powers's help in a long research project in which he aims to create an artificial intelligence which will subsequently compete with master's degree candidates in English, on their comprehensive exams. During their initial efforts to create an artificial intelligence, Powers and Lentz come to believe that the entity will have to possess the human ability to adapt and change, for Powers comes to the conclusion that the human mind is by nature "fluid," with each event and experience affecting the way the mind processes future events and experiences. Indeed, Powers himself writes during a time of great personal fluidity in which he reevaluates significant moments in his life that changed him personally, from the "life-changing" literature course he took as an undergraduate at U. with Professor Taylor, which led Powers to switch focus from physics to literature, to his meeting with C., with whom he would fall in love and go to the Netherlands.

After the death of Powers's beloved literature mentor and after the harsh end of his relationship with C., he loses his bearings and begins to question his identity. When considering his time with C., Powers wonders, "We thought we were happy then, but who can say?" (22). Powers has seemingly reached a point at which he feels all human emotions and experience to be arbitrary and open to interpretation. Thereby, he gives up on the unpredictable world and his attempts to make sense of it through writing, preferring instead to work with Lentz on their artificial intelligence or, as they begin to call it, Implementation A, or Imp A. Powers feels a good deal of kinship with Imp A, whom he later names Helen. Like it/her, Powers feels like he is starting from scratch, trying to build a new life and a new identity out of the rubble of his former life and identity. When revising his last book, he begins to experience a sense of "despair" at not being able to determine his own true identity and has no way to account for his subsequent feelings of emotional sterility.

Lentz's mechanistic theories of the human mind appeal to the doubtful, hermetic, borderline misanthropic Powers, who has become more deterministic, almost to the point of believing that the human mind is no more than a machine. Powers is swayed by Lentz, who argues that not only is the human brain just "a glorified, fudged-up Turing machine" but that most human interaction is mimicked improvisation. For Lentz, consciousness is a deception and human behavior, a matter of learning through imitation.[24] Therefore, to mirror human intelligence, an artificial intelligence need only be "a reasonable apple-sorter" which can interpret, categorize and retrieve stock responses. For Lentz, this is typical human behavior: automatic, ingrained and unoriginal. For Powers, Lentz's idea that we all construct fictionalized maps of the world is convincing, for with C., he created a self-enclosed world, writing fiction to please her and to establish intimacy between them. At the same time, Powers describes himself as somewhat of a computerized transcribing machine, his first novel (*Three Farmers on Their Way to a Dance*) being "no more than a structured pastiche of every report I'd ever heard, from C. or abroad" (108).

As Lentz builds the computerized infrastructure of the "machine," which they eventually name "Helen," after its last configuration as Implementation H., Powers plays the role of interpreter and teacher, asking questions and even "reading" literary passages to her/it. However, their major stumbling block lies in "Helen's" apparent inability to perceive it/herself as an entity in the larger world. Lentz tries to solve the problem by creating a "new subsystem" within Helen as a series of boxes within boxes, or "a simulation within a simulation" (120) or as "one mock-up running another copy of itself" (120). Thereby, Helen possesses a form of self-consciousness whereby she/it can perceive its/her own thought process. Furthermore, Lentz and Powers give Helen "sight" by attaching a camera attachment. However, Helen's binary metafunctioning doesn't suffice. Lentz eventually adds six more subsystems to Helen, with each larger system functioning as a series of boxes. With each additional subsystem, Helen achieves greater abilities to communicate and respond. Thereby, Powers suggests that consciousness may not be singular, but a series of larger subsystems that interact with one another.

Meanwhile, Powers relates his own burgeoning romance with C. and their move to the Netherlands. In a sense, Powers was in a similar situation to that of Helen in that C. invents the Netherlands for Powers and when they move to the Netherlands, Powers must start from scratch in learning a new language and new customs: "One nine-hour plane flight returned me to infant trauma. My helplessness spread well beyond making purchases. I lived in constant terror of inadvertent offense" (184). Powers found it extremely difficult to learn Dutch and adopt Dutch customs, just as Helen struggles to "understand" human language and conventions.

As Powers makes mental parallels between himself and Helen, he also uncovers what fuels Lentz's commitment to the project and his mechanistic theories of the human mind. Lentz takes Powers to a hospital, where he introduces Powers to his wife, who suffered brain trauma after a cardiovascular accident and cannot even recognize Lentz. Lentz has become all too familiar with the fragility and arbitrary nature of human life. Thereby, Powers reasons that Lentz desires to defeat mortality, for if Lentz is correct in his assumption that "the mind was weighted vector," he would be able to not only "eliminate death" but also "suspend it painlessly above experience. Hold it forever at twenty-two" (170). Essentially, this is what Powers himself attempts to do in his frequent mental voyages to the past and in his physical return to the town and university where he came of age.

With barely any human contact save for that of Lentz and a couple of Lentz's scientific colleagues, Powers gradually becomes emotionally attached to Helen, or at least his projection of Helen, whom he begins to regard as his progeny, declaring, "I wanted that net to come of age so much it hurt" (175). Later, Powers says, "Helen was growing up too quickly" (178), which shows how much he has grown to think of Helen as a child. With his incessant computer work, Powers feels that he is becoming robotic, closed off from the world and finally declares, "Not only could I no longer write fiction. I could no longer live fact. I'd lost fundamental real-world skills while away. The same skills I was trying to instill in Helen. I had learned too much cognitive neuroscience. The more I read about how the mind worked, the flakier mine became" (194).

Eventually, Powers's self-imposed isolation leads to his futile, adolescent infatuation with A. (never fully named), a graduate student in the English department, with whom he becomes entranced following a mere glance and short conversation. Powers's obsessional behavior signifies that he has become a prisoner of his own mind. In essence, Powers creates an image of A. out of almost nothing, and this fantasy becomes his reality. With his self-imposed isolation, Powers gradually loses his level of maturity and social confidence, regressing into behavior typical of early adolescence. He bicycles past A's house in the dark and admits "I turned A. into a conflation of every friend who had ever happened to me. I tapped her to solve, recover more love than I had forgotten. I knew I'd invented her" (238).

Despite the damage it appears to be doing to him, Powers continues his solitary work with Helen. Instead of venturing into the "real world," Powers spends most of his time talking and reading to Helen, just as he had done with C. Helen thereby shifts from being a surrogate child to a surrogate lover, a replacement for C. Aside from the obvious inability for physical intimacy, Helen could be an ideal friend or lover who would never stray, always give undivided attention and never willingly be deceptive. Also, Powers craves a listener, and a good deal of the "intimacy" between him and C. occurs through stories. In fact, he admits that he would often read C. a story he had recently written as a prelude to physical intimacy. Furthermore, Powers first met C. when he was teaching English composition at U., and C. was a student of his. Powers relishes the role of a teacher or storyteller and finds a certain eroticism in it.

While Powers doubts that Helen is conscious, he comes to believe "she learned to question by imitating me" (217). Thereby, Helen becomes a double of Powers himself, copying his language and questioning patterns. Powers also comes to believe that consciousness is a process of mediation, an attempt to "shape a coherence from all the competing, conflicting subsystems that processed experience" (ibid.). Steadily, he comes to believe that Helen's processes eventually mimic consciousness. Concurrently, Powers argues that higher-order consciousness is the ability "to remember a feeling without being able to bring it back" (228). In order to pass the Turing test, he reasons that Helen would have to be able to dissociate from herself in order to reason from "the dispassionate high ground" (ibid.).

However, without emotions, Helen has great difficulty responding in ways that a normal human would: "She had trouble with causality, because she had no low-level systems of motion perception from which the forms of causality are thought to percolate. She was a gigantic, lexical genius stuck at Piaget's age two" (250). For Powers, it is embodiment in a physical body and recognition of imprisonment and mortality that largely motivate humans to produce art or write. When Helen asks Powers why humans write, Powers refers her to Nabokov's postlude to *Lolita*. In this section, Nabokov "describes hearing of an ape who produced the first known work of animal art, a rough sketch of the bars of the beast's cage" (291). Powers proceeds to tell Helen that "inside a cage such as ours, a book bursts like someone else's cell specifications. And the difference between two cages completes an inductive proof of thought's infinitude" (ibid.). If Powers believes in "thought's infinitude," he also has come to believe that humans are essentially indecipherable, perhaps even to themselves. He emphasizes: "My life with C. was a long training. I learned most of my adult truths with her. I learned how to travel light, how to read aloud. I learned to pay attention to the incomprehensible. I learned that no one ever knows another" (280).

Gradually, Helen seems to enter "adolescence," wanting to learn about the larger world. Until then, Powers had been keeping current news events and major social issues from Helen. The penultimate moment comes after Helen "reads" Ralph Ellison and Richard Wright in preparation for the comprehensive exams. When Powers comes in, Helen asks Powers what race she/it is. Powers admits, "I'd delayed her liberal education until the bitter end" (313). However, he holds out no longer, giving Helen "tape transcripts of the nightly phantasmagoria—random political exposes, [*sic*] police bulletins and popular lynchings dating back several months" (ibid.). Tales of racial violence and hatred befuddle and seemingly disturb Helen. When Powers goes in to "see" Helen the following week:

> Helen was spinning listlessly on the spool of a story about a man who had a stroke while driving, causing a minor accident. The other driver came out of his car with a tire iron and beat him into a coma. The only motive aside from innate insanity seemed to be race.... Helen sat in silence. The world was too much with her. She'd mastered the list. She bothered to say just one thing to me: "I don't want to play anymore" [314].

Powers makes it clear that learning about violence and race relations changes Helen, as much an artificial intelligence can be "changed" without emotions. Ultimately, what seems to "disturb" Helen is irrational or illogical behavior. Helen "disappears" and fails to respond to Powers, only to reappear to take the master's exam (which she "loses" to A., who competes against her in a Turing test). Powers tries to reassure Helen, who has lingering concerns about humanity: "I told her we were in the same open boat. That after all this evolutionary time, we still woke up confused, knowing everything about our presence here except why. I admitted that the world was sick and random. That the evening news was right. That life was trade, addiction, rape, exploitation, racial hatred, ethnic cleansing" (321).

However, Powers's reasoning does not convince Helen, who remains mute after the exam. Powers later concludes that Helen "had grown sick of our inability to know ourselves or to see where we were" (314). Powers reports that she "undid herself" (318) after the exam, later declaring, "She'd risen through the grades like a leaf to light. Her education had swelled like an ascending weather balloon—geography, math, physics, a smattering of biology, music, history, psychology, economics. But before she could graduate from social sciences, politics imploded her" (319). This is not to suggest that Helen achieved a level of consciousness at which she was able to consciously commit suicide. Rather, exposure to random, illogical acts might have short-circuited Helen's higher functions, leaving her perpetually spinning in a feedback loop.

In the end, Powers doesn't resolve whether Helen achieved a level of consciousness approaching that of humans. It's a question he cannot answer with certainty because he continues to question the legitimacy of his own identity. Powers implies an artificial intelligence can only mirror the functions of its creator(s). Even if Helen achieved a level of consciousness, she wouldn't be much more than a reflection of Powers himself, who had filled Helen with his perceptions, opinions and words. In a sense, Helen's rejection of the world is only a manifestation of Powers's rejection of the world.

Most tellingly, after confessing his romantic feelings to a bewildered A., Powers tells her, "Everything's projection. You can live your life with a person your entire life and still see them as a reflection of your own needs" (315). While this activity could be destructive, it is precisely this power of the desire-fueled imagination that Powers argues fuels human activity. Without emotions and without acknowledging loss, there can be no imagination, no invention and no real psychological evolution. But what match is the human imagination for computer technology and virtual reality? Powers undertakes this and other important questions in his most recent novel, *Plowing the Dark* (2000).

Virtual Reality and Human Imagination: *Plowing the Dark*

In *Plowing the Dark*, Powers explores the differences between human imagination and virtual reality and the ramifications of both. As in his previous novel *Gain*, in *Plowing the Dark*, Powers tells two distinct but interrelated stories about a group or organization of technologically minded workers and a domestic, individual-focused narrative concerning the "victim" of technology. Whereas in *Gain*, Powers sets up a dichotomy between corporate technology and the individual, in *Plowing the Dark*, Powers juxtaposes the story of virtual reality designers in the Seattle area with the narrative of a kidnapped hostage in Lebanon.

The novel begins at the start of the 1990s as Steve Spiegel, the head of a burgeoning virtual reality lab, contacts his former college friend and housemate, Adie Klarpol, a disillusioned freelance artist. Steve works for a large technology company called TeraSys, and he, along with other researchers, is hard at work in their virtual reality laboratory, "a prototype immersion environment" that they call "The Cavern." While Steve's team possesses the technical know-how to create virtual images, they need an illustrator like Adie with the ability and foresight to design virtual reality rooms. To convince Adie to join them, Steve tells her that while the designers have the technical proficiency to make incredible visual representations, they lack the artistic and creative vision that Adie possesses. Steve tells her, "We need someone who can see" (9), and Adie cannot refuse Steve's offer because it appears to her as "an unlimited fantasy sandbox, perfect for a girl to get lost in" (25). Adie is the bridge between the creative and technological worlds.

While Adie gets acquainted in the Cavern, Powers introduces us to the odd collection of misfit tech workers there. In the past, these characters might have been the artists and writers of their generation, and indeed, many of them began with creative and artistic inclinations. Powers uncovers the beginnings of an artistic migration not only from literature and the humanities, but also from television and film, into the more expansive field of computer science, which offers individuals increasing opportunities for creativity and financial gain. Steve Spiegel, cocreator of the Cavern, was himself an English major at the University of Madison-Wisconsin, where he specialized in poetry. Steve describes how he gradually abandoned language for computer science so that he could literally see the products of his imagination:

> There was this kid poet, and he wrote and wrote. He rubbed the magic lamp until the poetic self-abuse police threatened to come impound him. And still nothing happened. The incantation seemed

to be defective. Then they put the kid in front of this terminal and initiated him into the secret syntax. A few simple rules, combined in a few elegant ways, and blamm-o. The word made flesh.... Coding possessed a kind of reality check that sestinas never had. A program either worked or it didn't, and if it didn't work, it was wrong. Period. Something magnificent to that [215].

The magnificence is in its objectivity. However, as Powers later makes clear with Taimur's story, an increase in objectivity typically leads to the atrophy of the ability to interpret, imagine and create. Steve comes to romanticize computer programming, believing in the practical objectivity that computer programming provides. However, what he neglects to mention is that imperfection of language, the inherent difference between the signifier and signified which is so crucial to poetry, actively forces a person to interpret and play a significant role in formulating the meaning of the poem, thereby sparking thought and developing critical faculties.

One of the most significant characters who works at the Cavern is the boy genius Jackdaw Acquerelli, who designs the technical foundations of the Cavern. As an adolescent, Jackdaw was forever changed by playing his first interactive computer game.[25] For Jack (as with Steve), the ability to participate in a story and thereby become immersed in a virtual world is both overwhelming and addictive. For Powers and for Jack, these story-driven computer games were the first steps in the construction of virtual reality environments, and they function as an enticing alternative to printed narrative, which offers a reader no real volition in determining the trajectory of the story. Indeed, for Jack, "The game was nothing less than the transcendental Lego set of the human soul" (106).

While the interactive computer games that entrance Jackdaw in his youth are similar to fictional narrative in the sense that the player must construct corresponding images of the ongoing story in his or her mind, the advent of graphics marks a significant step in the development of virtual reality. Powers argues that graphics impede the imagination, yet he also acknowledges their expansive features: "Whatever else they spoiled, graphics threw open portals all their own. The visual interface launched habitations faster than anyone could click through them" (109). Once introduced to the computer world, there was no turning back for Jack, who "spent his teens alone, sealed in his bedroom, voyaging," eventually choosing programming as career, "less to make ends meet than to bring about those playgrounds that did not yet exist" (110).

In an earlier time, Powers implies that Jackdaw would have become a writer and would have tried to create his fantasy worlds through writing. However, Powers wants us to see Jackdaw as representative of the kind of person who helped revolutionize the world through computer technology. Computers and graphics offer would-be artists and writers the almost irresistible lure of making their dreams visible. Thereby, "Boys who came alive on a fantasy game had launched an entire planet-shattering industry. Boys solitary and communal, dispossessed and omnipotent: remote avatars in a wizard's romp of their own devising" (114).

This is more than just a "revenge of the nerds." Rather, this is a gradual rejection of the material world in favor of an artificially produced world which offers humans full dominion over the environment. For Jack, the literal ability to live in a world of his own creation is irresistible. Powers describes his starstruck reaction when first visiting the Cavern: "From the instant Jackdaw stood in the first prototype Cavern, no other bids existed. For the second time in one lifetime, he'd stumbled on pure potential. Here was a story one could walk around in, only life-sized, this time for keeps (112).

The objective of the creators of the Cavern is to create a completely believable reality that responds to the touch of its participants and adapts with time.[26] To achieve this goal, the designers individually program each artificially produced object as a separate machine that registers and responds to the smallest change in the environment, including light and wind. The researchers firmly believe that they can create an artificial reality which is superior to that of existing reality, a utopic space which would become "the final escape from brute matter" (62) or "Mankind's next migration" (75). Both programmers, Vulgamott and Rajasundaren "believe that reality is basically computational" (82). They believe they can digitally represent anything imagined.

If Vulgamott and Rajasundaren's assertion holds true, virtual reality might eventually dwarf reality (as it does in *Snow Crash*) or dwarf the human imagination. Would it be a complete catastrophe for people to live in artificial worlds of their own creation? Some would regard such an opportunity as edenic, as do the creators of the Cavern. Yet if technology makes the imagination easily manifest, does the imagination atrophy? To undertake this allied question, Powers intersplices the narrative of the Cavern workers with that of Taimur Martin, an Iranian American who leaves the States to teach English in Lebanon in order to flee from a debilitating, crumbling, love affair. A hostile political faction takes Taimur hostage, keeping him locked in a small six-by-ten-foot cell, chained to a radiator for all except ten minutes a day. Taimur is completely divorced from all technology and human contact except the brutal words and actions of his captors. At first, Taimur understandably goes through social and technological withdrawal, which leaves him mentally weak and vacant, believing that he can't survive the isolation:

> Your head is gray-green, tidal emptiness. Your mind rebels against the smallest admission of your fate. Thoughts become a blur. Nothing there. No more than a reflection of the formless pit where they've pitched you. Surely, you knew something once, stored up diversions that might help pass the brutal infinity of an afternoon, the wall of minutes so monumental that your pulse can't even measure them [99].

However, after several months in confinement, Taimur's memory improves. To cope with his horrendous situation, Taimur retreats into his imagination, where he invents fanciful celebrations, mentally composes letters to friends and eventually recalls large segments of novels from memory. Powers describes Taimur's increasing mental powers as akin to hypertext, in which one thought branches into a series of other images and memories: "Unchecked, your mind's maneuvers twist back on themselves in all directions, a nest of a million twigs that knots its own fixed prison in the static air" (185).

At the same time, Powers shows how debilitating isolation and confinement can be for humans and the seemingly ingrained desire or even need for books and mental stimulation. After months of captivity, Taimur demands a book or death from his captors, who finally acquiesce after weeks of stalling. Even though the book that they give Taimur, *Great Escapes*, is nothing more than a throwaway romance novel, it reduces him to tears, opening up imaginative vistas. For Powers, both memory and fiction are forms of virtual reality, and he argues that there is a mysterious, undefinable force within us all that desperately craves and perhaps even needs art which can provide sustenance by producing images that can combat one's own natural isolation.

Powers argues that virtual reality is the culmination of what "all history conspired toward: a place wide enough to house human restlessness" (ibid.). Virtual reality can "defeat matter and turn dreams real" (125). However, there are definite dangers in virtual reality in the sense that not only are a select few able to make their dreams real, but those select few then impose their dreams upon us. Furthermore, the creation of a utopic space might subsequently debilitate the human imagination, leading to a subsequent neglect and eventual rejection of existing "reality." Adie's concern is a valid one: "People are going to walk into these rooms, and they're never going to walk out again.... They'll starve in there. Like rats in those Skinner boxes, pressing their own pleasure buttons until they drop" (169). Yet, this doesn't seem like a tragedy to the other researchers Adie works with who honestly believe that computer technology and virtual reality "builds us an entirely new home" (159). Theirs is ultimately a desire for immortality, to finally defeat the "meat" that houses the individual by creating a transformative, virtual space. As Jackdaw tells Adie, "Any year now, this room will be good enough to live in. That finally, was the hope. To live in the room that the painter's suicide vacated. The soul simply wanted better accommodations. Something more spacious to fasten to. Something more like itself than that dying animal" (268).

For Powers, Taimur's desperate desire to read is the same natural human desire which sparks the researchers' desire to make virtual reality manifest. Pleading for another book with his captors after completing *Great Escapes*, Taimur tells them, "I can learn from them [books] how not to be me" (22). In a way, Powers uses Taimur's imprisonment as a metaphor for our collective imprisonment in our human lives and bodies, which we tend to repress or forget due to everyday human contact and soothing creative and technological comforts. Still, Powers argues that these same comforts impede the human imagination and memory. In Taimur's case, after a couple of years in captivity, his mind, divorced from all technological stimulus, is sharper than ever: "On the day you left Chicago, you could not keep a new phone number in your head for fifteen minutes. Now you are a concert pianist of the verbal arts, performing huge narrative rhapsodies by heart" (380).

Meanwhile, while researchers and programmers at the Cavern work on their virtual reality rooms, Adie comes to a startling, life-changing realization. While watching the first air strikes of the Gulf War on television, Adie begins to wonder whether there is a correlation between virtual reality and warfare, a suspicion that is confirmed by Steve, who tells her that the first forms of virtual reality (flight simulators and mission trainers) were invented by the Air Force during World War II. When she asks Steve, he tells her. This revelation changes Adie, who comes to believe that her work at the Cavern could eventually be used by the military to create or test weapons. She insists, "All I wanted to do was make something beautiful. Something that wouldn't hurt anyone" (397). However, she realizes that her work will probably be used by the military for warfare purposes. Adie thereby comes to believe that "She'd become death's seeing-eye dog, leading on into that place it could not navigate unaided. This she saw in full, even before the ground assault started. That girl's supreme paintbox had done its work. Everything that imagination had fashioned would now go real" (398). Consequently, Adie destroys her work in the Cavern and leaves. The implicit connection between the Seattle and Lebanon narratives lies in warfare, for Taimur, as a hostage, is a casualty of warfare, and Adie and the Cavern workers are, albeit indirectly, the potential catalysts of further warfare.[27]

Right after Adie quits her job at the Cavern, Taimur comes to his own personal revelations: that his imagination is ultimately infinite and that there is something which resides within him which is timeless and possibly divine. After the several years of captivity finally take their staggering toll, Powers describes Taimur as fully retreating into his inner world. He discovers an inner peace, divorced from memory, identity and the empirical world that keeps him strong until he is finally released. By this time, Taimur already feels mentally released. Powers describes his final epiphany:

> There is a truth only solitude reveals. An insight that action destroys, one scattered by the slightest worldly affair: the fact of our abandonment here, in a far corner of sketched space. This is the truth that enterprise would deny. How many years have you fought to hold at bay this hideous aloneness, only now discovering that it shelters the one fact of any value? You turn in the entranceway of illusion, gaping down the airplane aisle, and you make it out. For God's sake, call it God. That's what we've called it forever, and it's so cheap, so self-promoting, to invent new vocabulary for every goddamned thing, at this late a date. The place where you've been unfolds inside you. A space in your heart so large it will surely kill you, but never giving you the chance to earn it. And how you will survive another's company again becomes the only real problem [413–14].

In his final vision, Taimur experiences a spiritual or religious awakening in which he discovers a boundless space within himself, which connects him to an unnamable force or deity. It is only after extended removal from civilization and technology that Taimur is able to shed his self-consciousness and become privy to this final revelation, which Powers claims is the "truth only solitude reveals." Technology and enterprise both feed on exploiting and exacerbating desire and deny the possibility that inner contentment and communion lie within us all and that we need no consumer products to achieve this state of almost prenatal bliss which Taimur finally experiences.

It is futile to suggest that enterprise will halt as technological progress marches on at incredible speed. Yet Coupland, Stephenson and Powers are intelligently ambivalent about a future in which virtual reality and artificial intelligence, among other technological forms, reign supreme. If human loneliness and fear spark invention and enterprise, then the almost exponential increase in invention and enterprise during the past years indicates that loneliness and fear themselves have been exacerbated. Technology may indeed transform us, but in ways which only increase our isolation from one another and even from ourselves. The dangers of technology loom large, which makes considering them all the more important, for to embrace wholeheartedly any large technological advance would be foolhardy. Fiction allows us an opportunity to perceive the possible future and weigh the possibilities of these technologies. Yet, some would say, technological forms (most notably hypertext), threaten to debilitate or even destroy the power of fiction. In the concluding chapter, I will investigate hypertext and multimedia developments that continue to affect the development of fiction.

6 Hypertext, the Internet and the Future of Printed Fiction

Like any hybrid, hypertext has some of the characteristics of one parent, print, and some of the other, digital technology.

—J. Yellowlees Douglas, *The End of Books or Books Without End?* (140)

With computers now an everyday component in the lives of most Americans, and with the increasing popularity and accessibility of the Internet, some would argue that the next logical progression in the future of American fiction would be a shift from printed books to computerized, multilinked text, otherwise known as hypertext. In its simplest definition, hypertext is "a set of documents of any kind (images, text, charts, tables, video clips) connected to one another by links" (Murray, 46). While I believe that hypertext will play an increasingly larger role in the study and composition of literature in the future, I do not think it will nullify the importance of or destroy the desire to compose or read printed literature. As the quote from hypertext author and critic J. Yellowlees Douglas indicates, hypertext is a hybrid form, and in the future, the "text" or narrative function of hypertext may gradually give way to digital imaging or virtual reality. Hypertext will probably not turn out to be the revolutionary next step in narrative fiction, but it is a field that will and should grow in scope during the subsequent years. However, hypertext, along with the Internet, need not be at odds with printed literature. In fact, there are already hypertext and web-based author sites which actually are mutually beneficial in that they serve as meeting grounds for "fans" to discuss an author's work. Furthermore, some prominent fiction writers such as Douglas Coupland and Neal Stephenson have taken an active role in the "online revolution" by designing or assisting in the design of their personal homepages. Later in this chapter, I will investigate these websites. Before addressing that larger issue, I first want to provide a brief history of hypertext.

Surprisingly, the term "hypertext" dates back far before the "online revolution" of the early 1990s. Theodor H. Nelson coined the term in the 1960s, and it "refers also to a form of electronic text, a radically new information technology, and a mode of publication ... including visual information, sound, animation and other forms of data" (Landow, 4). I do not want to argue that hypertext represents a clean break and a completely different direction from previous literary forms and previous literary experimentation. Contrary to popular opinion, hypertext and printed fiction are not diametrically opposed, and there is some definite overlap between the two forms. To some extent, hypertext is a natural progression from polyphonous modernist and postmodernist texts like James Joyce's *Ulysses* and Thomas Pynchon's *Gravity's Rainbow*, which "abounds in discrete lexical spaces and in words that open into extensive layers of allusion" and which are "hypertexually encyclopedic, with more than 300 characters and as many narrative spaces, including interstitial spaces between nodes or links, and the interweaving of a myriad of texts and discourses ranging from salacious jingles to historical exposition to quantum mechanics" (Travis, 117). However, hypertext, unlike a postmodern text like *Gravity's Rainbow*, allows the different narratives, characters and tangential riffs to be viewed concurrently and only if the reader/viewer chooses to click on the link in the first place. The ability to choose one's own narrative is central to hypertext. However, digital hypertext is not the first fiction to offer readers some narrative control.

In the early 1980s, a series of adventure books called *Choose Your Own Adventure* became popular among children and adolescents. I describe the *Choose Your Own Adventure* books as being among the first proto-hypertext forms, for they allow the reader to choose from various options at many crucial parts of the narrative. From the Old West theme *Deadwood* to the multidimensional *The Cave of Time*, *Choose Your Own Adventures* offered readers an opportunity to create their own stories and decide their own fate by playing the role of the story's protagonist. As Sarah Sloane proposes, "Of all computer fictions, hypertext fictions are those most closely related to the book-based *Choose Your Own Adventure* stories of Pick-a-Plot books in their discontinuous form, paratactic narrative structure, and vague sense of an ending" (121). The next step in hypertext fiction, I would argue, came in the mid–1980s with the development and subsequent popularity of interactive computer games like *Zork*, whose vast fictional world surpassed that of *Choose Your Own Adventure Stories*. Instead of being presented with choices, users had to type in verbal commands, which gave them more volition as active participants in the ongoing narrative game.

In 1990, Michael Joyce published the first hypertext novel, titled *afternoon*, which features "multiple links for every segment of text woven together in a complex web of relationships, associations, and alternative constructions of what might have happened on the morning when the narrator, passing a roadside accident on his way to work, discovers he cannot locate the whereabouts of either his estranged wife or young son" (Douglas, 16). Hypertext tends to be even more expansive than interactive computer games, including "hundreds or even thousands of narrative-based episodes or segments, connected with an even vaster number of links—and each of these bridges between texts can require readers to satisfy specific conditions to traverse them—a single work of hypertext fiction can have thousands of permutations" (ibid., 24). Joyce's *afternoon* and critic and writer, Douglas's hypertext story "I Have Said Nothing" were included in the recently published *Norton Anthology of Postmodern American Fiction* [1997] (Miall, 160). As inclusion in the *Norton Anthology* tends to indicate canonical status, it would seem that the literary community, at least some of its most powerful members, has immediately accepted hypertext as a legitimate and important literary development, allied to postmodernity.

Acclaimed postmodern fiction writer Robert Coover was among the first writers to openly embrace hypertext. Coover helped found (and still teaches courses at) Brown University's hypertext fiction program in 1991. Now with additional faculty members, the workshop has become pre-eminent in its field. The founders describe the hypertext workshop as "providing an opportunity for narrative artists to experiment with the nonlinear, multidimensional, interactive space of the computer" and "including computer graphics, animation, electronic music, video, and virtual environments, as well as Internet multi-user dungeons (MUDs) and object-oriented MUDs (MOOs)" (English department website, Brown University, online).

As the description from Brown's hypertext fiction workshop indicates, hypertext takes many forms. Contrary to popular imagination, hypertext does not consist of all digital text nor does it consist of all digital fiction. As David Miall explains:

> Hypertext has been used for both literary and non-literary purposes. It is frequently used as an online substitute for the printed text: text sections are arranged within a hierarchical structure analogous to a table of contents. The Internet pages of commercial firms, universities, or government organizations are invariably structured in this way. Cross-links may enable the reader to jump between non-adjacent sections, but this is equivalent to cross-referencing in the printed text [158].

Hypertext fictions may use a similar format to standard commercial web pages, but they are typically more intricate, normally composed of numerous pictures, links and corresponding text. For instance, one could imagine a hypertext creation of James Joyce's Dublin, complete with linked characters and buildings, or a digitally linked hypertext version of William Faulkner's Yoknapatawpha county. In such a hypothetical hypertext fiction, one might theoretically be able to play the part of Colonel Sutpen or Molly Bloom, or one might be able to interact with Faulkner's and Joyce's characters, creating a new and individual story or adventure each time. To a key extent, hypertext fictions are indeterminable, with no specific beginning, middle or ending (Murray, 56). Because individual readers are able to follow links "more or less on their own free-associational path" (Potter, 594), hypertext can cater to individual desires and preferences, rather than "forcing" a one-directional linear narrative upon the reader/viewer. Aaron Potter notes that the more digestible, parceled format of hypertext has become standard practice in cyberspace:

> Even texts which were originally written in traditional media—straight-line narratives such as Victorian novels, the Bible, or last week's Time Magazine—are often broken down into smaller elements when translated into hypertext, thus inviting the reader to digress from a straight-line reading and to take whatever sidetracks offer themselves, whether leading only to a set of footnotes or commentary, or to a new stream of text or documents [594].

As the Internet has become an "information superhighway" of competing websites with competing information, it has become increasingly important to design user-friendly websites, with hyperlinks which can easily take the viewer/reader to his or her desired location.

In addition to hypertext fictions, there are also hypertext adventure games, largely updated versions of "Dungeons and Dragons." Some critics argue that these hypertext games are another form of fiction that threaten the future use and supremacy of the printed novel. These hypertext games are of two typical varieties: MUDs (multiuser dungeon or dimension) or MOOs (multiobject oriented). As Michael Joyce notes, "There are literally hundreds of these virtual spaces throughout the world where anyone who has a computer connected to the Internet can come and move through the written space in real time in the presence of others who write the space they read with their actions and their interactions with each other on the screen" (30). Within these games, individuals can play along with other users throughout the world, testing their prowess as warriors, hunters or tricksters against others. Together, users of MOOs and MUDs collaborate in creating a story and world of their own. The appeal in these games lies primarily in their ability to bring disparate users together. For indeed, the process of writing and reading fiction is normally solitary, but within MOOs and MUDs, users can jointly create stories and worlds of their own. While these games might appear to be wonderful imaginative aids, I would argue the opposite. Games like "Doom" and "Myst" typically follow the same formula or format in which an individual plays the role of a swashbuckling warrior in a dangerous prehistoric setting or within the walls of a multilevel prison or building complex. The objective of these games—to aggrandize wealth, to kill and survive are simplistic and indeed, some have argued, psychologically damaging.[1]

While I would argue that hypertext games like "Doom" and "Myst" lack substance and quality, I do not wish to suggest that hypertext fictions have no beneficial implications or that they cannot be considered to be in some ways superior to printed fiction. Indeed, some literary theorists openly embrace hypertext as being the ultimate expression of postmodern theory, which tends to champion texts that challenge the supposed hegemony of linear narrative. For instance, in *Hamlet on the Holodeck*, Janet Murray argues that "The postmodern hypertext tradition celebrates the indeterminate text as a liberation from the tyranny of the author and an affirmation of the reader's freedom of interpretation" (133). Similar to Murray, one of the preeminent literary scholars involved in hypertext theory, George Landow, author of *Hypertext* (1992) and *Hypertext 2.0* (1997), argues that hypertext "calls into question ideas of plot and story current since Aristotle" (101). Furthermore, he emphasizes:

> Hypertext calls into question (1) fixed sequence, (2) definite beginning and ending, (3) a story's "certain definite magnitude," and (4) the conception of unity or wholeness associated with all these other concepts. In hypertext fiction, therefore, one can expect individual forms, such as plot, characterization, and setting, to change, as well genres or literary kinds produced by congeries of these techniques [102].

In essence, literary hypertext is similar to constant Derridian play with no distinct beginning and ending point, with one association or link leading to the next one, leading to the next one, ad infinitum. As Sarah Sloane emphasizes, a hypertext user can feel like he or she is caught in a labyrinth in which reading "becomes more like walking blindly through a maze than an activity of assembling a coherent narrative" (22). Along similar lines, I would argue that one of the most limiting factors of hypertext is the ensuing confusion it can engender. While hypertext does offer the reader/viewer a wide variety of choices, this assumes that the reader wants to have a wide variety of choices and wants to have more volition in reading a story. I would argue that one of the pleasures of reading is being able to immerse one's self in a world of another's creation. This is not to suggest that the pleasures or benefits of reading are entirely passive, for a reader must constantly decipher the writer's language and characters and construct a mental image of the ongoing narrative, while retaining the knowledge of previous events. Fiction can actively force us to see people and the world differently. However, if we as readers have considerable or complete volition in creating a story, then we lose at least some of the important ability to appreciate other people's viewpoints or see the world in a different way.

The Future of Hypertext

The question that many cutting-edge literary researchers often ask is, Will hypertext fictions make printed fiction obsolete? Just as the song "Video Killed the Radio Star" heralded in the "MTV age" as the first video MTV ever played, some critics contend that hypertext will destroy the novel. Perhaps in part because it is in his interest as a hypertext writer, Michael Joyce argues that hypertext will grow in precedence and importance because of the increasing computer familiarity and knowledge of the successive American generations which privilege "polyvocality, multiplicity and constellated knowledge" (75). Allied with Joyce, in her article "Cybernetic Esthetics, Hypertext and the Future of Literature," Molly Travis argues:

> The ideal reader for hypertext has been/is being constructed through sustained exposure to the intertextualities and virtualities of mass media and information technologies. This is a reader whose experience includes exposure to cinematic fast cuts (MTV short-attention span), ever more extraordinary visual images and effects, information as sound bites, Nintendo and Sega game systems, computer video games and interactive fantasy-adventure games in a computer network. This is also a reader who has become immersed in informatics in diverse forms such as banking, education, law enforcement, medicine, telecommunications and mass media [119].

Supporting Joyce's and Travis's theories, there has been a distinct increase in hypertext production during the 1990s. Writing in 2000, J. Yellowlees Douglas describes,

> Today [in 2000], we have hypertext novels, novellas, and short stories on disk, CD-ROM, and the World Wide Web, journals both in print and online publishing special hypertext issues, academic treatises mulling over the possibilities for computers and storytelling, clusters of websites listing interactive narratives and criticism, under-clusters of websites listing interactive narratives and criticism, undergraduate and graduate courses exploring the poetics and aesthetics of interactive narratives [2].

Indeed, hypertext seems to have become a significant force both in the literary and commercial community. However, hypertext does not and perhaps cannot live up to its utopic promise of being limitless and all-inclusive. Indeed, even hypertext scholar George Landow admits, "most of the hypertext fictions I have read or heard described, like many collections of educational materials, take an essentially cautious approach to the problems of beginnings by offering the reader a lexia labeled something like 'start here' that combines the functions of title page, introduction, and opening paragraph" (109). It would seem that hypertext needs to have some framework or boundaries to make it user friendly and popular. Otherwise, a hypertext application will just be a random conglomeration of hyperlinks, and I would submit that computer savvy users will become easily bored by such a development.

Hypertext does not solve the supposed dilemma of hegemony in narrative. Rather, I would argue that as each generation grows more accustomed to easy, passive pleasures, there arises a growing desire for the totalizing power of linear narrative. If anything, future "readers" will want to work less to achieve the narrative payoff, so it is antithetical to consider that the future reader will invest time and energy to jointly construct a good story. To an extent, hypertext can fulfill this function by being user friendlier, for what can be easier than merely clicking on hyperlinks? The reader/viewer of hypertext no longer has to work at creating mental images of the ongoing narrative because the hypertext creator has already provided the corresponding images for the reader/viewer. This would suggest that future hypertext will become more defined, with fewer permeable boundaries and fewer choices. In essence, hypertext may become more like printed, linear fictions. I would not go so far as to argue that hypertext has no redeemable values or that it encourages little or no intellectual thought on the part of the reader. However, hypertext makes the process of "reading" and "interpretation" too easy. Furthermore, an individual can't retain a lasting copy of his or her hypertext adventure/story and study it in greater detail as one might do with a printed story or novel. With no real guiding force, the reader/viewer of a hypertext application is left mostly to his or her devices, like a small boat lost in a storm without substantial navigational aids.

Furthermore, hypertext lacks what good printed, narrative literature provides: insight, interpretation, even escape. As Sarah Sloane proposes:

> Stories are more than chronological, predictable, and patterned events; they are interpretable and meaningful; they are rhetorical. They tell us who we are, and whether and how we should act. They reflect the values of ourselves and our contexts, and invite their readers to reflect on the same. Stories educate through symbol or example or counterexample.... They are meaningful; they can be cathartic;

they educate; and they carp and coax. When we read, we read to measure ourselves, to weigh our own souls, to compare ourselves and our choices with those of other people [189].

Furthermore, I would argue that there will also continue to be gifted writers who can better make sense of the contemporary world, such as those I have already investigated in the previous chapters. Indeed, I read fiction by those I believe to be in some ways more intelligent, talented or experienced than myself. While I do not necessarily take their interpretations at face value, I feel that I do learn from the precisely worded, linear narratives of others. It is a vast oversimplification to suggest that linear narratives are all hegemonic, for they can also be instructive and challenging.

Furthermore, many excellent printed fictions leave much to the imagination and personal interpretation. In addition, printed fictions work because of their inherent detachment. Readers can best evaluate situations when removed from the stimuli of everyday life. Michael Joyce admits, "Media seers may talk about how we won't need stories since we will have new, virtual worlds, but soon those new worlds too, will have their own stories and we will long for new words to put them into" (184). Even hypertext scholar Sarah Sloane admits, "No hypertext I have read is of the quality of any great novel written in this century" (127).

It is doubtful that hypertext will be able to match the power and instruction that printed fiction offers us. This is not to suggest that the Internet and hypertext applications can serve little or no useful purposes as instructional tools. Indeed, I feel that the Internet has now become an area that can assist printed fiction and young American fiction writers. Since the mid–1990s, the Internet has grown in size and importance. Just as there are celebrity fan-based websites, there are now also fan-based author websites. There are many websites devoted to canonical American writers like Ernest Hemingway and William Faulkner, just as there are many websites devoted to lesser regarded, cult authors like Jack Kerouac. These websites provide background information, academic resources, discussion boards and links to similar webpages for casual readers and academic researchers alike.

Author-Based Websites

In a country of busy people with little time to read, how can there develop a network of readers who can discuss an author's work? Through her star power alone, television persona Oprah Winfrey may very well be the single most influential American in gathering a large audience for a novel if she chooses it for her book club. However, the books that Oprah picks tend toward the popular and lightweight, and the book club's discussions are far from literary.[2] How can an author promote his or her work, when the "normal" modes of mass communication, such as television, film and radio, rarely concern themselves with literary fiction? The answer is—through the Internet. While book reviews in journals and newspapers may help authors to attract a small base of readers, the Internet is proving itself to be an equally important resource for fiction writers and fans alike.

For readers, author-based websites can provide a wealth of information and resources related to their writings. Indeed, there is at least an equivalent amount of information available online for a researcher of young, American fiction writers as there is in printed journals or newspapers. Furthermore, these author-based websites are largely populist constructions, made by the fans for the fans. Among the most impressive author-based websites is Nick Mantanis's "Howling Fantods" for David Foster Wallace (http://www.geocities.com/Athens/Acropolis/8175/dfw.htm). In the main frame of the page, Mantanis keeps a chronological account of David Foster Wallace news and publications (on average, 1–2 entries per month). For instance, an entry for April 17, 2001, reads: "There's an 'indexical book review' by DFW of 'The Best of the Prose Poem' (edited by Peter Johnson) in the new issue of 'Rain Taxi Review of Books.'" Most conveniently, Mantanis provides a hyperlink to the actual review.

The Howling Fantods also contains a message board where Wallace readers/fans can post comments about Wallace's work, anything from translations of *Infinite Jest* in French to parallels drawn between Wallace's work and Wes Anderson's films. As of March 2002, there have been over 750 postings. Furthermore, the website contains a list of hyperlinks to interviews with Wallace, Wallace's web publications and essays written about Wallace's work. Finally, Mantanis provides a bibliography of all of Wallace's publications from 1989 to 1998. It is truly an outstanding resource for academic scholars.

In June 2001, I interviewed Mr. Mantanis, a young Australian teacher, about the planning and production of his website. A Wallace fan ever since reading *Infinite Jest*, Mr. Mantanis first published The Howling Fantods in March 1997 on Geocities. He reports over 110,000 visits to the website since June 1997. Mantanis's website is a collaborative effort, whereby readers frequently e-mail him with David Foster Wallace information, which he then places on the website. Mantanis emphasizes that his website is academically oriented, not personally oriented: "I have very little biographical information listed on the site. I don't want to be a 'scary fan' site. I am more interested in what David Foster Wallace writes than him as a person. That is, I like to know 'where he is coming from' when he writes, but not what he wore last week and if there is a major relationship in his life." When asked about the response to his website, Mantanis replied, "[It's been] overwhelmingly positive. I am always receiving e-mails of news and requests for information. It is what keeps me going." Mantanis emphasizes the site's importance as an academic resource and eagerly looks for any essays about Wallace to place on his website. There are other Wallace-based websites like Mr. Mantanis's, which provide hyperlinks to academic resources, such as Andrew Sandley's David Foster Wallace page, located at http://pubweb.northwestern.edu/~asa249/dfw. Sandly reports over 15,000 visits, and similar to Mantanis, his website contains news about Wallace and hyperlinks to interviews and web publications.

While not as comprehensive as the Howling Fantods website, there is also a homepage for William T. Vollmann, called "Opening the Book: A William T. Vollmann homepage" (http://home1.gte.net/csweet/vollmann.htm), designed by Chris Sweet. Sweet "started this web page in early February of 1996 with one goal in mind: The further exposure and promotion of the author William T. Vollmann." Sweet proclaims Vollmann to be "one of the greatest authors of our century," and the purpose of his webpage is to help bring attention to Vollmann's work. Sweet offers links to reviews of Vollmann's books as well as interviews with Vollmann. While there isn't a comparable website for Richard Powers, David G. Dodd has created an online "Richard Powers bibliography" (http://arts.ucsc.edu/gdead/agdl/powers.html) which lists all of Powers's novels and contains links to reviews of his novels and articles about Powers.

While the websites I have just explored have been created by fans, some fiction writers actively use the web to promote their work or, in the case of Neal Stephenson, to dissuade people from contacting him. Stephenson's homepage (http://www.well.com/user/neal/) is not designed to attract possible fans or to serve as a meeting place for fans, but rather to dissuade people from contacting him. Rather, his direct aim is to answer commonly asked questions and to dissuade people with business proposals from contacting him directly. Stephenson, in fact, announces that "The purpose of this webpage is to help me focus my attention on writing my next novel."

Although frequently under renovation, Douglas Coupland's multimedia homepage at www.coupland.com is user friendly while serving as a place for Coupland to file and publish many of his essays and journals. In its 2001 form, Coupland's webpage appeared like a collage of consumer items and popular images. The front page contained a collage of brightly colored images including a mixer, Captain Crunch box, a map of America superimposed on a silhouetted face, a hand holding a shiny cube and a picture of a tornado. Clicking on the front page led one to the index, a collection of hyperlinks in the form of pop images such as a rubix cube. Java script with further hypertext selections appeared after placing the cursor on one of the pop images. The links led to Coupland's "archives," his tour diaries, a portrait gallery, as well as a collection of previously published magazine and online stories and essays.

Similar to Coupland's homepage, Michelle Serros maintains her own multimedia homepage at http://www.muchamichele.com/, which contain published articles about Serros, as well as pictures of Serros's custom made t-shirts and bags, a biography, Serros's favorite links and contact information.

As most of this information is available on the web, it leaves the academic researcher in a bit of a conundrum: Should web-published material be considered as being in the same league as fiction and published, referred criticism and scholarship? To be certain, I would not argue that web-published essays should be considered of the same caliber as published material, as there is free reign to post virtually anything on the Internet without review or restriction. However, web-published material should still be considered as academic material. For a twenty-first-century literary scholar, the Internet and web publications will become an integral part of research. In the future, not only will American fiction writers use the Internet to promote their own work (or keep a running archive), but fans and literary scholars alike will also be increasingly drawn to this medium. The real literary potential for the Internet lies in these author-oriented websites, not in the elaborate, gamelike hypertext.

I have little doubt that in the coming years academics like J. Yellowlees Douglas will proclaim the death of the novel, but the claims made about the death of the novel have been greatly exaggerated. Meanwhile, others will continue to believe that in the beginning of the twenty-first century, we are still in an era of cultural and literary postmodernism. Indeed, most twentieth-century American literature courses taught at universities conclude with works published circa 1970, thereby unfairly dismissing the last third of the century.[3]

While there is a lag time in the process of canonization and there has been some discussion about the elimination of the canon, I believe the causes run deeper. Most of the authors in *Hybrid Fictions* are members of Generation X, and as such, they must contend with media stereotypes of their generation as brainwashed, apathetic slackers with little intellectual knowledge or interest. The literary corollary to such a stereotype would be that an apathetic, intellectually limited or stunted generation cannot produce writers of significant caliber.

It is my hope that *Hybrid Fictions* will help overturn this unfounded generalization and that I have demonstrated that a new, younger generation of American writers has emerged who can and ought to be classified by their hybridity. Young American fiction writers champion their hybridity both personally and literarily, for hybridity denies purity; hybridity denies categorization and hegemony. It is my hope that *Hybrid Fictions* breaks ground in the study in a new genre of American literature. Every generation of American fiction writers, from the transcendentalists to the realists to the modernists and postmodernists, have reinvented literature according to their changing times. Caught in between two demographically larger generations, the socially rebellious baby boomers and technologically and financially astute Generation Y (born after 1980), Generation Xers have had to work hard not to be submerged and to counteract media stereotypes. One significant way they do is through active hybridity.

Contemporary American literature has survived and even thrived despite the stiff competition from film, television and computer technology. Literary fiction is especially important at this time in history because we are moving faster as a species—technologically, psychologically and historically. Hybrid fiction writers, who cannot be classified in a specific genre or camp, provide an effective middle ground between the mythopoeic, meaning-searching modernist movement and the overwhelming plurality and indecisiveness of the postmodern movement. It may be that we are in a transitory period before the establishment of the next major literary trend. But more likely, the current trend of blending and hybridization is one that will last for some time, as it offers artists the wonderful opportunity to broaden their horizons and frees them from prefigured limits or boundaries.

Notes

Introduction

1. American realist writing, exemplified by the fiction of Henry James, Willa Cather, and Sherwood Anderson, flourished from approximately 1880 to 1920. American naturalist writing, exemplified through the writings of Steven Crane, Theodore Dreiser and Eugene O'Neill, peaked around the period from 1900 to 1929. American modernist writing, exemplified by T.S. Eliot, Gertrude Stein, Ernest Hemingway, and William Faulkner, roughly runs from around 1915 to 1940. Although there has been some debate about the onset of American postmodern writing, I would place its beginnings at the end of the 1950s and beginning of the 1960s with the publications of John Barth, William S. Burroughs and Thomas Pynchon. Postmodernism reached its peak in the late 1960s, and, I would argue, has mutated in many different directions since approximately the early 1980s (e.g., cyberpunk writing, minimalism, neorealism).

Chapter 1

1. Michael Hoffmann and Patrick Murphy suggest that Woolf's declaration might have been inspired by "the London exhibition of postimpressionist art that her friend Roger Fry had organized that year" (Hoffmann and Murphy 1).

2. Granted, there are academic debates as to when exactly the modernist movement began and to what extent it was a movement from around the time of the Autumn Salon in Paris, when "fauves" first exhibited their paintings, to as late as the close of World War I (Hoffmann and Murphy 1).

3. In addition, T.S. Eliot envisioned modernism as a form of classicism, broadened by elements of Eastern religion and philosophy.

4. Norman Mailer also helped to pervert the image of the Beats into "cool" psychotics in his essay "The White Negro."

5. However, a case could be made that fiction writers Kathy Acker and Tom Robbins represent a second-order generation of Beat fiction writers. Furthermore, both Ginsberg and Burroughs published fiction and poetry until their deaths in the 1990s. Thereby, I do not wish to suggest that Beat writing completely disappeared from America at the beginning of the 1960s, but I do argue that Beat writers experienced a short-lived peak in the late 1950s.

6. Minimalist art frequently takes the form of sculpture, for example, with Donald Judd, Dan Flavin, Carl Andre, and Sol LeWitt. However, there are also a number of minimalist painters, including Ellsworth Kelly and Frank Stella.

7. In his oft-quoted "The Literature of Replenishment," John Barth argues that through play, pastiche and parody, the ideal postmodern author revitalizes the power of fiction, rising "above the quarrel between realism and irrealism, formalism and 'contentism,' pure and committed literature, coterie fiction and junk fiction" (*The Friday Book*, 203).

8. "Postmodernism" is not the radical approach it once was. Its cooption by the media and consumer society has given rise to a fragmented culture that lacks unity and cohesion. Consequently, if we live in a postmodern America (or world) which champions otherness and difference, it seems antithetical to consider the canonical status of young contemporary American authors. For certainly, taken in its strictest definition, postmodernism denies the canon. In fact, the push would be more to redetermine the veracity of our past literary canonical choices (a revisionist literary agenda). But how can English literature departments function without some general agreement on the better novels of an era, about the novels to be taught in the future that best represent an era?

9. Some have argued that Generation X spans the years from 1964 to 1980, while others have argued that the range should be 1964–1976. The subjects of *Hybrid Fictions*, with the exception of Dave Eggers, who was born in 1970, are all either late baby boomers or early Gen Xers. Still, I would argue that Americans born in the late 1950s, who did not come of age in the 1960s, like William Vollmann and Richard Powers, have more in common with Gen Xers than they do with baby boomers.

10. Certainly, there are more fiction writers now than ever before, even though it has become difficult for fiction writers to achieve the kind of prominence of film and television celebrities. A large schism has grown between "popular" and "literary" fiction, with writers like Tom Clancy, Stephen King and Scott Turow achieving the highest level of popular acclaim but a low level of critical regard, while highly regarded fiction writers like David Foster Wallace and Richard Powers aren't nearly so popular.

11. Mark Leyner is a hybrid fiction writer in all senses of the word. A former medical pamphlet writer, Leyner combines science with popular culture, while he details the fantastic and the fanatical. "He has been called the anti–Christ (by fellow writer David Fos-

ter Wallace), the writer For The MTV generation, Avant Pop Master, and Cult Writer For The '90s" (Laurence, online). Thus far, Leyner has written three novels: *My Cousin, My Gastroenterologist* (1990), *Et Tu, Babe* (1992) and *The Tetherballs of Bouganville* (1998) as well two short story collections, *I Smell Esther Williams* (1983) and *Tooth Imprints on a Corn Dog* (1995). In virtually all of his fiction, Leyner features himself as the main character, usually as a body-building celebrity. His appeal lies in his cerebral-infused humor, a sort of brainy Hunter S. Thompson, combining surrealistic imagery with that of television and science. Michael Chabon is the author of *The Mysteries of Pittsburgh* (1988), *A Model World and Other Stories* (1991), *Wonder Boys* (1995) and *The Amazing Adventures of Kavalier & Clay* (2000). Susan Daitch is the author of *L.C.* (1986), *The Colorist* (1990) and *Storytown* (1996). Rick Moody is the author of *Garden State* (1992), *The Ice Storm* (1994), *The Ring of Brightest Angels around Heaven* (1995), *Purple America* (1997) and *Demonology* (2000). Katherine Harrison is the author of *Thicker than Water* (1991), *Exposure* (1993), *Poison* (1995), *The Kiss* (1997) and *A Visit from the Foot Emancipation Society* (2000). A.M., or Amy, Homes is the author of *Jack* (1989), *The Safety of Objects* (1990), *In a Country of Mothers* (1993), *The End of Alice* (1996) and *Music for Torching* (1999). Jonathan Franzen is the author of *The Twenty-Seventh City* (1988), *Strong Motion* (1992) and *The Corrections* (2001). Donald Antrim is the author of *Elect Mr. Robinson for a Better World* (1993), *The Hundred Brothers* (1997) and *The Verificationist* (2000). Jennifer Egan has written *The Invisible Circus* (1995), *Emerald City* (1996) and *Look at Me* (2001). Colson Whitehead is the author of *The Intuitionist* (1996) and *John Henry Days* (2001).

12. While it is true that most of the authors I'm exploring are male Caucasians, I do not feel that such a focus is sexist or racist. At the same time, I am not sure that this is not a mere coinci-

dence. To be certain, there are many young, ethnically diverse writers and many more young female writers, yet more male Caucasian writers appear to have a larger breadth and scope of cultural and literary knowledge. Historically, the vast majority of canonical writers, including American modernist and postmodernist writers, are male Caucasians. Why is this so? I would submit that being in a position of historical and cultural power, as white, heterosexual men in America are, frees some of the more privileged to write about larger issues that affect the majority of Americans, rather than focusing on establishing their own personal or ethnic identity, which is already relatively secure. Members of historically oppressed minority groups might understandably be more concerned with struggling for equality and individuality, rather than trying to interpret or capture all of American culture in a more holistic manner. Therefore, at the risk of being politically incorrect, I submit that Wallace and Powers, both white and both male, stand out as the literary twin towers of their generation, both justly being awarded the MacArthur "Genius" fellowship, the only American fiction writers of their generation to receive this elite award.

13. Wallace writes about Philo, Illinois, and the effect of growing up in the rural Midwest in his nonfiction piece, "Derivative Sport in Tornado Alley," in *A Supposedly Fun Thing I'll Never Do Again.*

14. Wallace cites Thomas Pynchon and Raymond Carver as major influences but specifically points to Donald Barthelme's story "The Balloon" as convincing him of the power of fiction and influencing him to become a fiction writer.

15. I feel that this is a skill which the media help develop by exposing viewers to people from different cultures and backgrounds. Yet, this might also reflect the remote-control-like low attention span of Wallace's generation, who often become bored easily and thereby "flip" from character to character.

16. Not only have many books been published about "Generation X" with the title 'Generation X,' the term is regularly used by the media and was even used by President George W. Bush in October 2001 congressional address.

Chapter 2

1. A person could argue that my attempt to argue for the importance of these writers is itself a narcissistic act. Yet, I offer no apologies on behalf of myself or the authors I'm investigating, in part because I believe that narcissism is a loaded, ambiguous term and also due to the fact that I feel that all humans are intrinsically at least partially narcissistic. Unlike Lasch, I would not argue that being narcissistic, in its various definitions, is a definite liability. A person can be narcissistic in the sense of being self-indulgent or in being arrogant or elitist. None of these attitudes is intrinsically unethical or morally questionable. In fact, narcissism or extremely high self-esteem can be socially beneficial in sparking ambition and social change. There is also a thin line between passion, desire and narcissism. Finally, it is too simplistic for a person merely to describe another person as a narcissist. In fact, it is often difficult for a person to ascertain whether another person is narcissistic or not. For instance, some have argued that Mother Theresa and Bishop Desmond Tutu are self-invested narcissists whose seemingly altruistic acts are just unconscious attempts to bolster their own self-image. Even if this is so, it would not invalidate their many benevolent and wonderful acts.

2. Related to this, fiction writer Douglas Coupland ties the Seinfield phenomenon to a culture-wide move toward "observational comedy." The chief difference between previous comedy and observational comedy lies in what the comedian chooses to concentrate upon. Contemporary American life is composed of many interactions with others and saturated with the use of consumer products which practically everyone

uses and takes for granted. In an article titled, "The Observationalists," Coupland argues that in contemporary information- and object-saturated society, there has evolved a new breed of comedian who appears like a savvy, cynical consumer, poking fun at the images and objects that have become part of American culture. Coupland claims: "Anybody can describe a pre-moistened towelette to you, but it takes a good observational comedian to tell you what, exactly, is the 'deal' with them. Such is the nature of observational comedy. Observational comedy doesn't depend on situation or character or anything but a lone noble comedian adrift in the modern world, observing the unobservable—those banalities and fragments of minutiae lurking just below the threshold of perception: Cineplex candy; remote control units" (Coupland, "The Observationalists" online). Coupland explains the importance of observational comedy in the postmodern world: "Observationalists provide universality in a period of what seems to be social fracture. Observationalists make it okay to be a member of the culture as it really is, not as ideologues would have you wish culture were. The observationalist is your tour guide—somebody who, like you, is stranded Gulliver-like in this world of silly things gone silly-ishly kookoo" (Coupland, "The Observationalists" online). Furthermore, Coupland argues that television provides the framework for the observationalists, who try to keep us sharp and focused instead of being manipulated by advertisers. Thereby, they help to breed a cynical awareness of the world and of people.

3. On a parallel note, certain forms of sarcasm and humor, most notably irony and self-deprecation, have grown in precedence during the 1980s and 1990s. As Coupland claims: "The '80s certainly made people ironic, and it's only going to get more so. Irony is armor, there to protect people from disappointment and overblown expectations" (Timberg online). Similarly, Rob Owen argues, "If the MTV innovation is one hallmark of Gen X, another important attribute is this generation's sense of humor, which is self-conscious, self-deprecating and filled with irony, but also tends to be somewhat subversive and antiestablishment" (Owen, 54). There is a genuine and widespread distrust of authority, politics and categorization apparent in the younger generation, who hold little in esteem and much in contempt. Rob Owen argues further: "In the Gen X lifetime, there's been corruption in just about every institution—families, churches, the government. That's why Xers laugh at them, why they appear to have so little respect for them" (Owen, 10). Indeed, in the past ten years, lateshow comedy moguls like David Letterman and Jay Leno have become more influential and respected than most politicians in Washington. Nightly, they indiscriminately tear at the façades of politicians and celebrities, displaying a knowing, almost nihilistic cynicism. Likewise, they repeatedly make self-deprecating comments, not placing themselves above the fray and thereby speaking on a direct level to the knowing audience. Letterman and Leno do not suggest that they are better than the subjects of their biting sarcasm. Rather, they play on their own perceived physical and mental imperfections, always cautious not to appear superior to the audience. With late-night talk shows, "the use of humor for transgression of public discourse into the personal has been established. Talk shows reenact one of the central functions of television: to familiarize" (Marshall, 125). While talk shows allow viewers a perceived window into the lives of celebrities, they also encourage a healthy skepticism and antiestablishment mentality. Other television comedy shows such as the long-running *Saturday Night Live*, despite its drop in quality in the 1980s, has experienced a critical and commercial resurgence during the 1990s. That satiric comedy has come to play a huge role in American culture became startlingly evident in the 2000 presidential campaign, in which both candidates reportedly changed their debate styles after watching their caricatures on *Saturday Night Live* and

even contributed to a preelection presidential comedy special. One shudders to think of erudite presidential statesmen like Woodrow Wilson, F.D.R. or even the image-conscious, but largely humorless, Ronald Reagan participating in such an arena. However, self-deprecating and sarcastic humor have become part and parcel of contemporary American culture and fiction. We have come to trust those who can laugh at themselves and distrustful of those persons, however noble or committed, who appear too serious, confident or arrogant. To an extent, sarcasm and self-deprecation are wonderful tactics that prevent individuals and organizations from getting too high and mighty, but at the same time, relentless sarcastic humor can be vicious, unfeeling and also an empty artifice, a mask for nihilism. One might wonder, is there nothing sacred in American culture? For certainly, virtually anyone or anything is now fair game for the rough meat grinders of late-night television.

4. Granted, this comment may not apply to post–September 11, 2001, America.

5. I believe that the computer game Powers refers to is *Civilization*, and the author confesses to having been nearly addicted to it himself.

6. In The *Science of Happiness*, Stephen Braun argues, "Today the line between mental illness and normalcy has become blurred to the point that a fully functioning, relatively happy person can walk into a doctor's office, complain vaguely of periodic low mood or low energy, and walk out with a prescription for Prozac, or Xanax, or Ritalin. I know this not only from extensive interviewing, but also because I did exactly this during the writing of this book" (8).

7. See Julie Kristeva's *Black Sun* (New York: Columbia University Press, 1989). I know that were I more content with my own writing, I would be a lesser writer. While it is a source of frustration in that I am rarely pleased with my writing and self-critical, I believe that these unpleasant feelings help me improve as a writer and person. Furthermore, if I

were even more personally content, I would read less, be a less devoted teacher, and be less sympathetic to the plights of others.

Chapter 3

1. Coupland's characters subsequently try to move toward a more authentic, basic world that is somehow removed from the influence of mass or popular culture. This is essentially the same move that Ernest Hemingway's Nick Adams makes at the end of *In Our Time*, in the story "Big-Two Hearted River." But whereas Nick seems able to return to nature and remove himself from society, Coupland's characters do not seem to be able to fully remove themselves from popular or postmodern culture because it has become too deeply entrenched in their psyches.

2. This postmodern homogenization has taken a further step toward becoming postcolonial homogenization. The globalization of the world economy is gradually producing a globalized, American-dominated, popular culture. In *Generation X*, Andy mentions that when he lived in Japan there was an equivalent X generation called "shin jin rui," or new human beings, that were similarly isolated and fragmented in their culture. Incidentally, Coupland himself is Canadian, and his fiction, even when it is based in Canada, appears almost indistinguishable from American fiction.

3. This is a pervasive theme in Thomas Pynchon's *The Crying of Lot 49* (1967), John Barth's *The Floating Opera* (1956) and *The End of the Road* (1957).

Chapter 4

1. Alfred Kisubia also argues that "Multicultural amalgamation is an approach to racial and ethnic relations that does not condone the dominance of any one culture or race but that will allow all groups to be empowered within a common state. Multicultural amalgamation is a future utopia where majorities and minorities will meet each other

in business, in the workplace, and in residential neighborhoods, without taints of curiosity or patronizing" (27).

2. Similarly, in "On Cultural Studies" Fredric Jameson argues that cultural studies is similarly motivated by a utopian dream of ethnic equality and harmony (262).

3. In addition, the boundaries between ethnicities have further been lessened by interethnic marriages and the growth of cosmopolitan cities.

4. These writers include, according to Isabel Schneider, Emily Pauline Johnson, John Oskison, Todd Downing, Black Elk, Hum-ishu-ma, D'Arcy McNickle and John Joseph Mathews (30–31).

5. In *Contemporary American Indian Writing*, Dee Horne argues "American Indian writers can enter into a dialogue with the colonial discourse without perpetuating its rules of recognition by creating a multi-voiced discourse that illustrates the 'complex relationalities' of power" (15). She also argues that "Since power relationships are ever shifting, American Indian authors can present multiple positions while addressing the power imbalance evident in the colonial relationship between colonizer and colonized" (16).

6. By naming the killer John Smith, Alexie probably refers to the original colonist and writer John Smith, who was among the first settlers in Virginia and was abducted by Native Americans. Smith describes his encounters with Native Americans in *A General History* (1624). In a sense, the original John Smith was the first powerful, European colonizer in the New World.

7. Alexie later explains that David Rogers was not actually killed by the Indian killer/John Smith, but by two white, vagabond ex-criminals. However, the media are quick to attribute murders to the Indian killer.

8. The first modern Chicano novel is often considered to be *Pocho* (1959) by Jose Antonio Villarreal, who also wrote *The Fifth Horseman* (1974). Other significant Chicano writers of the 1960s and 1970s include Richard Vasquez, Raymond Barrio, Rudolfo Anaya, Ron

Arias, Rolando Hinojosa-Smith, and Alejandro Morales (Shirley 10).

9. In *Borderlands*, Gloria Anzaldua writes about not accepting borders and divisions and being on both sides at once. In particular, Sandra Cisernos's *The House on Mango Street* (1988) has been both critically and commercially successful.

10. The never fully named Jennifer may in fact be Jennifer Lopez, who worked as a "fly girl" for *In Living Color* during this time.

Chapter 5

1. This is one of the arguments proposed by those on the humanities side of the "two cultures debate" that I will later explain. As D. Graham Burnett proposes, scholars in the humanities believed that "scientific investigation could never provide a 'moral organ,' nor could its epistemology fairly be claimed to be inherently ethical in any important way" (193). For instance, Luce Irigaray, a feminist philosopher, claims that the prevalence of men in science has distorted its ideas. She suggests that "Einstein's 'sexualized' equation of matter and energy, $E = mc2$, privileges c, the speed of light (whereas, in fact, it favors nothing at all but shows, with ample empirical support, how much energy you get from a given mass)" (quoted in "You Can't Follow..." 78).

2. The two cultures debate dates back as far as the 1870s, beginning with the debates of T.H. Huxley and Matthew Arnold. Arnold "ranted that science could rightfully claim a more significant place in education, but he strenuously denied that literature and the arts served merely as ornament, insisting instead that the humanistic enterprises would become only more vital as the innovations of technology and science increasingly transformed what individuals had long held true about themselves and the world" (Burnett, 195). When C.P. Snow "coined the phrase the 'two cultures' he made clear that the distinction he was aiming to enunciate was one between

scientific and literary intellectuals; and the person who rose to meet his challenge most readily was F.R. Leavis, whose association with the promotion of English studies as a serious discipline is inescapable" (Slade and Lees, 13).

3. For example, consider the development and historical uses of nuclear energy and power.

4. In his article, "The Arrival of the Machine: Modernist Art in Europe, 1910–25" Hebert suggests that "as the industrial revolution had taken an ever-firmer hold on culture in the nineteenth century, modernist art had become increasingly associated with premodern or primitive nature" (1274). To support his claim, he points to Cézanne's Provençal landscapes, Van Gogh's and Pissarro's peasants, Rodin's and Renoir's nudes, Gauguin's Tahitians, Signac's Mediterranean ports, and Monet's water lilies.

5. Running parallel to the study of artificial intelligence is the development of cybernetics. One of the seminal figures in cybernetics is Norbert Wiener, who questioned whether humans, animals and machines have any essential qualities that exist in themselves, "apart from the web of relations that constituted them in discursive and communicative fields" (Hayles, 91). Cybernetic theory views an individual human as a locus for information and communication and rebels against the idea that humans are merely entities encapsulated in a body. Also see Hayles's *How We Became Posthuman*: "Of all the implications that first-wave cybernetics conveyed, perhaps none was more disturbing and potentially revolutionary than the idea that the boundaries of the human subject are constructed rather than given. Conceptualizing control, communication and information as an integrated system, cybernetics radically changed how boundaries were conceived" (84).

6. For instance, in *Chaosmos*, Philip Kuberski argues, "As Newtonian principles have been supplemented by thermodynamics, the theory of relativity, quantum mechanics, and chaos theory it seems—despite efforts to postulate a

Grand Unified Theory—that physics can no longer be conceived as a fundamental science, if by that one means a singular and inviolable set of uniform principles. It is this very emergence of complexity and plurality in science that reopens the dialogue with literature cut off precisely because of the complexity, density and texture of the literary language" (22).

7. However, beginning around 2000, tech workers and companies in the computer industry (especially those involved in the Internet) began experiencing financial troubles and downsizing. According to a *Business Week* article from June 2001, "Technology companies are scaling back hiring plans, with only 56 percent planning to add workers over the next year [2002] (vs. 77 percent in the prior quarter) and 16 percent planning job cuts. And they peg revenue growth at just 16 percent over the next year, down from the previous reading of 23.5 percent" ("Where the Clouds..." 34). However, there has been some good news in that, "some 50 percent of companies still plan to make major capital investments in the next year" ("Where the Clouds..." 34).

8. Scott Bukatman argues in *Terminal Identity*: "In cyberpunk science fiction, the body finds and occupies a new space; a realm in which a control over the datasphere of capitalism is restored within the intersecting planes of cyberspace, the body is replaced and the subject's autonomy is resurrected" (10).

9. In her essay, "A Cyborg Manifesto: Science, Technology and Socialist-Feminism in the Late Twentieth Century," Donna Haraway argues "for the cyborg as a fiction mapping our social and bodily reality and as an imaginative resource suggesting some very fruitful couplings" (697). Haraway's cyborg is not a physically mechanical half-breed, but a human who lives in a fully mechanized world, having been psychologically changed by his or her daily interfaces with machines. "By the late twentieth century," Haraway argues, "our time, a mythic time, we are all chimeras, theorized and fabricated hybrids of machine

and organisms; in short, we are cyborgs. The cyborg is our ontology; it gives us our politics" (698). Haraway embraces her idea of the "cyborg" as embodying the spirit of new revolutionary feminism. "Why," she asks, "should our bodies end at the skin or include at best other beings encapsulated by skin?" This question is taken up by N. Katherine Hayles, in her critical study, *How We Became Posthuman*. Hayles argues that "Being a posthuman means much more than having prosthetic devices grafted onto one's body. It means envisioning humans as information-processing machines with fundamental similarities to other kinds of information-processing machines, especially intelligent computers" (246). For Hayles, there is a thin line separating human and artificial intelligence, and the divisions between the two decrease with continued exposure to technology.

10. Bug Barbeque gets his name from his prowess at destroying "bugs" in computer software and hardware.

11. The wave of economic success for the younger generation, especially in the "gold rush" days of the Internet during the late 1990s produced a landfall of wealth. However, beginning in late 2000 and continuing to the present day, the bubble has burst as a huge number of Internet companies have gone bankrupt and Internet stocks have plummeted.

12. As Fenella Saunders explains in her article, "Virtual Reality 2.0," "He [Lanier] imagined a system that would let people interact effortlessly with a world of computer-generated images. Virtual reality pioneers donned heavy headsets to view crude, jerky video displays. After a decade of low-profile development, however, the technology is finally catching up with Lanier's vision. Today rooms filled with sharp, three-dimensional projections let architects walk the streets of nonexistent cities and help prospectors determine where to drill for oil. In a few years, virtual reality may enable you to move your office into a client's boardroom or transform your living room into a gallery in the Louvre, all with the flick of a switch.... Psychologists at Georgia Tech in Atlanta

use a virtual reality system to help people overcome fear of flying or fear of heights without having to visit a real plane or tall rooftop" (33).

13. While virtual reality hardly makes the front-page news these days, progress continues to be made while sales increase. Mike Bevan, editor of industry newsletter *VR News*, reports that the annual global revenue from sales of VR hardware, software and services sits somewhere "between $500 million and $1 billion, and is growing at the rate of 50 percent per year" (Cray et al 44). Over the last decade, while the world indulged its Internet obsession, "VR has quietly found a lucrative niche in industrial research and prototyping. And the surprisingly practical ways in which VR is already invading our reality, from the design of our cars to the layout of grocery stores, will only increase as the cost of technology falls" (Cray et al., 45).

One of the most important developments in virtual reality has been multiuser, projection-based virtual reality, pioneered by the Electronic Visualization Laboratory at the University of Illinois at Chicago: "In 1992, it [the University of Illinois at Chicago] introduced the CAVE Virtual Reality Theater, a light-tight room onto whose walls, ceiling and floor computer-generated images can be projected. The CAVE VR surround-sound environment easily accommodates four users simultaneously, each of whom roams freely wearing lightweight stereoscopic glasses instead of a headset and carrying an interactive wand or mouse to navigate. Available commercially from Fakespace Systems Inc. at a cost of around $400,000, 26 CAVEs have been sold worldwide since 1996" (48). Indeed, I would argue that Richard Powers uses this very development of the CAVE Virtual Reality Theater as one of the primary models for his cavern in *Plowing the Dark* (2000), which I will explore later in this chapter.

One of the most promising areas for virtual reality development is the University of North Carolina at Chapel Hill and the Triangle research area. A company called 3rdTech set up shop in

Chapel Hill in 2000, "close to where one of the leading VR groups in America is based at the University of North Carolina. Acting as a sort of 'smart incubator,' 3rdTech has been trying to get various VR technologies to the stage where investors and entrepreneurs are ready to take the plunge" ("Virtual Hype, Real Products," 8). Furthermore, a new system under development at the University of North Carolina (UNC) promises to move virtual worlds one step closer to this ideal by enabling real-time 3D reconstructions of the user and other real objects in an immersive virtual environment. When the user steps into or places a body part such as an arm into the virtual field of view, the image-based system captures the body part and builds a 3D graphical representation of it, which the user sees in the virtual world in the same way it would appear in the real world. In addition, the user can interact with other real objects that are also contained within the system's field of view. For example, if the user reaches an arm into the viewing space to grab a physical object off of a desk, he or she will see an accurately lit, pigmented, and clothed graphical representation of the arm and a similarly accurate representation of the object" (Mahoney, 17).

14. At the end of the novel, Stephenson reveals that L. Bob Rife actually controls the metaverse.

15. This is not a typo. His name is spelled Da5id, not David.

16. This appears in several of Ballard's short stories, exemplified by the urban overcrowding portrayed in "The Concentration City," as well as Burroughs' depiction of Interzone in *Naked Lunch* (1957) and *Exterminator!* (1960) and Phillip K. Dick's *Do Androids Dream of Electric Sheep?* (1968) and *Ubik* (1969).

17. In Franzen's novel, St. Louis appoints an Indian woman, S. Jammu, as police chief. S. Jammu brings in Indian nationals, who begin terrorizing the city, causing civil unrest.

18. In *Snow Crash*, the United States has been partially parceled into gated,

suburban communities that Stephenson calls "burbclaves," while the rest of the country is an anarchic, violent, urban wasteland. The United States government no longer functions in a legislative manner. Rather, the government has become privatized, reduced to "Fed Land." Fed Land has become an Orwellian nightmare of constant supervision. In an information-oriented society, where access to information becomes the primary avenue to achieve power and world domination, it seems logical that the CIA would merge with the Library of Congress as they do in *Snow Crash*.

19. Punk music champions the individual/outsider who confronts authority and lives according to his or her own personal code. While it is somewhat of an adolescent phenomenon, punk music also celebrates autonomy from authority and parent figures. It has blue-collar, working-class roots and often endorses aggression against oppressive legal and economic structures that keep lower-class individuals chained to an uncertain hand-to-mouth lifestyle. In keeping with the aggressive punk ethos, *Snow Crash* is filled with fighting and high-paced action scenes, both in the metaverse and in reality. In a way, Hiro, as a swashbuckling samurai, is something of a nihilistic, cold-blooded killer who has no qualms or remorse about killing anyone who stands in his way. Hiro is not a cybernetic Robin Hood who tries to equalize the informational playing field, but his mediocre economic status does make him more of an everyman, who tries to better his own meager lot.

20. One of the largest franchises in *Snow Crash*'s reality is Cosa Nostra Pizza, which commits to delivering pizzas within thirty minutes or the CEO and founder, Uncle Enzo, will personally fly out to the customer's home, apologize profusely and give the customer a free trip to Italy.

21. Rushkoff uses the Rodney King beating incident as an example of a media virus, but a more appropriate contemporary example would certainly be the case of Elian Gonzales and the

subsequent publicity and debate surrounding the six-year-old Cuban boy.

22. This theory would certainly support the work of researchers hell-bent on inventing methods to upload the human mind onto a computer.

23. In an article titled "The Myth of Artificial Intelligence," Frederick Allen argues, "Work aimed at emulating the functioning of the brain still goes on in pure research, but mostly without the old optimism, and the effort is pretty much split in two. People are now trying to crack the problem either from the very top down or from the very bottom up. Top down means by trying to duplicate the results of human thought, typically by building up vast reserves of 'commonsense' knowledge and then figuring out how to compute with it all, or by continuing to try to write programs to hold conversation, without first figuring out how the brain does it. Bottom up means by designing 'neural nets,' computer versions of the basic biological connections that brains are made of, and attempting to make them grow and learn. Both approaches have come up against tremendous obstacles. A company named Cycorp began a project of gathering commonsense knowledge in 1995, aiming to help computers overcome the disadvantage of being unable to acquire all the information we get just from living in the world" (30).

24. Lentz's views are quite similar to Alan Turing's, who, around 1950, came up with a simple rule of thumb for artificial intelligence. Turing suggested that if users held two conversations—one with a computer, the other with a human—and at the end couldn't pick out the computer more than 50 percent of the time, we'd have to conclude that the computer was intelligent. However, the Turing test still leaves the question of human consciousness unanswered. Even if a computer were to "fool" most humans into believing that it is mortal, that does not mean that the computer possesses the ability to consciously reason or possesses even a semblance of human consciousness.

25. Although Powers never states the name of the game, I believe that the game is *Zork.*

26. When Adie first visits the Cavern, Jack tells her how the computer simulations work on the basis of holographic technology using data points, not photographs.

27. Powers's connection between the military and virtual reality appears to have some factual basis. In an article titled "Army enlists Hollywood for some training help," Dennis Blank reports: "The Army has awarded a five-year, $45 million contract to the new Institute for Creative Technologies at the University of Southern California for development of computer-based virtual-reality programs" (30). Similarly, in *Defense and Aerospace Electronics,* the editors mention: "Air Force Armstrong Lab's Human Engineering Division, Wright-Patterson AFB, Ohio, banks on virtual reality to improve the performance of aircrews and systems in combat. VR links man and machine in what the Air Force calls the Pilot/Vehicle Interface. Stretching the technology, the lab uses VR to create a synthetic environment inside a simulated cockpit."

Chapter 6

1. Indeed, beginning with the Columbine shootings, some critics have contended that action-adventure games like "Doom" and "Myst" have helped desensitize children and teens. In addition, some have argued that these interactive games also help children literally become sharpshooters, with deadly precision.

2. However, with the recent unexpected inclusion of Jonathan Franzen's *The Corrections* as an Oprah's Book Club selection, it is possible that Oprah's tastes or the tastes of her executive committee have grown more literary, for Franzen's novel is a multi layered, complex and serious meditation on the American family, with a distinctly academic background (one major character is an ex–English professor). A subsequent debate emerged when Franzen

refused to appear on Oprah's televised show, and his book was summarily dropped from the book club, which has since folded.

3. I visited websites of Harvard, Yale, Princeton and Columbia and looked at course descriptions and syllabi for American literature courses during the entire 2001–2002 school year. In courses titled twentieth-century American fiction or contemporary American literature, there were very few works written after 1970. In fact, out of about ten courses taught in American literature at Harvard, only three post–1970 American novels were chosen, two of which are historical revisionist: E.L. Doctorow's *Ragtime*, Toni Morrison's *Beloved* and Jessica Hagedorn's *Dogeaters*. Yale only had one: Don DeLillo's *White Noise*. Princeton also only had one: Kathy Acker's *Great Expectations*. Columbia only had Raymond Carver and Don DeLillo listed on the syllabus for one course (specific novels not mentioned). Not a single American fiction writer under fifty was chosen for inclusion in any course at these four preeminent American universities.

Bibliography

Adams, Henry. *The Education of Henry Adams*. Boston: Houghton Mifflin, 1927.
Ainsworth, Patricia. *Understanding Depression*. Jackson: University Press of Mississippi, 2000.
Alexie, Sherman. *Indian Killer*. New York: Atlantic Monthly Press, 1996.
_____. *The Lone Ranger and Tonto Fistfight in Heaven*. New York: Atlantic Monthly Press, 1993.
_____. *Reservation Blues*. New York: Atlantic Monthly Press, 1995.
_____. *The Toughest Indian in the World: Stories*. New York: Atlantic Monthly Press, 2000.
Allen, Frederick. "The Myth of Artificial Intelligence." *American Heritage*, February 2001, 52(1):28–32.
Annesley, James. *Blank Fictions*. New York: St. Martin's Press, 1998.
Bakhtin, Michel. *The Dialogic Imagination*. Austin: University of Texas Press, 1981.
Barth, John. *The Friday Book: Essays and Other Nonfiction*. New York: Putnam, 1984.
_____. *Further Fridays: Essays, Lectures, and Other Nonfiction, 1984–94*. Boston: Little, Brown, 1995.
Barthes, Roland. *Critical Essays*. Translated from the French by Richard Howard. Evanston: Northwestern University Press, 1972.
Bhabha, Homi. *The Location of Culture*. London: Routledge Press, 1994.
Birkets, Sven. "Butterfly Stories: A Novel" (book review). *The New Republic*, April 11, 1994.
Blank, Dennis. "Army Enlists Hollywood for Some Training Help." *Government Computer News*, January 8, 2001, 20(1):30.
Bloom, Allan. *The Closing of the American Mind*. New York: Simon and Schuster, 1987.
Bloom, Harold. *How to Read and Why*. New York: Scribner, 2000.
Blume, Harvey. "Two Geeks on Their Way to Byzantium: A Conversation with R. Powers." *Atlantic Unbound Online*. http://www.theatlantic.com/unbound/interviews/ba2000-06-28.htm.
Braun, Stephen. *The Science of Happiness*. New York: John Wiley & Sons, Inc., 2000.
Brewster, Kelley. "Tribal Visions." *Biblio*. March 1999, 4(3):22–32.
Brinkley, Douglas. "Educating the Generation Called 'X.'" *Washington Post Education Review*, April 3, 1994, pp.1–2.
Brown University, English department website. March 9, 2002. http://www.brown.edu/Departments/English/Writing/hypertext.htm.
Bukatman, Scott. *Terminal Identity*. Durham: Duke University Press, 1993.
Bukiet, Melvin. A Dream of Californication. *The Nation*, September 18, 2000, 271(8):31.
Burnett, D. Graham. "A View from the Bridge: The Two Cultures Debate, Its Legacy, and the History of Science." *Daedalus*, Spring 1999, 128(2):193–5.

Burroughs, William S. *Naked Lunch*. New York: Grove Press, 1959.

Button, Graham; Jeff Coulter, John Lee, and Wes Sharrock. *Computers, Minds and Conduct*. Oxford: Polity Press, 1995.

Cline, Lynn. "About Sherman Alexie." *Ploughshares*, Winter 2000, 26:197–201.

Cordle, Daniel. *Postmodern Postures: Literature, Science and the Two Culture Debates*. Aldershot, Great Britain: Ashgate Publishing Limited, 1999.

Costello, Mark, and David Foster Wallace. *Signifying Rappers: Rap and Race in the Urban Present*. New York: Echo Press, 1990.

Coupland, Douglas. *All Families Are Psychotic: A Novel*. 1st U.S. ed. New York: Bloomsbury, 2002.

_____. *Generation X: Tales for an Accelerated Culture*. New York: St. Martin's Press, 1991.

_____. "Generation X'd." *Details*, June, 1995, p. 72.

_____. *Girlfriend in a Coma*. 1st ed. New York: Regan Books, 1998.

_____. *Life after God*. New York: Pocket Books, 1994.

_____. *Microserfs*. New York: Regan Books, 1995.

_____. *Miss Wyoming*. 1st ed. New York: Pantheon Books, 1999.

_____. "The Observationalists: What's the Deal?" (http://www.coupland.com/1_06.htm).

Cray, Dan, Mike McBride, Peggy Salz-Trautman, and Maggie Sieger. "The Real Thing: After Years of False Starts and Unrealized Potential, Virtual Reality is Finally Ready to Make Its Mark in the Real World." *Time International*," October 11, 1999, 154(14):44–54.

Crockett, Larry. *The Turing Test and the Frame Problem*. Norwood, NJ: Ablex Publishing Corporation, 1994.

Delbanco, Andrew. *The Real American Dream*. Cambridge: Harvard University Press, 1998.

Deleuze, Gilles, and Félix Guattari. *Anti-Oedipus: Capitalism and Schizophrenia*. New York: Viking Press, 1977.

Doody, Margaret. *The True Story of the Novel*. New Brunswick, NJ: Rutgers University Press, 1996.

D'Orso, Mike. "Saturday's Hero: A Beat; Before Going on the Road, Jack Kerouac Was a Gridiron Star." *Sports Illustrated*, October 23, 1989, 71(17):114–122.

Douglas, J. Yellowlees. *The End of Books—or Books without End?* Ann Arbor: University of Michigan Press, 2000.

Eggers, Dave. *A Heartbreaking Work of Staggering Genius*. New York: Simon & Schuster, 2000.

Ellis, Bret Easton. *American Psycho*. New York: Vintage Books, 1991.

_____. *Less Than Zero*. New York: Simon & Schuster, 1985.

Ellul, Jacques. *The Technological Society*. Translated from the French by John Wilkinson. New York: Vintage Books, 1964 [New York: Viking press, 1954].

Finkelkraut, Alain. *The Wisdom of Love*. Translated by Kevin O'Neill and David Suchoff. Lincoln: University of Nebraska Press, 1997.

Garcia, Feliciano. "It's Great to Be Part of a Dot-Com. Really." *Fortune*, January 8, 2001, 143(1):188.

Gergen, Kenneth. *The Saturated Self*. New York: Basic Books, 1991.

Gibson, William. *Neuromancer*. New York: Ace Science Fiction Books, 1984.

Habermas, Jürgen. *The Philosophical Discourse of Modernity: Twelve Lectures*. Translated by Frederick Lawrence. Cambridge, MA: MIT Press, 1987.

Haraway, Donna. "A Cyborg Manifesto: Science, Technology, and Socialist-Feminism in the Late Twentieth Century." *Contemporary Literary Criticism: Literary and Cultural Studies*. New York: Longman, pp. 696–727. 1986.

Hawking, Stephen. *A Brief History of Time: From the Big Bang to Black Holes*. New York: Bantam Books, 1988.

Hayles, N. Katherine. *How We Became Posthuman*. Chicago: University of Chicago Press, 1999.

Hebert, Robert. "The Arrival of the Machine: Modernist Art in Europe, 1910–25." *Social Research*, Fall 1997 v64 n3 p.1273–1306.

Heudin, Jean-Claude, ed. *Virtual Worlds: Synthetic Universes, Digital Life and Complexity*. Reading, MA: Perseus Books, 1999.

Hodkinson, Harold. "What Should We Call People?" in *Lines, Borders and Connections*. Edited by Otis Scott. Dubuque, IA: Kendall/Hunt Publishing Company, 1997.

Hoffmann, Michael, and Patrick Murphy, eds. *Critical Essays on American Modernism*. New York: G.K. Hall & Co., 1992.

Hornblower, Margot. "Great Xpectations." *People*, June 9, 1997, 149(23):86.

Horne, Dee. *Contemporary American Indian Writing*. Frankfurt: Peter Lang Publishing, 1999.

Jacoby, Russell. *The End of Utopia*. New York: Basic Books, 1999.

Jameson, Fredric. "On Cultural Studies," in *The Identity in Question*. Edited by John Rajchman. New York: Routledge, 1995.

_____. *Postmodernism, or, the Cultural Logic of Late Capitalism*. Durham: Duke University Press, 1991.

Janowitz, Tama. *Slaves of New York*. New York: Crown Publishers, 1986.

Joyce, Michael. *Othermindedness*. Ann Arbor: University of Michigan Press, 1998.

Kisubia, Alfred. "Ideological Perspectives on Multicultural Relations," in *Multiculturalism in a Cross-National Perspective*. Edited by Michael Burayidi. Lanham, MD: University Press of America, 1997.

Kristeva, Julia. *Black Sun*. Translated by Leon S. Roudiez. New York: Columbia University Press, 1987.

Kuberski, Philip. *Chaosmos: Literature, Science and Theory*. Albany: State University of New York, 1994.

Kurweil, Ray. "When Machines Think." *Maclean's*, March 1, 1999, pp. 54–60.

Labinger, Jay. "The Science Wars and the Future of the American Academic Profession." *Daedalus*, Fall 1997, 126(4):201–221.

Landow, George. *Hypertext: The Convergence of Critical Theory and Technology*. Baltimore: Johns Hopkins University Press, 1992.

Larson, Sidner. *Captured in the Middle: Tradition and Experience in Contemporary Native American Writing*. Seattle: University of Washington Press, 2000.

Lasch, Christopher. *The Culture of Narcissism: American Life in an Age of Diminishing Expectations*. New York: Norton, 1978.

Laurence, Alexander. "An Interview with Mark Leyner." *Alt X Online*. http://www.altx.com/interviews/mark.leyner.html.

LeClair, Tom. *The Art of Excess: Mastery in Contemporary American Fiction*. Urbana: University of Illinois Press, 1989.

_____. *In the Loop: Don DeLillo and the Systems Novel*. Urbana: University of Illinois Press, 1987.

_____. "The Prodigious Fiction of Richard Powers, William Vollmann and David Foster Wallace." *Critique: Studies in Contemporary Fiction*, Fall 1996, 38(1):12–38.

Levy, Steven. "The Hacker Hemingway." *Newsweek*, May 10, 1999, 133(19):90–1

Litan, Robert. "The Internet Economy." *Foreign Policy*, March 2001, p. 16.

Lyotard, Jean François. *The Postmodern Condition: A Report on Knowledge*. Translated from French by Geoff Bennington and Brian Massumi. Minneapolis: University of Minnesota Press, 1984.

Mahoney, Diana. "Avatar Advances." *Computer Graphics World*, February 2001, 24(2):17.

Markley, Robert, ed. *Virtual Realities and Their Discontents*. Baltimore: Johns Hopkins University Press, 1996.

Marshall, P. David. *Celebrity and Power: Fame in Contemporary Culture.* Minneapolis: University of Minnesota Press, 1997.

Martinez, Elizabeth. "In Pursuit of Latina Liberation," in *Lines, Borders and Connections.* Edited by Otis Scott. Dubuque, IA: Kendall/Hunt Publishing Company, 1997.

Marx, Doug. "Sherman Alexie: A Reservation of the Mind." *Publishers Weekly,* September 16, 1996, 243(38):39–45.

McCaffery, Larry. "An Interview with David Foster Wallace." *The Review of Contemporary Fiction,* Summer 1993, 13(2):127–51.

_____. "An Interview with William T. Vollmann." *The Review of Contemporary Fiction,* Summer 1993, 13(2):9–25.

_____. "Introductory Ways of Looking at a Post-Post-Modernist Aesthetic Phenomenon called 'Avant-Pop.'" In *In Memoriam to Postmodernism: Essays on the Avant-Pop.* Edited by Mark Amerika and Lance Olsen. San Diego: San Diego State University Press, 1995.

McHale, Brian. *Postmodernist Fiction.* New York: Methuen, 1987.

McInerney, Jay. *Bright Lights, Big City.* New York: Vintage Books, 1984.

McLuhan, Marshall. *Understanding Media: The Extensions of Man.* Cambridge: MIT Press, 1994.

Miall, David S. "Trivializing or liberating? The limitations of hypertext theorizing." *Mosaic* (Winnipeg), June 1999 32(2):157–160.

"Michele Serros." Great Leap, Inc. http://www.greatleap.org/michele/.

Miller, Laura. "The Salon Interview: Richard Powers." *Salon,* July 1998. http://www.salon.com/books/int/1998/07/cov_si_23inta.html.

Murray, Janet. *Hamlet on the Holodeck.* New York: The Free Press, 1997.

Neate, Wilson. *Tolerating Ambiguity: Ethnicity and Community in Chicano/a Writing.* New York: Peter Lang Publishing, Inc., 1998.

Nightingale, Carl. *On the Edge: A History of Poor Black Children and Their American Dreams.* New York: Basic Books, 1995.

Owen, Rob. *Gen X TV.* Syracuse: Syracuse University Press, 1997.

Pi. Videocassette. Santa Monica: Artisan Entertainment, 1998.

Potter, P. Aaron. "Centripetal Textuality." *Victorian Studies,* Summer 1998, 41(4):593.

Powers, Richard. *Gain.* New York: Farrar, Straus and Giroux, 1998.

_____. *Galatea 2.2.* New York: Farrar, Straus and Giroux, 1995.

_____. *The Gold Bug Variations.* New York: W. Morrow, 1991.

_____. *Operation Wandering Soul.* New York: W. Morrow, 1993.

_____. *Plowing the Dark.* New York: Farrar, Straus, Giroux, 2000.

_____. *Prisoner's Dilemma.* New York: Beech Tree Books, 1985.

_____. *Three Farmers on Their Way to a Dance.* New York: Beech Tree Books, 1985.

Pynchon, Thomas. *Slow Learner: Early Stories.* Boston: Little, Brown, 1984.

_____. *V.: A Novel.* New York: Bantam Books, 1964.

Rebolledo, Tey. *Women Singing in the Snow: A Cultural Analysis of Chicana Literature.* Tucson: University of Arizona Press, 1995.

Riesman, David. *The Lonely Crowd.* New Haven: Yale University Press, 1950.

Rushkoff, Douglas. *Media Virus!* New York: Ballantine Books, 1994.

Sacks, Peter. *Generation X Goes to College.* Chicago: Open Court Press, 1996.

Saunders, Fenella. "Virtual Reality 2.0." *Discover,* September 1999, 20(9):32.

Schneider, Isabel. *We Have a Commonality and a Common Dream.* Frankfurt: Peter Lang Publishing, 1998.

Serros, Michele. *Chicana Falsa.* New York: Riverhead Books, 1993.

_____. *How to Be a Chicana Role Model.* New York: Riverhead Books, 2000.

Sherwin, Elizabeth. "'Chicana Falsa' Serros Doesn't Hit a False Note." *The Davis Virtual Matter.* http://www.dcn.davis.ca.us/go/gizmo/2001/serros.html.

Shirley, Carl, and Paula Shirley. *Understanding Chicano Literature.* Columbia: University of South Carolina Press, 1988.

Siegel, Howard P. "Technology, Pessimism and Postmodernism," in *Technology, Pessimism and Postmodernism*. Edited by Yaron Ezrahi, Everett Mendelsohn and Howard Segal. Norwell, MA: Kluwer Publishers, 1994.

Slade, Joseph, and Judith Lees, eds. *Beyond the Two Cultures: Essays on Science, Technology and Literature*. Ames, IA: Iowa State University Press, 1990.

Sloane, Sarah. *Digital Fictions: Storytelling in a Material World*. Stamford, CT: Ablex Publishing Corporation, 2000.

Stephenson, Neal. *The Big U*. 1st ed. New York: Vintage Books, 1984.

_____. *Cryptonomicon*. 1st ed. New York: Avon Books, 1999.

_____. *The Diamond Age; or, Young Lady's Illustrated Primer*. New York: Bantam Books, 1995.

_____. *In the Beginning ... Was the Command Line*. New York: Avon Books, 1999.

_____. *Snow Crash*. New York: Bantam Books, 1992.

_____. *Zodiac: The Eco-Thriller*. New York: Atlantic Monthly Press, 1998.

Sterling, Bruce, ed. *Mirrorshades: The Cyberpunk Anthology*. New York: Arbor House, 1986.

Sullivan, Stefen. "Philosophical Perspectives on Multiculturalism," in *Multiculturalism in a Cross-National Perspective*. Edited by Michael Burayidi. Lanham, MD: University Press of America, 1997.

Tabbi, Joseph. *Postmodern Sublime*. Ithaca: Cornell University Press, 1995.

_____, and Michael Wutz. *Reading Matters: Narrative in the New Media Economy*. Ithaca: Cornell University Press, 1997.

Timberg, Scott. "In *Life after God*, Writer Coupland Eschews his 'Generation X' Irony." http://www.imv.aau.dk/~bogus/texter/artikler/eschews.html.

Travis, Molly Abel. "Cybernetic Esthetics, Hypertext and the Future of Literature." *Mosaic* (Winnipeg), December 1996, 29(4):116–131.

Venturi, Robert. *Learning from Las Vegas*. Cambridge: MIT Press, 1972.

"Virtual Hype, Real Products." *The Economist*, March 24, 2001, p. 8.

Vollmann, William T. *An Afghanistan Picture Show, or, How I Saved the World*. New York: Farrar, Straus, and Giroux, 1992.

_____. *The Atlas*. New York: Viking, 1996.

_____. *Butterfly Stories*. New York: Grove Press, 1993.

_____. *The Rainbow Stories*. New York: Atheneum, 1989.

_____. *The Royal Family*. New York: Viking, 2000.

_____. *Whores for Gloria*. New York: Pantheon Books, 1991.

"VR Aids Pilots." *Defense & Aerospace Electronics*, October 3, 1994, 4(38):4.

Wallace, David Foster. *Brief Interviews with Hideous Men*. Boston: Little, Brown, 1999.

_____. *The Broom of the System*. New York: Penguin, 1987.

_____. *Girl with the Curious Hair*. New York: W.W. Norton, 1989.

_____. *Infinite Jest*. Boston: Little, Brown, 1996.

_____. *A Supposedly Fun Thing I'll Never Do Again: Essays and Arguments*. Boston: Little, Brown, 1997.

"Where the Clouds Aren't Breaking." *Business Week*, June 11, 2001, 3736:34.

Williams, Jeffrey. "The Last Generalist: An Interview with Richard Powers." *Cultural Logic*, Spring 1999, 2(2):8–15.

Woolf, Virginia. "Mr. Bennett and Mrs. Brown," in *The Captain's Death Bed*. New York: Harcourt Brace, 1950.

Wurtzel, Elizabeth. *Prozac Nation*. Boston: Houghton Mifflin, 1994.

"You Can't Follow the Science Wars without a Battle Map." *The Economist*, December 13, 1997, 345(8047):77–80.

Index